IMAGES
of America

PATROL AND RESCUE BOATS ON PUGET SOUND

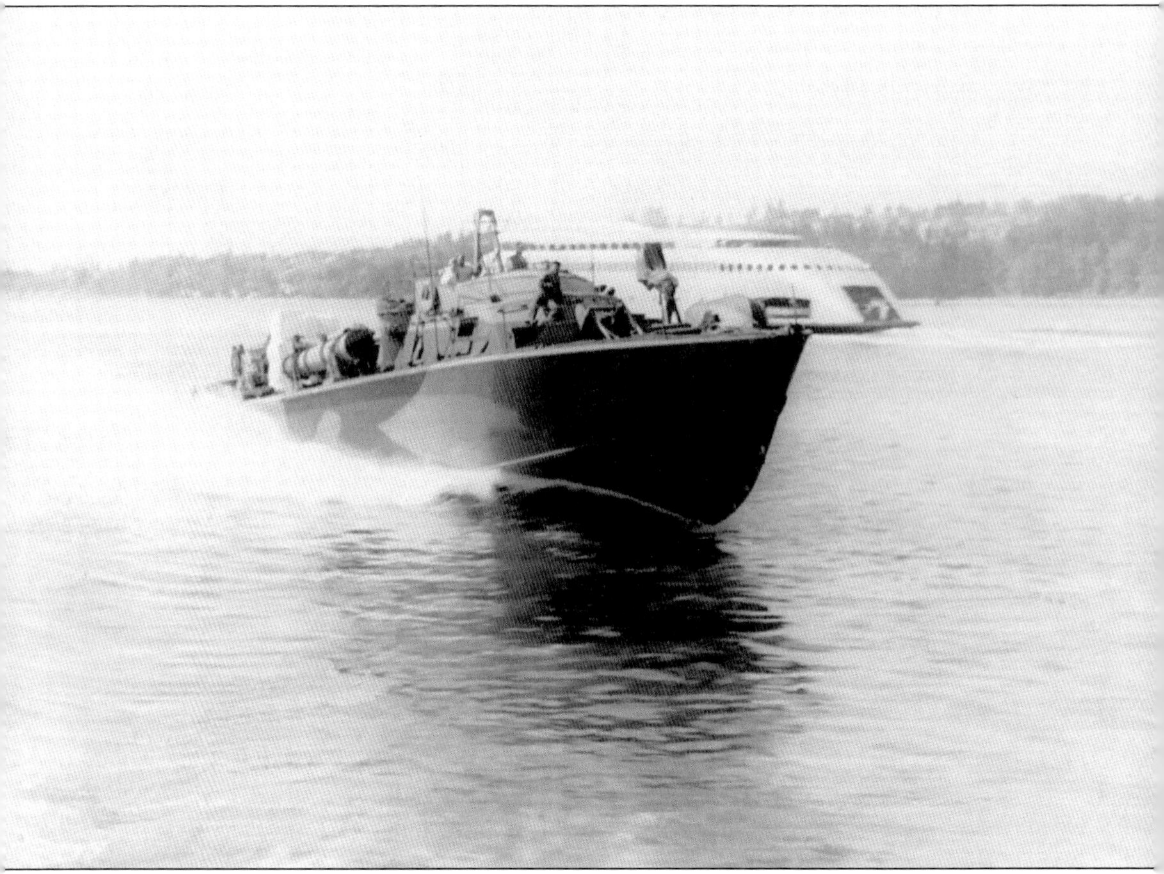

FIGHTING AND FERRY BOATS. It is little known that the fast, legendary patrol torpedo (PT) boats that fought bravely in the South Pacific and elsewhere during World War II also plied the waters of Puget Sound. This rare, previously unpublished photograph from World War II Navy PT crewman Frederick (Fred) Gilmartin shows his speeding 78-foot PT-646 passing in front of the widely known ferry boat *Kalakala* in the summer of 1945. The ferry was on its normal route between Seattle and Bremerton, home of the Puget Sound Navy Yard, and the PT boat was on a test run. Toward the end of the war, PT boats produced by Higgins Industries of New Orleans, Louisiana, were transported to Puget Sound by the Navy's PT Ferrying Command for transfer to Russia as part of the federal government's Lend-Lease program. This initiative was designed to support the wartime efforts of US allies. (Courtesy Fred Gilmartin, Ed.D., US Navy PT Ferrying Command.)

ON THE COVER: One of the most widely produced patrol boat designs from the 1930s through World War II was the Coast Guard's 38-foot picket boat, shown in this dramatic bow-on view at full speed. More than 530 were built by boatyards throughout the nation; Ballinger Boat Works of Kirkland, near Seattle, produced the third largest number, 68. These picket craft fit patrol needs on Puget Sound perfectly. As described in *U.S. Coast Guard Cutters and Craft of World War II*, the 38-footers were a cabin-type patrol craft "tailored to meet the practical requirement for policing and patrolling harbors, shallow inlets, and protected bodies along the coasts." (Courtesy National Archives, Pacific Alaska Region, Seattle.)

IMAGES
of America

Patrol and Rescue Boats on Puget Sound

Chuck Fowler, Dan Withers,
and Combatant Craft of America

ARCADIA
PUBLISHING

ISBN 978-0-7385-7581-0

Published by Arcadia Publishing
Charleston, South Carolina

Printed in the United States of America

Library of Congress Control Number: 2011925403

For all general information, please contact Arcadia Publishing:
Telephone 843-853-2070
Fax 843-853-0044
E-mail sales@arcadiapublishing.com
For customer service and orders:
Toll-Free 1-888-313-2665

Visit us on the Internet at www.arcadiapublishing.com

To military veterans Bill Somers, Harry Wiedmaier, and Bud Tretter, and also to Roxane Withers, whose extraordinary efforts to preserve patrol and rescue boat history honor all who served.

Contents

ACKNOWLEDGMENTS

Producing this book has been an honor and a privilege. But we have not been alone in this effort, and some colleagues and friends merit special recognition.

First among these is Bruce "Chip" Marshall, whose knowledgeable and dedicated research assistance in the Washington, DC, area has been vital. In addition, retired Coast Guard captain Gene Davis, director of the Coast Guard Museum Northwest in Seattle, has been a constant source of excellent images and information, as have Dr. Robert Browning and Christopher Havern of the Coast Guard Historian's Office in Washington, DC. William (Bill) Galvani and Danelle Feddes at Navy Museums Puget Sound, including the Puget Sound Navy Museum at Bremerton, as well as Ed Finney and Rob Hanshew, Photographic Section, US Navy History and Heritage Command, have also given valued research assistance.

Others who have helped us are Kathleen Crosman, National Archives, Alaska Pacific Region, and Carolyn Marr, Museum of History and Industry (MOHAI), both in Seattle, as well as Alyce Guthrie and Allyson Bethune at PT Boats, Inc., the national PT boat veterans organization. Additional professionals who made our efforts much easier were Loita Hawkinson, Kirkland Heritage Society; Marsha Moratti, Jefferson County Historical Society Research Center, Port Townsend; Jeff Jewell and Todd Warger, Whatcom Museum of History and Art, Bellingham; Robert Schuler, Tacoma Public Library Northwest Room; and Tom Rogers, Tacoma Sea Scouts. More historical images were provided by Leroy Hurt, Booz Allen Hamilton, US Coast Guard RB-M Acquisition Project Resident Office at Kvichak Marine Industries, Kent; and Jason Solomon of SAFE Boats International. Dedicated volunteers at the Puget Sound Maritime Historical Society who gave essential assistance were Ron Burke; Lisle Rose, Ph.D.; Karl House; and Jack Carver.

Three World War II veterans were particularly helpful in providing outstanding rare photographs from their personal collections: C.W. (Bill) Somers; Fred Gilmartin, Ed.D.; and Harold (Hal) Turner. Retired Coast Guard rear admiral John Lockwood, former District 13 commander, has given ongoing encouragement and support.

The inspiration for this book came from individuals and groups, including World War II crash boat skipper and veteran Bill Somers and many members of the Army Air Force/US Air Force Crash Rescue Boat Association and the West Coast Crash Rescue Boat Association, particularly Bud and Jerry Tretter and Don Lashua. Another group that gave support was the Coast Guard 83-Foot Sailors Association, including Wendel (Wink) Weber, Dick Craig, Myron (Tike) Hillman, and Ed Young. Others also deserve special mention, namely those affiliated with Save the PT Boat, Inc., in Portland, Oregon, including Harry Wiedmaier, Ken Nissen, Jim Brunette, John Akin, Jerry Gilmartin, Bob Alton, Dale Billups, and Chuck Kellogg.

Four others involved in major patrol and rescue boat restoration projects deserve our thanks as well: Randy Cunningham of the World War II Army Air Force P-619 crash rescue boat, veterans Heinz Hickethier and Bob Brower of the Gamewardens Association, Vietnam War PBR (patrol boat river), and Mike Granat, Bellingham International Maritime Museum.

Finally, our appreciation goes to Donna Libert, Tiffany Frary, Jim Kempert, former editor Sara Higginbotham, and former publisher Devon Weston at Arcadia Publishing for their understanding and support through the entire book development process.

Introduction

Largely because of the widely publicized World War II exploits of US Navy lieutenant, PT boat commander, and later president John F. Kennedy, the small, fast PT boats have earned a legendary place in the nation's military maritime history.

Through this wartime episode and many lesser but still dramatic stories, military historians and enthusiasts are very familiar with PT boat activities during World War II. But relatively few people are aware that these famed boats also operated on Puget Sound waters, far away from active combat zones in the South Pacific, Alaska, Europe, and the Mediterranean. This fascinating story—and the Pacific Northwest history of other Navy, Coast Guard, Army, and Air Force patrol and rescue boats—is chronicled in this book.

Although relatively well known, PT boats appear only as blips on the radar screen of military sea services history. However, fast patrol boats and rescue craft have been essential in periods of both war and peace both in Puget Sound and worldwide. The proud but largely unknown crews who have operated them have given dedicated, often courageous service to our nation.

While a few larger patrol vessels, such as torpedo destroyers and hydrofoils, are mentioned in this book, they appear only if they were built or served on the sound. Generally, only patrol and rescue boats about 100 feet long or less are featured.

As defined by naval historian Norman Friedman in his major reference volume *U.S. Small Combatants: An Illustrated Design History*, patrol boats are "small, usually high speed military craft which operate relatively close to the shore," whether these be in ocean coastal areas or inland waters such as Puget Sound.

In a broader military context, Friedman notes that patrol boats "lie outside the mainstream of U.S. naval strategy, outside the balanced fleet of capital ships [battleships and aircraft carriers], escorts and submarines designed to project U.S. power abroad." Historically, patrol boats tended to fill "extemporized roles in wartime and to be discarded in peacetime."

However, in the 1980s, the 1990s, and the first decade of the 2000s, as enemy threats came to the nation's home shores, fast response patrol boats have increasingly become vital to protecting our national security. In an age of international terrorism, patrol boats and their crews have become maritime mainstays of our homeland security forces. And in 2010, projecting the nation's military maritime power at home and overseas required a balanced force, including major ships such as aircraft carriers, destroyers, and submarines and also small, fast patrol and rescue boats.

The earliest US naval presence in the Puget Sound region began in 1841, when the large sailing ships of Navy lieutenant Charles Wilkes first explored the sound for scientific and political purposes. Following initial voyages to the area in 1792 by Capt. George Vancouver and early settlement by the British, Wilkes's six-ship US Exploring Expedition fleet and its crews helped secure the area for the United States. In 1853, as American settlers increasingly populated the region, it would become the territory of Washington.

In 1854, a year after the territory was created, the first true patrol boat was dispatched to the new territory by the US Department of the Treasury. The 94-foot Revenue Cutter Service schooner *Jefferson Davis* was assigned to combat the smuggling of goods into the region, which was robbing the federal government of needed customs duty revenue.

The federal government also sent US Navy ships to Puget Sound to protect citizens of the rapidly growing settlements along its shores from attack by threatening Indian tribes. The sloop-of-war USS *Decatur* arrived in Seattle in October 1855, to be followed by the Navy's first steam-powered patrol vessel in the sound, the auxiliary sail-rigged vessel USS *Massachusetts*. Four decades later, power plant technology improved, and the Navy awarded a contract to Seattle's Moran Brothers Shipyard to build the first high-speed patrol boat in the region, the USS *Rowan*. More powerful steam engines in the late 1800s and then gasoline and diesel engines beginning in the early 1900s permitted the design, construction, and use of smaller, faster patrol boats.

The increasing international strategic and domestic importance of the Pacific Northwest, as well as new shipbuilding and engine technology, led to the establishment of the first permanent naval installation in the region. In 1891, Lt. Ambrose Barkley Wyckoff convinced the Navy and Congress to establish the Puget Sound Naval Station at Bremerton, later renamed Navy Yard Puget Sound, and in 1945, Puget Sound Naval Shipyard (PSNS). And while PSNS focused mainly on constructing and repairing major ships, they and civilian shipyards in Seattle and elsewhere in the sound also built smaller patrol boats.

There was no real strategic need for speedy small craft in the sound and off Washington State coasts until the impact of indirect but growing enemy threats began with the Spanish-American War in 1898 and continued through World War I. Summing up this historical shift, Friedman noted that the development of small patrol boats "was driven by two quite separate factors; technology, particularly the technology of high speed, and national strategy."

In 1920, the number of patrol boats and their operation began to increase in the region when the 18th Amendment to the Constitution, which authorized Prohibition, became law and was implemented by the Volstead Act. The US Coast Guard was given the new, expanded responsibility of preventing rum-running boats from smuggling illegal liquor into the United States on the Atlantic coast, in the Gulf of Mexico, and along the Pacific coast, including Washington State and Puget Sound. Prohibition ended in 1933 with the repeal of the 18th Amendment; however, the 14-year period produced major design and engine technology advances that proved valuable when the Navy's famous PT and similar boats, as well as fast Coast Guard and Army Air Force rescue craft, were built during World War II. In important combat and support roles throughout the world, all of these tough, speedy small boats were essential to the United States's ultimate victory.

From the launching of one of the first US Navy torpedo boats, the USS *Rowan*, in 1896 to the Coast Guard's Response Boat–Medium (RB-M) by Kvichak Marine in 2008, innovative Puget Sound boat builders have developed a significant share of the nation's fast patrol and rescue craft. Throughout this period, a full array of the nation's major patrol craft, including those of the Navy, Coast Guard, Army, and Air Force, has also operated on the sound. This important but little-known aspect of regional military maritime history is recorded in these pages.

This historical narrative of patrol and rescue boats is interrupted by the personal story of the rescue, restoration, and operation of one particular boat, the World War II–era Coast Guard CG-83527. The 83-foot-long boat, which served in Tacoma, Washington, and south Puget Sound from 1945 to 1962, was rediscovered in 2003 by Dan Withers, president of the nonprofit Combatant Craft of America, and his wife, Roxane. The boat is a surviving, important part of Pacific Northwest military maritime history. She is the last of the wooden Coast Guard cutters in military configuration and has an iconic place in both the region's and the nation's patrol boat history.

For the most part, the history of military patrol and rescue boats in the nation and Puget Sound has been hidden and unknown. This book, in factual narrative and rare, often dramatic images, seeks to reveal this fascinating story. It is a wartime and peacetime saga about the boats, their crewmembers, the boat builders, and those who restore, operate, and exhibit these proud vessels that symbolize the nation's fighting spirit of freedom.

One

Beginnings

Patrolling the Sound

Although the initial US Navy presence on Puget Sound began in 1841 with the arrival of Lt. Charles Wilkes's US Exploring Expedition fleet of sailing ships, it was not until 1898 that the first steam-powered patrol boat was built and operated on the sound's inland waters.

Because the nation expanded geographically from the Atlantic to the Pacific coast, enemy threats to the eastern seaboard from Europe in the late 1700s and throughout the 1800s drove earlier patrol boat development and operation. The first fast, smaller steam-powered patrol craft were designed, built, and placed in service on the east coast. Only later would these boats be constructed and operated by the Navy and Coast Guard on the more distant west coast, considered less vulnerable.

Two steam-driven torpedo boats, capable of a top speed of 27 knots (31 miles per hour), became the first patrol boats constructed and used in the Pacific Northwest. In 1898, the USS *Rowan*, Torpedo Boat No. 8, was built by Moran Brothers Company in Seattle, and the USS *Goldsbrough*, Torpedo Boat No. 20, was constructed by Wolff and Zwicher Iron Works in Portland, Oregon, in 1899. After commissioning and intermittent patrol duties off the Pacific coast from the Spanish-American War period up to World War I, they had both become obsolete, and were decommissioned and scrapped by 1919.

During the pre–World War I period and through the war, most patrol boats in Puget Sound were assigned to the US Revenue Cutter Service, which in 1915 became the Coast Guard. Instead of purpose-built military vessels, most were tugboats and fishing boats acquired and refitted for military service. In Puget Sound patrol boat history, the early Navy torpedo boats and adapted Coast Guard patrol vessels provided an important foundation for the innovative design, engineering, construction, and operational era ahead.

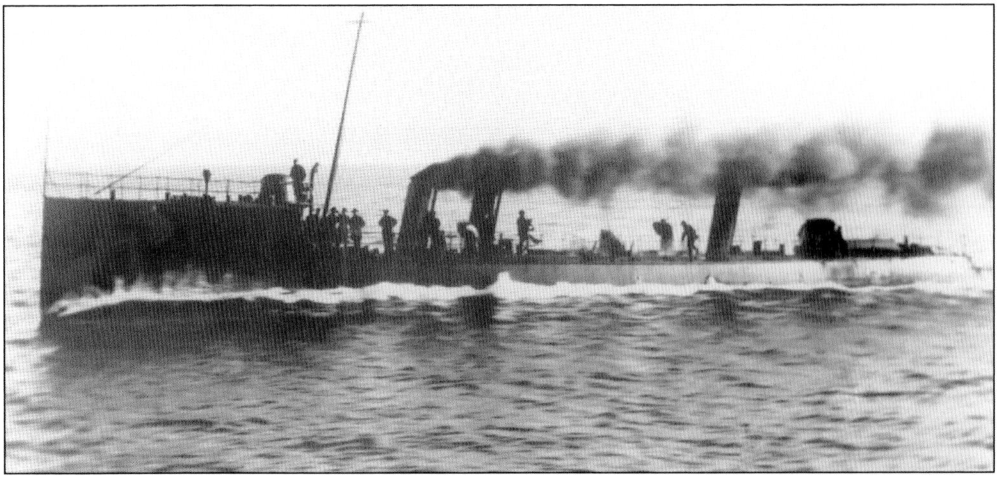

Patrol Steamer. Pictured above at high speed during sea trials on Puget Sound is the US Navy's USS *Rowan* (Torpedo Boat No. 8). Construction began in 1896, and she was launched in 1898. A large vessel at 170 feet long, the *Rowan* was the first steam-powered patrol boat built in the Puget Sound region. She was decommissioned soon after launching and assigned to Bremerton until called to active duty in 1908. The photograph below shows the vessel, also known as a torpedo boat destroyer, during a training run off the California coast about 1910 when assigned to the 3rd Torpedo Flotilla at Mare Island. She patrolled the Pacific coast from the Canadian border to Magdalena Bay, Mexico, for four years until decommissioned in 1912 and later sold for scrapping. (Above, courtesy Museum of History and Industry, MOHAI, Seattle, Puget Sound Maritime Historical Society, PSMHS Collection No. 10342; below, courtesy John Shaw, USS Rowan Reunion Association.)

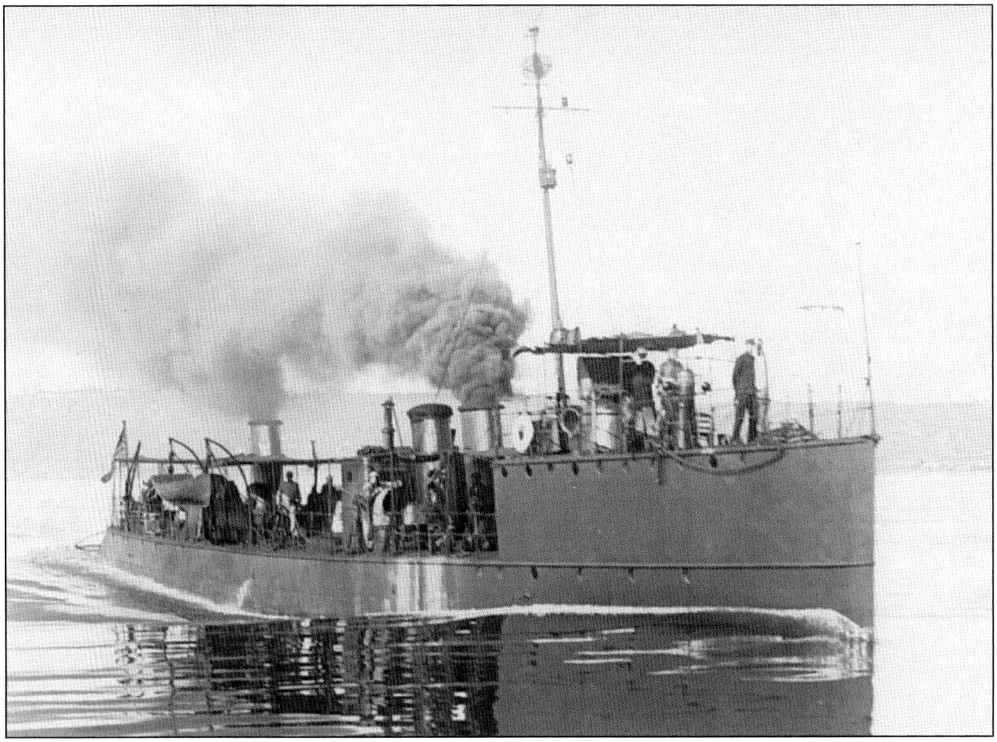

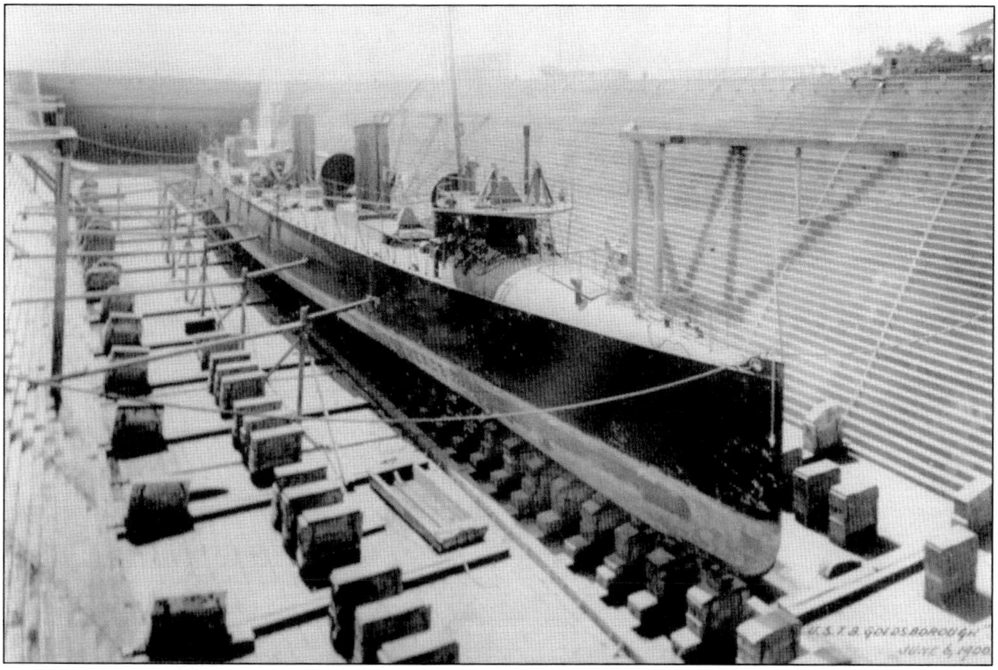

Torpedo Boat Too. Another early patrol boat, the USS *Goldsborough* (Torpedo Boat No. 20), also had a Pacific Northwest connection. Named after a Navy admiral and built by the Wolf & Zwicker Iron Works in Portland, Oregon, the *Goldsborough* was launched in 1899 and commissioned in 1908. She was based in San Diego and patrolled the coast of California and Mexico for six years until 1914. The torpedo boat was assigned to the Oregon State Naval Militia at Portland from 1914 to 1917 and then fully commissioned again for Pacific coast patrol duties during World War I. The *Goldsborough* is pictured below after decommissioning at the Puget Sound Navy Yard in Bremerton in 1919; she was scrapped soon after. (Above, courtesy NavSource; below, courtesy Puget Sound Navy Museum.)

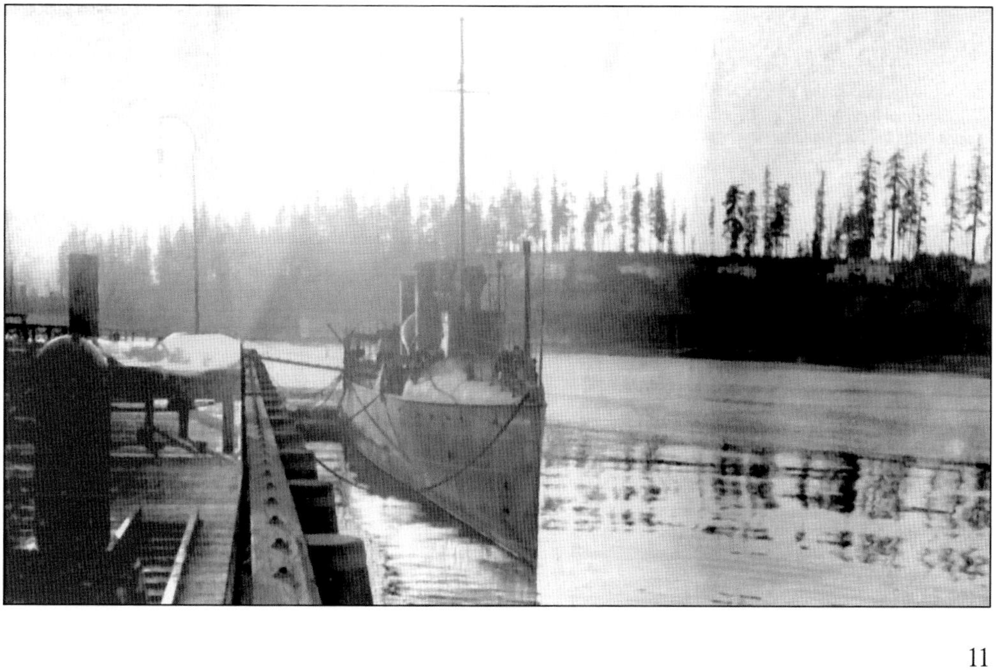

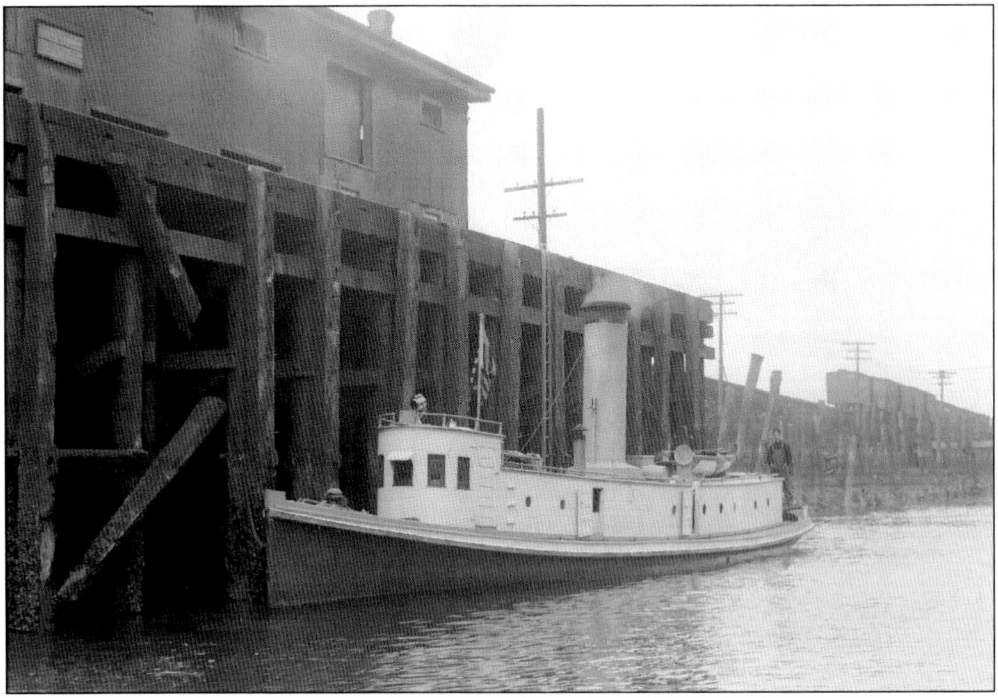

On Guard. The 65-foot-long *Guard* (pictured here) and the *Scout* were early US Revenue Cutter Service small patrol boats, both commissioned in 1896. The *Guard* patrolled Puget Sound waters from her station in Port Townsend and was assigned as a tender to the cutter *Grant*. After a grounding accident, she was decommissioned in 1912. (Courtesy Museum of History and Industry, Seattle, PSMHS Collection.)

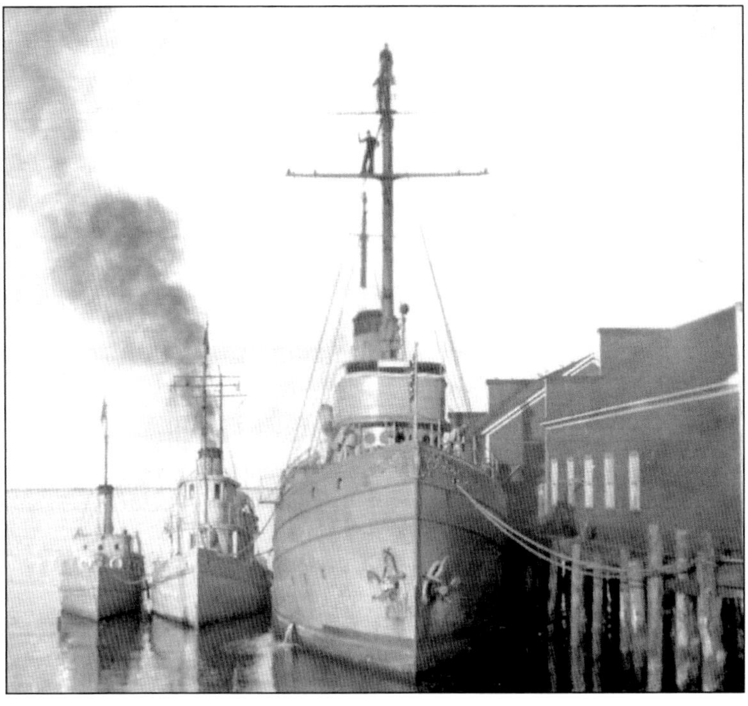

Rafted Revenuers. Three vessels of the US Revenue Cutter Service fleet are moored together in the early 1900s on Puget Sound. At left is the *Scout*, built in 1896; the long-serving cutter *Arcata* is in the center; and the 152-foot cutter *Snohomish* is at right. The *Snohomish*, built in 1908 and powered by a triple-expansion steam engine, made many significant rescues during her 26-year active-duty career. (Courtesy Coast Guard Museum Northwest.)

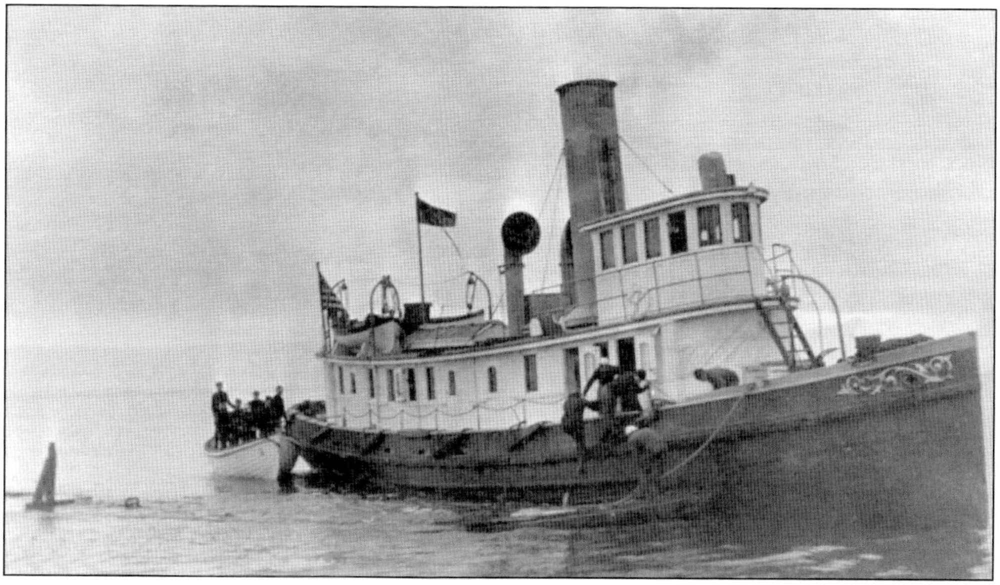

Cutter Crewmen Rescued. Crewmen from the 54-foot gasoline freighter *Rene* are pictured as they are rescued and assisted aboard the *Arcata* in January 1912. The disabled *Rene* capsized and sank off the Dungeness Spit while being towed by the *Snohomish*. The well-known 85-foot *Arcata* was built in San Francisco in 1903 and had a long Puget Sound and Pacific Northwest career before being decommissioned in 1936. (Courtesy Coast Guard Museum Northwest.)

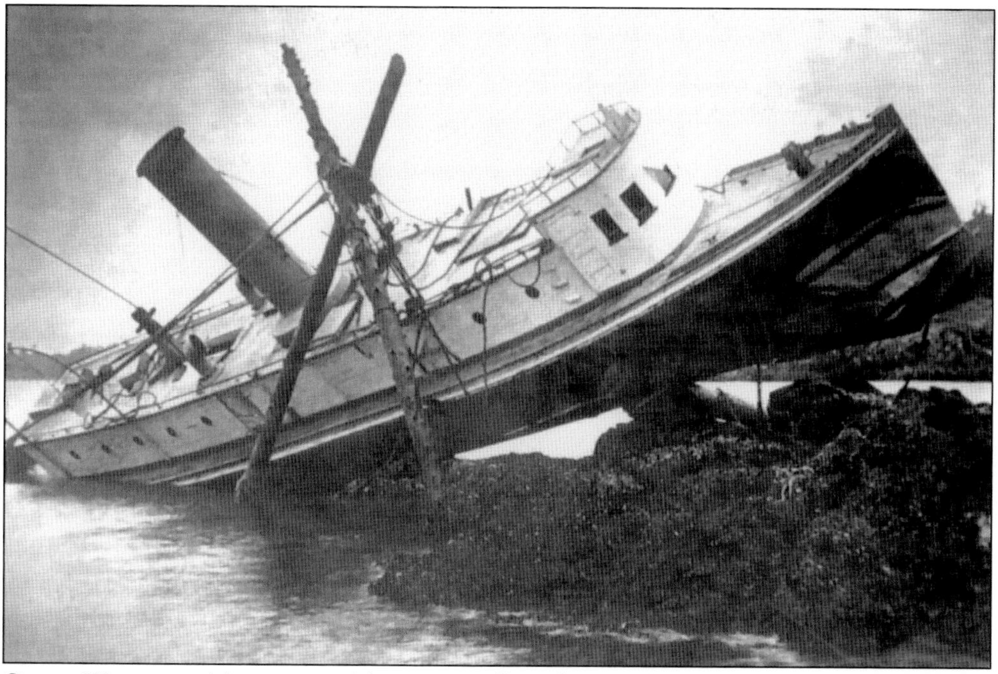

Guard Wrecked. After serving 16 years patrolling the sound, the *Guard* met a sad end when she was wrecked on the rocks at San Juan Island in 1912, decommissioned, sold, and replaced by another Revenue Service cutter of the same name. However, the wrecked 1896 *Guard* was refloated and rebuilt and became the commercial passenger and freight steamer *Georgia*. (Courtesy Coast Guard Museum Northwest.)

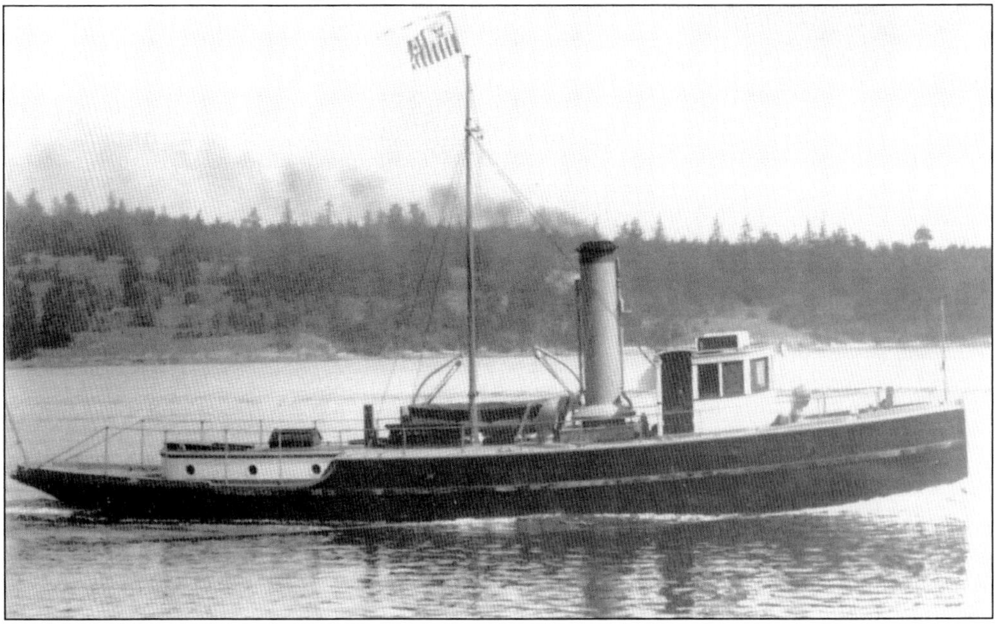

NEW *GUARD*. A new patrol boat named *Guard*, above, was commissioned by the Revenue Cutter Service in 1913. Sixty-seven feet long, the replacement vessel was powered by an oil-fired, triple-expansion steam engine that gave the small cutter a maximum speed of 10 knots. The *Guard* was stationed in Friday Harbor and later Seattle and served 40 years on Puget Sound before being decommissioned by the Coast Guard in 1943. (Courtesy Coast Guard Museum Northwest.)

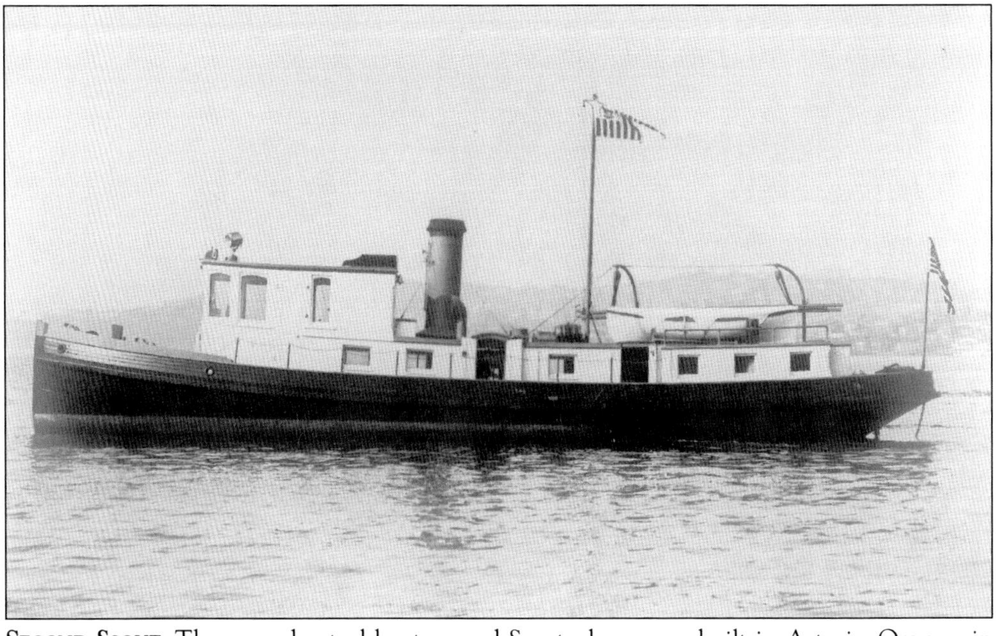

SECOND *SCOUT*. The second patrol boat named *Scout*, above, was built in Astoria, Oregon, in 1903, acquired by the Revenue Cutter Service from the Customs Service in 1914, and transferred to Seattle. The 61-foot vessel had a gasoline engine and carried a crew of six when she patrolled the waters of Puget Sound. *Scout* was decommissioned in 1930. (Courtesy US Coast Guard Historian's Office.)

Two

Prohibition through World War II 1920–1945

The post–World War I development of patrol and rescue boats nationally and on Puget Sound was driven more by US social and economic interests than military considerations. Promoted by increasingly pervasive temperance movements that began before the American Revolution, the 18th Amendment to the US Constitution was passed, and the Volstead Act was then approved by Congress to implement it. The act, prohibiting the production, distribution, sale, import and export, and consumption of alcoholic beverages, did more to accelerate the design and construction of fast patrol boats than any war or other military conflict. The nation's five-year-old Coast Guard was given the daunting responsibility of enforcing the new law at sea and stemming the tide of liquor smuggling, more popularly known as rum-running.

Because it needed faster small craft to patrol coastal areas and intercept high-powered rumrunner boats, the Coast Guard expanded and sought new design and propulsion solutions for its new patrol boats.

Prohibition-driven innovations during the 1920s and 1930s and growing threats from Germany in Europe and Japan in the Far East would produce some of the most important developments in fast combat and rescue boat history. These breakthroughs would lead to the creation of PT boats for the Navy and other speedy patrol and rescue craft for the Navy, Coast Guard, and Army Air Force.

Among these iconic military craft operating in Puget Sound during World War II were the Coast Guard's widely produced 38-foot picket boats, more than 60 of which were built in the Seattle area, and 83-foot patrol boats assigned throughout the region toward the end of the war.

Although little known because of wartime national security and secrecy restrictions, Navy PT boats plied Puget Sound waters from 1942 to 1945. Also, 85-foot and 63-foot Army Air Force crash rescue boats operated in the sound during the war. Built in California, the 85-foot boats were refitted at a Seattle shipyard in 1944 and subsequently assigned to aircrew rescue service in Alaska.

Overall, the basic design, engineering, and construction standards that evolved from the Prohibition period and were improved before and during World War II set the stage for decades of subsequent patrol boat development. This major aspect of military maritime history is mirrored in regional applications on Puget Sound.

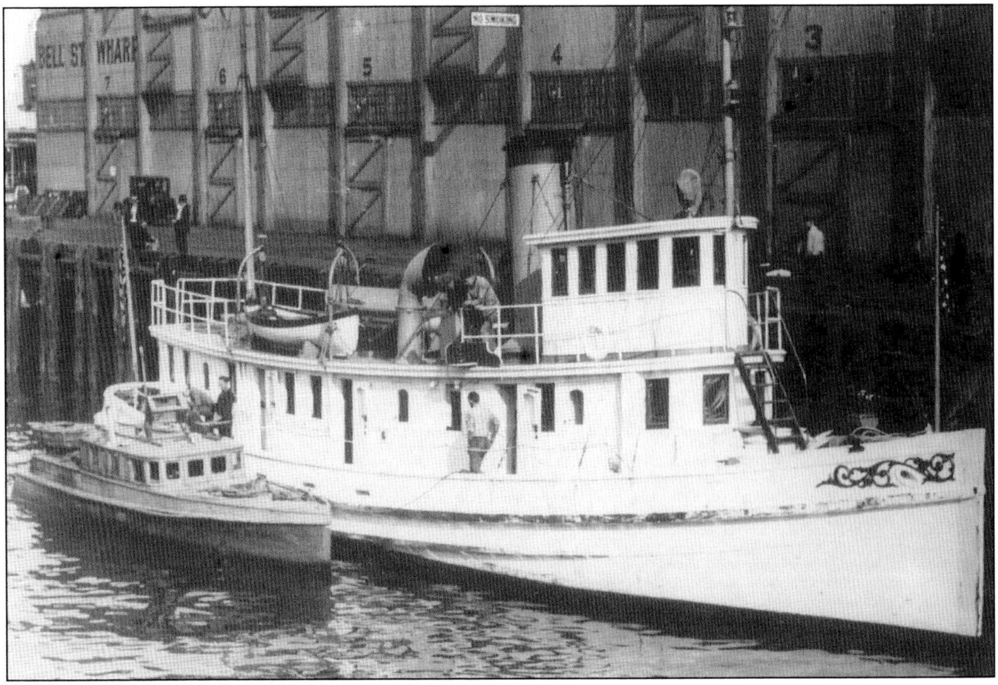

Revenue Cutter and Rumrunner. A seized rumrunner is pictured here rafted alongside the Revenue Cutter *Arcata* in Seattle. Although *Arcata*'s maximum speed of 11 knots (13 miles per hour) made chasing faster boats carrying illegal liquor a challenge, it was reported that her captain's masterful pursuit tactics more than made up for the difference. (Courtesy Coast Guard Historian's Office.)

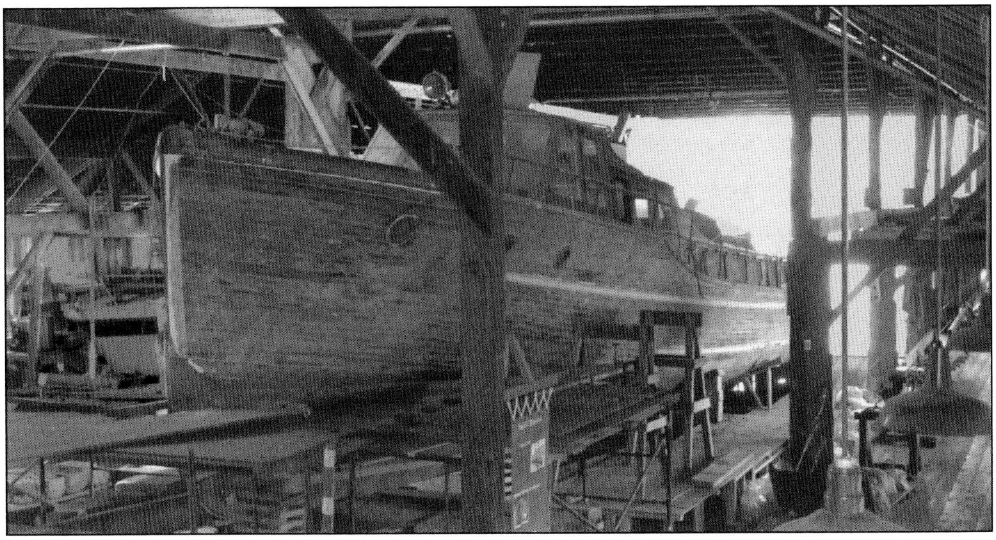

Rumrunner Under Restoration. The *Fleetwood*, shown here, is a Canadian-built rumrunner being restored at the Britannia Heritage Shipyard at Steveston Village in Richmond, British Columbia. Originally named *Skeezix*, the sleek 65-foot boat was built in Vancouver, British Columbia, in 1930, near the end of Prohibition. Built specifically to transport banned liquor across the US-Canadian border, she was powered by three engines, including twin 450-horsepower World War I Liberty aircraft power plants. (Photograph by Bryan Klassen, courtesy Britannia Heritage Shipyard.)

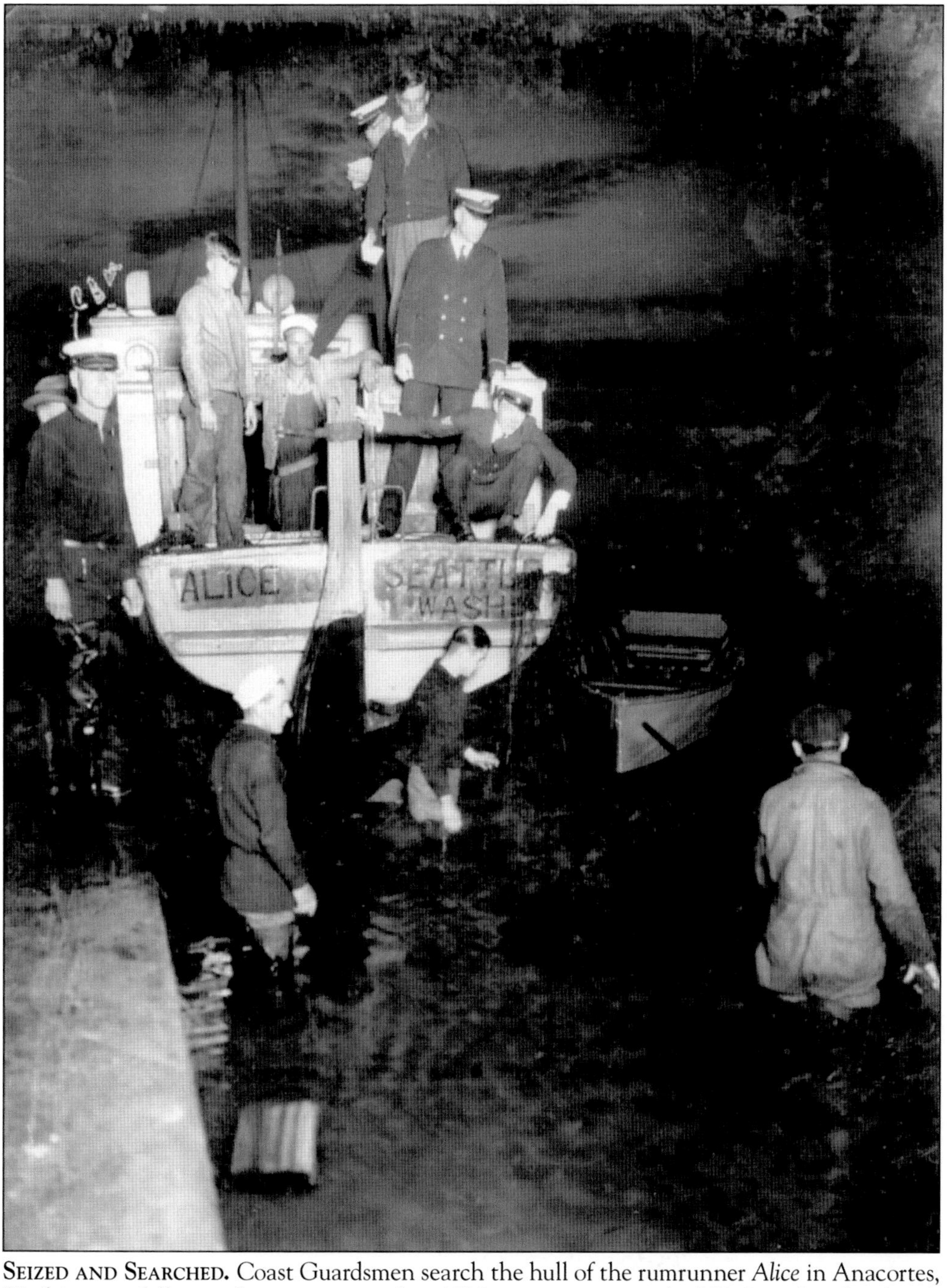

SEIZED AND SEARCHED. Coast Guardsmen search the hull of the rumrunner *Alice* in Anacortes, Washington, following her seizure in a late-1920s operation near the US-Canadian border. A unique vessel, the *Alice* was a converted former US Navy 50-foot motor sailer that had two special compartments built onto the hull below the water line to conceal shipments of prohibited liquor from Canada. (Courtesy Coast Guard Museum Northwest.)

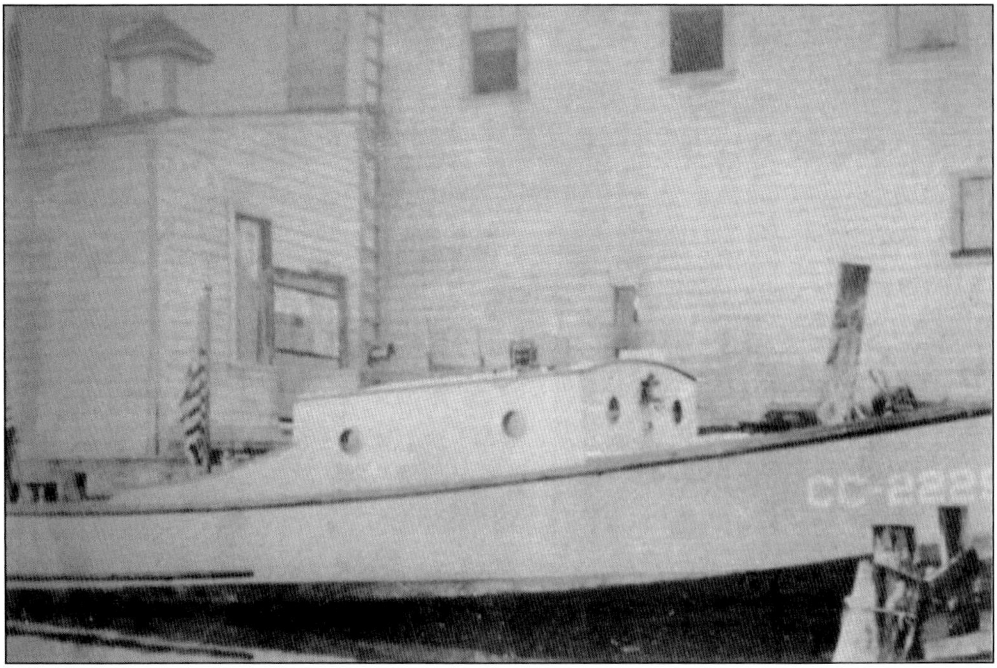

Cocky Picket Boat. Among the smaller Coast Guard patrol craft built to combat rumrunners during Prohibition was the 36-foot open-cabin picket boat shown here at the Puget Sound Navy Yard. The yard constructed three out of 30 of this type of picket boat, each powered by a six-cylinder gasoline engine of more than 150 horsepower, and capable of speeds up to 25 miles per hour. (Courtesy Coast Guard Museum Northwest.)

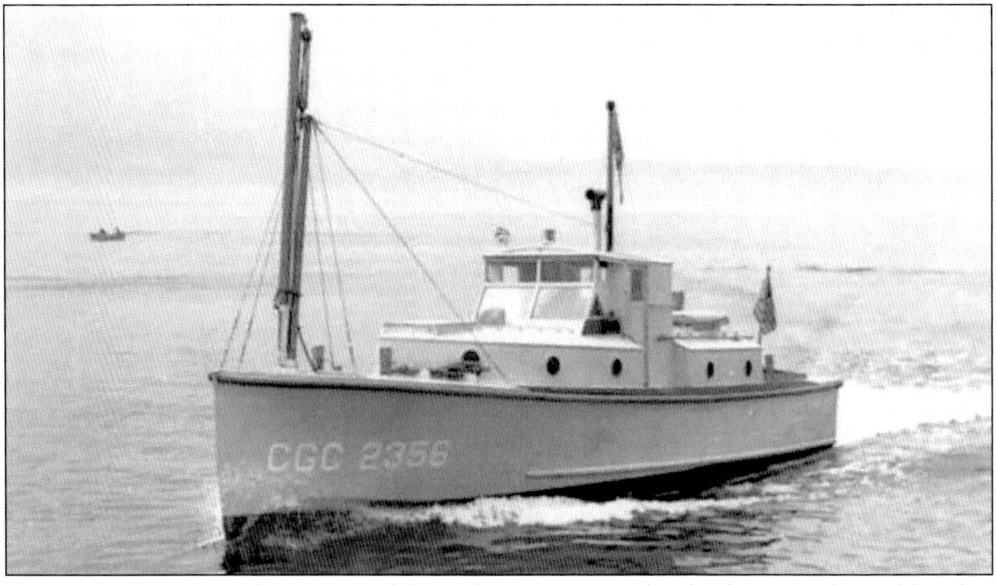

Double Trouble. Another version of the 36-foot Coast Guard picket boat was the double-cabin design, shown here with an enclosed bridge station. A total of 73 were built nationwide, including 10 at the Puget Sound Navy Yard. Powered by a similar six-cylinder gasoline engine, both models of these picket boats were based at Port Townsend to combat north Puget Sound rum-running. (Courtesy Coast Guard Museum Northwest.)

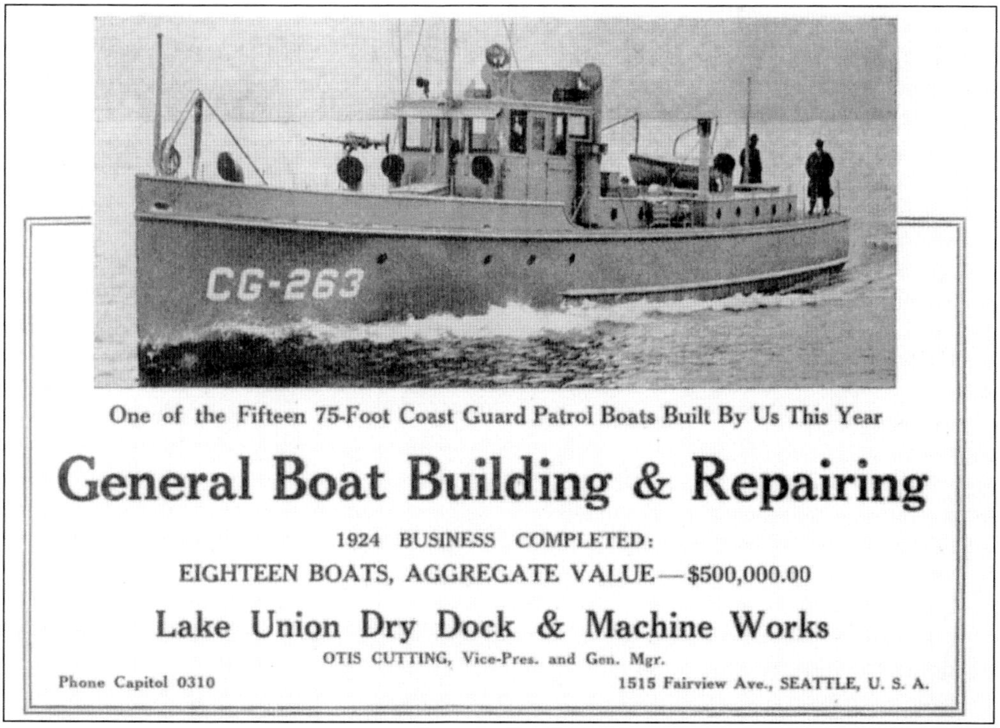

Advertising Achievement. A 1924 boating magazine advertisement for Lake Union Dry Dock & Machine Works in Seattle promotes achieving a proud production goal, building 18 total boats worth a half-million dollars, including 15 of the widely known 75-foot Coast Guard patrol craft. The backbone of the Prohibition-era patrol fleet, 203 of the so-called "Six Bitters" were built at boatyards across the nation. (Courtesy Mark Freeman Maritime Collection.)

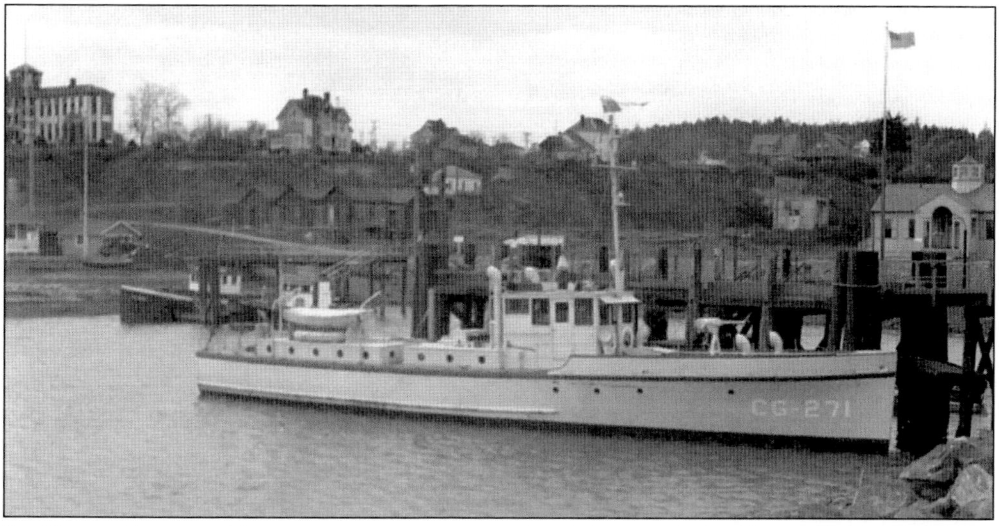

Six Bitter Station. Shown at its home station in Port Townsend, CG-271 was the ninth 75-foot patrol boat built for the Coast Guard by Lake Union Dry Dock in the mid-1920s. Powered by twin six-cylinder Sterling Viking gasoline engines of 400 horsepower each, they could reach a top speed of about 15 knots (17 miles per hour). These wooden vessels were durable and said to be relatively easy to maintain. (Courtesy Jefferson County Historical Society, No. 2.837.)

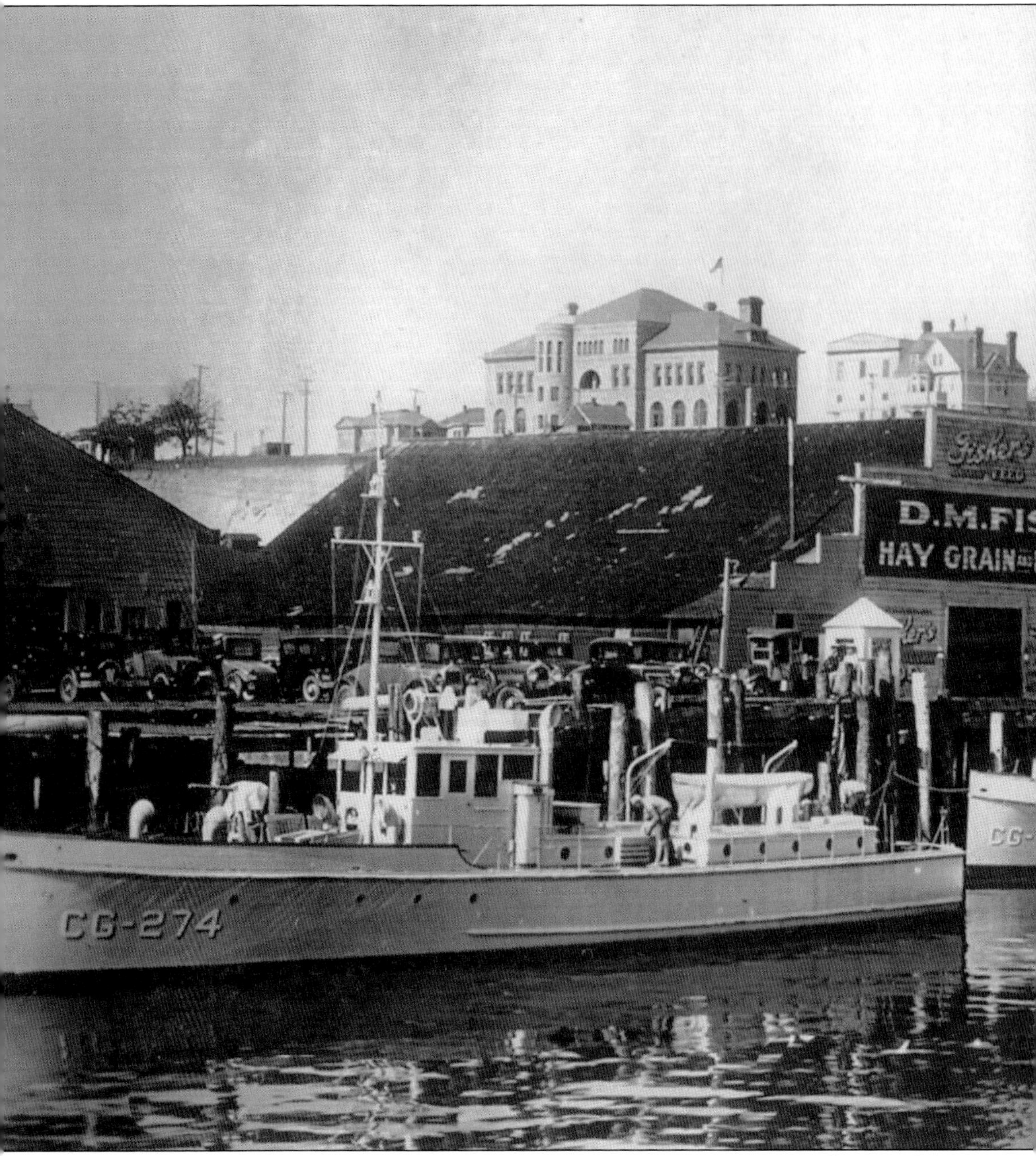

Formidable Fleet. The impressive Coast Guard fleet stationed at Port Townsend during Prohibition in the late 1920s is pictured at Fish's Dock on the downtown waterfront. Among the six patrol boats shown are three 75-footers at left and two enclosed double-cabin picket boats at far right. All were constructed by proud craftsmen in Puget Sound boatyards. Based at the entrance to Puget Sound, the fleet's craft as well as others patrolled west to Neah Bay and up to 20 miles offshore

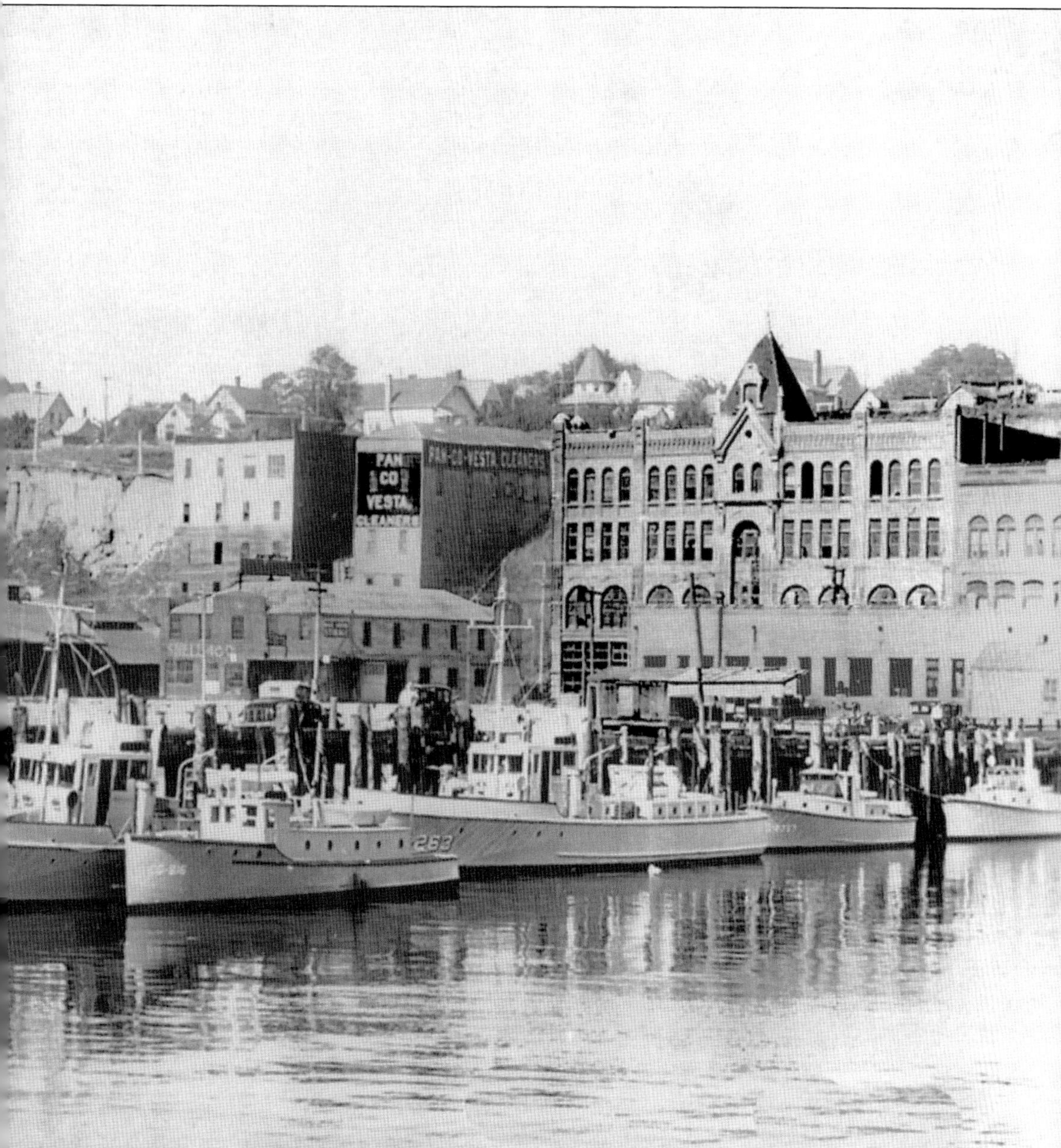

in the Pacific, through the San Juan Islands, and north to the Canadian border at Blaine. Some of the 75-footers served through World War II, but with the repeal of the 18th Amendment to the Constitution in 1933 and the end of Prohibition, most were sold by the federal government as surplus property. (Courtesy Jefferson County Historical Society, No. 2.41.)

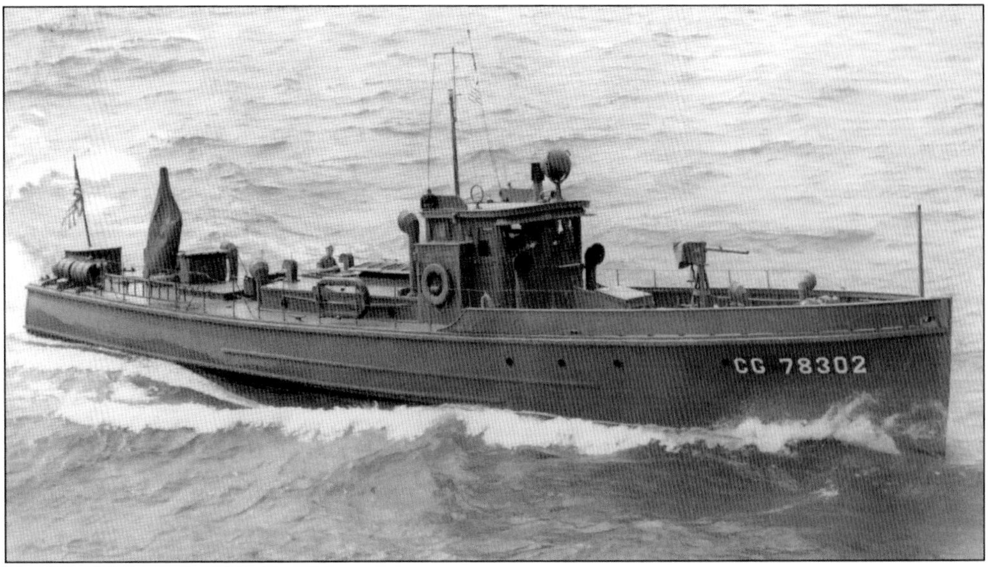

Wartime Profile. The 78-foot Coast Guard patrol boat that became the Tacoma Sea Scouts' *Charles N. Curtis* is shown in her World War II paint scheme. Before and during the war, she patrolled Puget Sound and also coastal Washington State from Port Angeles in the north to the Columbia River in the south. While in wartime service, she was armed with a .50-caliber machinegun, a one-pounder cannon, and two depth charge tracks. (Courtesy Tom Rogers, Sea Scout Ship 110.)

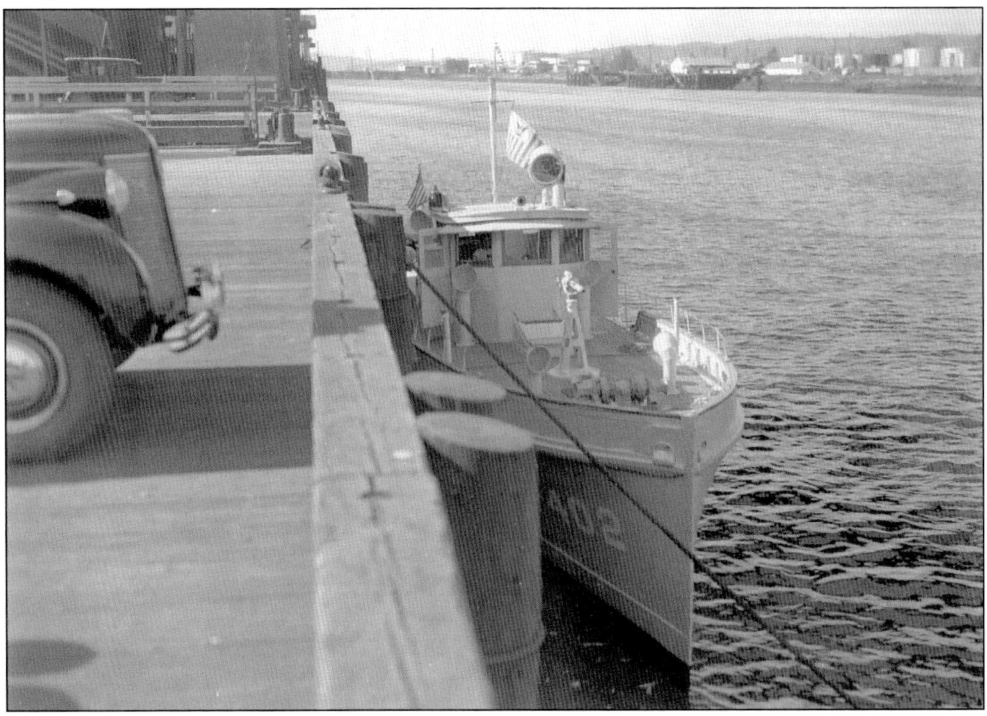

Pre-War in Tacoma. Built in Newport News, Virginia, and commissioned in 1931 to combat rum-running on the Atlantic coast, the then-numbered CG-402 was transferred to the Pacific Northwest for patrol duties in 1936. She is shown here in 1937 moored at the Coast Guard base at the Tacoma Municipal Dock on the City Waterway. (Courtesy Tom Rogers, Sea Scout Ship 110.)

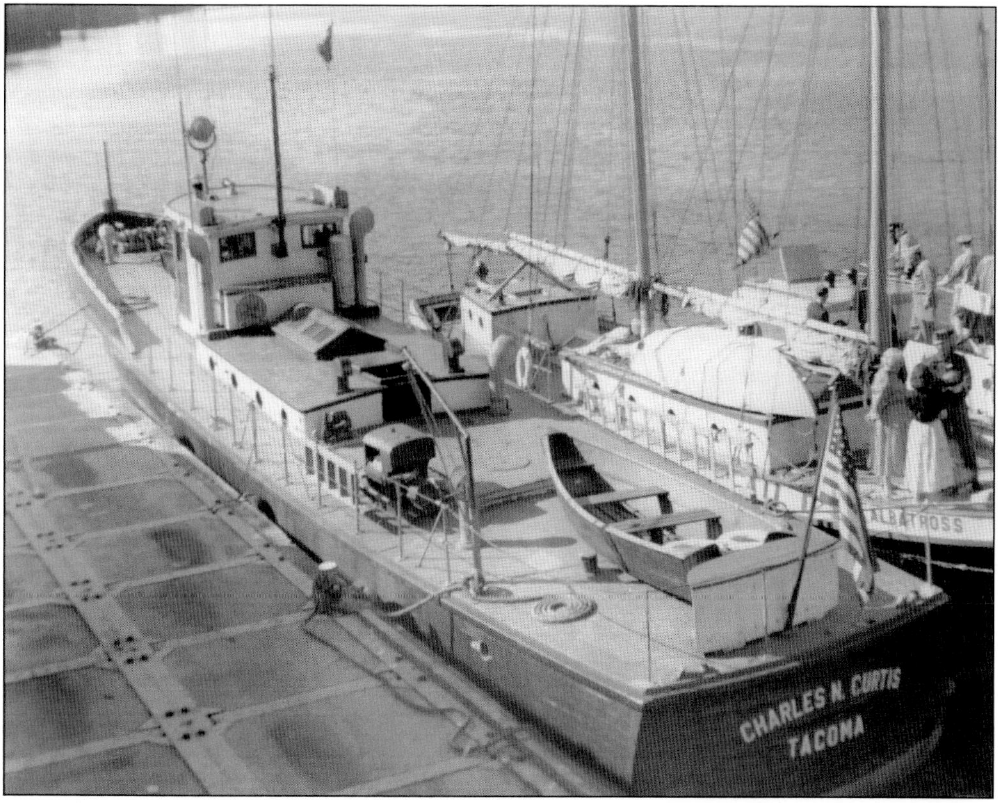

Early Sea Scout Days. At the end of the war, the newly numbered CG-78302 was decommissioned and acquired by the Mount Rainier Council of the Boy Scouts of America and assigned to its Tacoma Sea Scout unit. Renamed the *Charles N. Curtis* for the council's executive, she is shown here at the Sea Scout base at the Navy Reserve center on the Hylebos Waterway in 1948. (Courtesy Tom Rogers, Sea Scout Ship 110.)

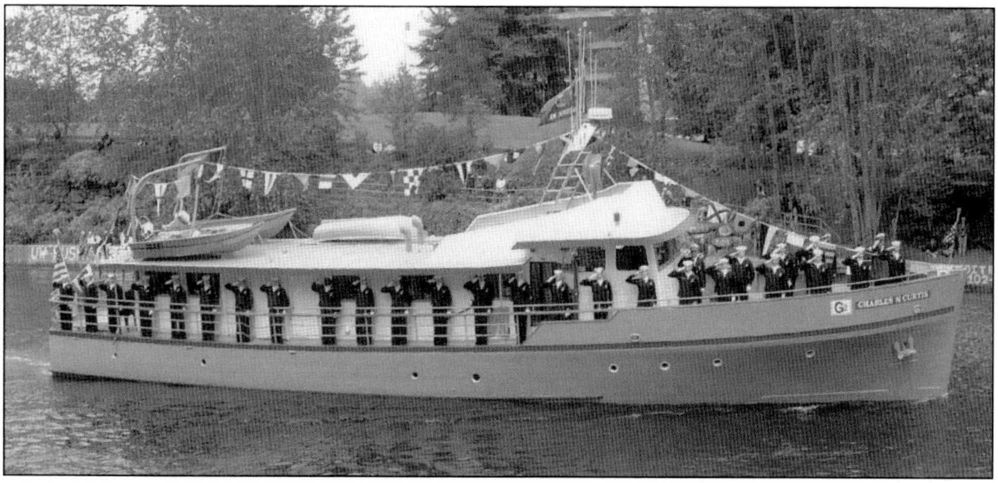

Opening Day Pride. The Sea Scout crew of the *Charles N. Curtis* is pictured lining the rail at attention during the Seattle Yacht Club's opening-day event in May 2005. The *Curtis* has been a perennial seamanship award winner at community festivities in Tacoma, Seattle, and throughout the Puget Sound region. (Courtesy Tom Rogers, Sea Scout Ship 110.)

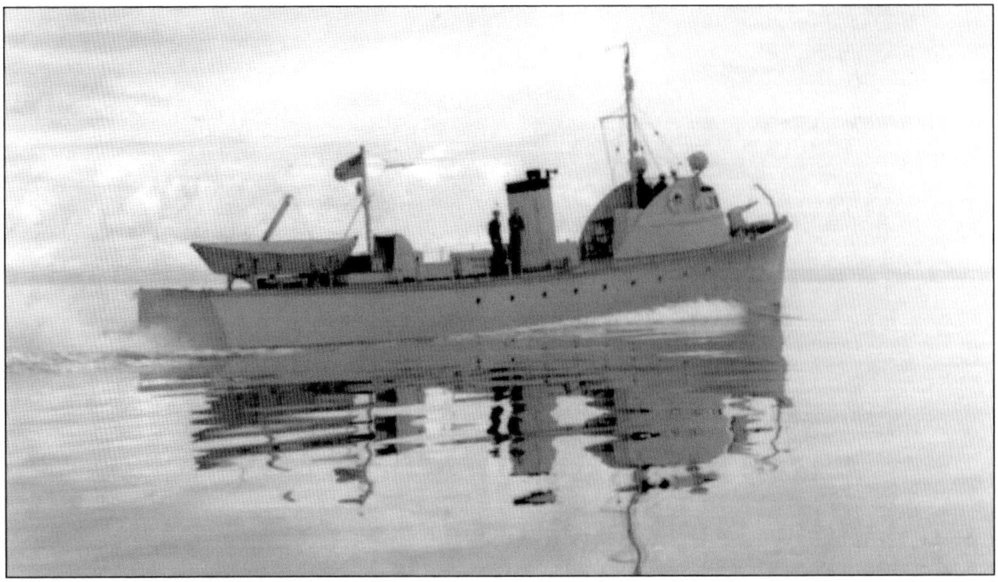

PLACID WATER PATROL. One of two 80-foot Coast Guard patrol craft assigned to Puget Sound before and during World War II is shown at slow speed and on calm waters. Nine of these vessels were built in 1937 at boatyards in Florida, Massachusetts, and California. Each of the boats constructed on the Pacific coast cost $55,000, including the hull, superstructure, and engines. (Courtesy Coast Guard Museum Northwest.)

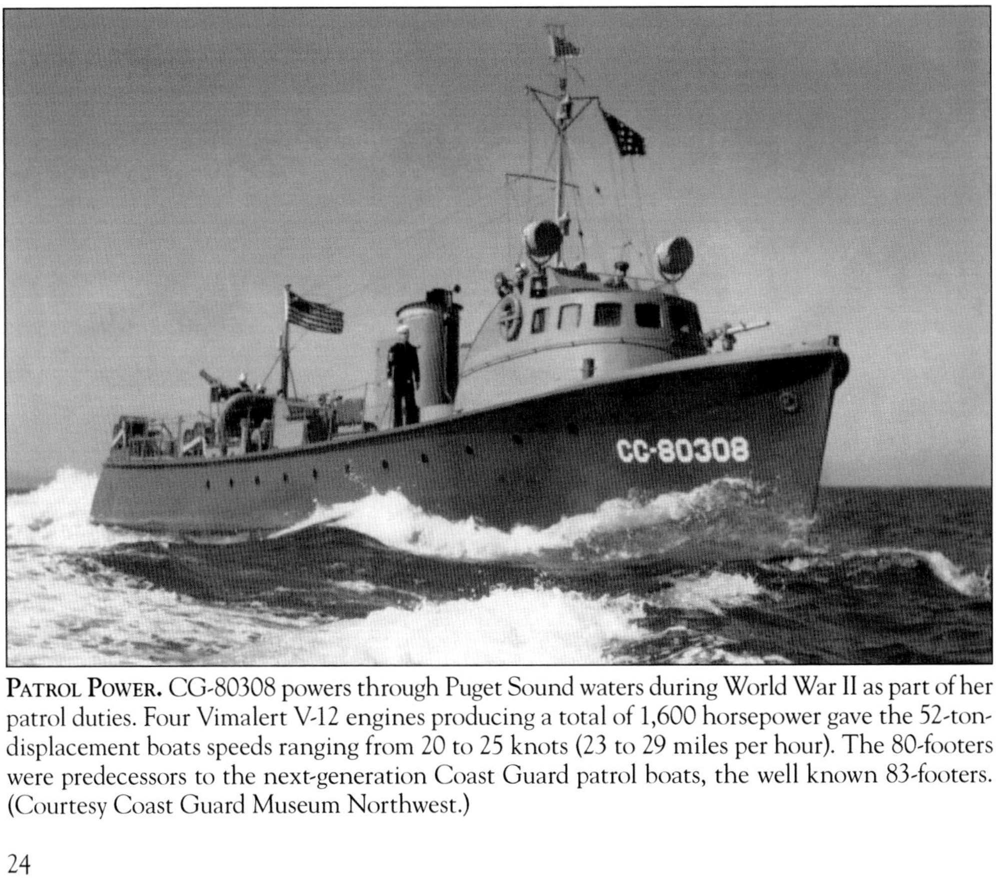

PATROL POWER. CG-80308 powers through Puget Sound waters during World War II as part of her patrol duties. Four Vimalert V-12 engines producing a total of 1,600 horsepower gave the 52-ton-displacement boats speeds ranging from 20 to 25 knots (23 to 29 miles per hour). The 80-footers were predecessors to the next-generation Coast Guard patrol boats, the well known 83-footers. (Courtesy Coast Guard Museum Northwest.)

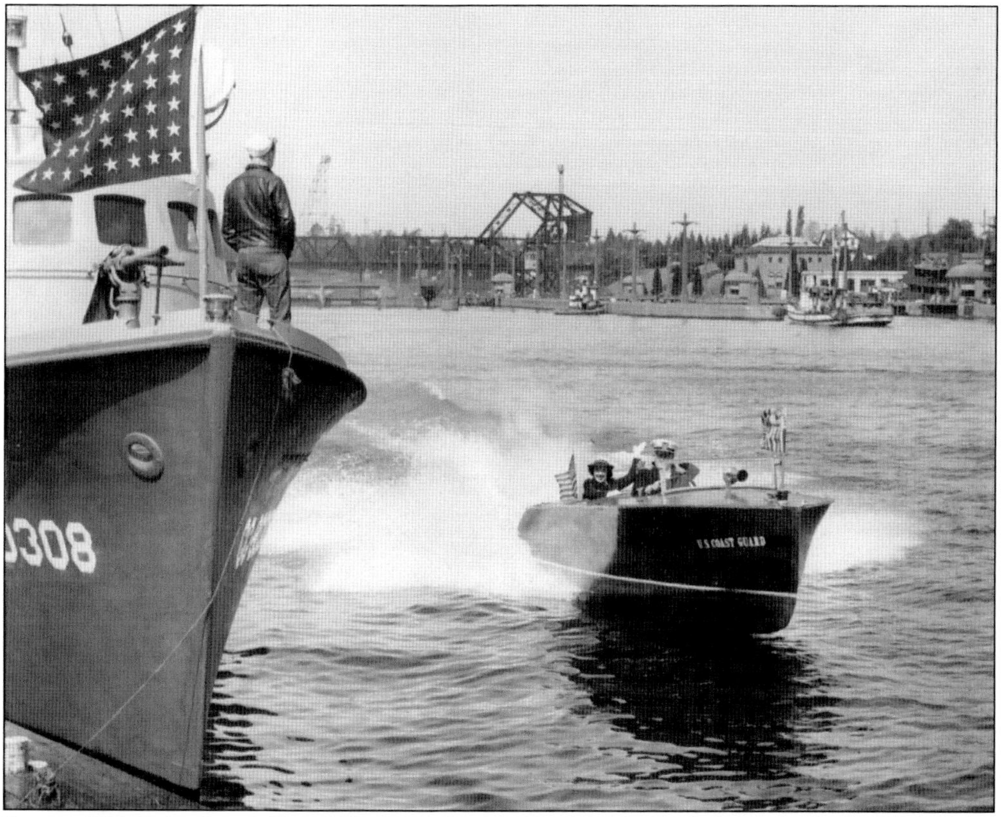

Speedy SPAR. In this publicity photograph, a Coast Guard speedboat carried a waving SPAR, a member of the service's World War II women's unit, as part of a wartime recruiting program. As more and more Coast Guardsmen were needed as frontline vessel crewmen and for shoreside duties, women were actively recruited for key support roles on the home front. (Courtesy Coast Guard Museum Northwest.)

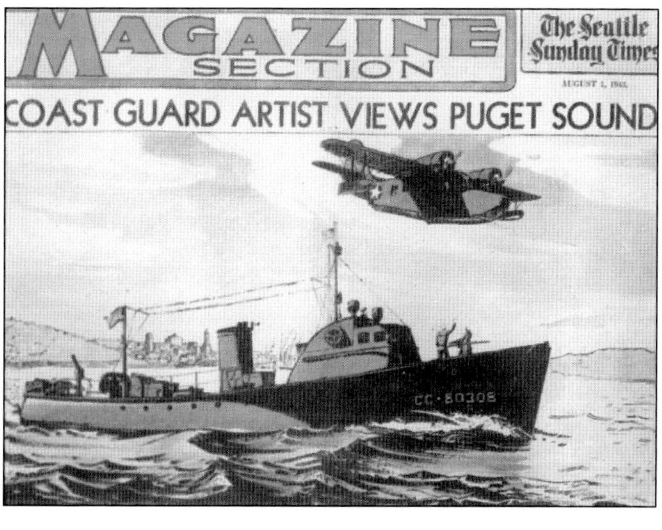
MAGAZINE SECTION

The Seattle Sunday Times

COAST GUARD ARTIST VIEWS PUGET SOUND

Active-Duty Artist. In 1943, during the mid-point of World War II, the *Seattle Times* published a full-page article prepared by Coast Guard staff and illustrated by a talented service member, Seaman Ken Riley. Here he depicts an 80-foot patrol boat on Seattle's Elliott Bay in the foreground and a Grumman JRF Goose amphibious patrol plane flying overhead. (Courtesy Coast Guard Museum Northwest.)

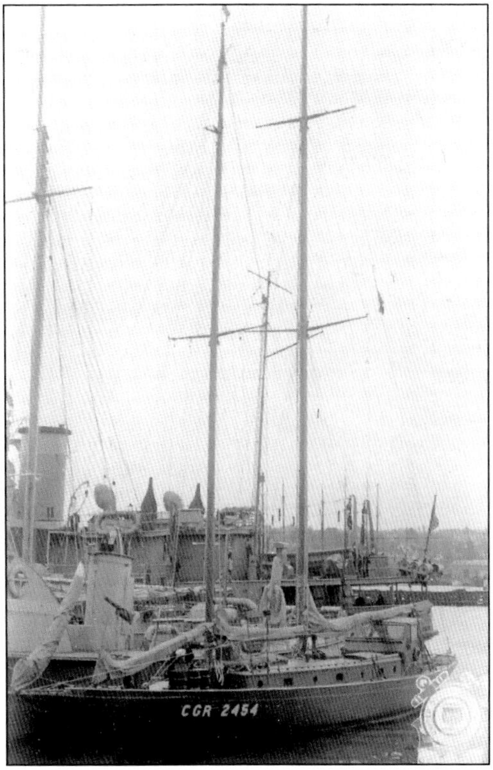

Sailboat Security. Among the many civilian vessels brought into Coast Guard Reserve patrol service during World War II through federal emergency legislation was the schooner *Red Jacket*, shown here in the foreground as CGR-2454. Owned, restored, and sailed as of 2010 by Terry and Renee Paine of Tacoma, during the war, the classic wooden sailboat was stationed at Friday Harbor and patrolled the waters around the San Juan Islands. (Courtesy National Archives, Alaska Pacific Region, Seattle.)

Ferry Lane Patrol. With a Black Ball Line ferry in the background, the former motor yacht *Dunlin* (CGR-777) is shown painted gray and patrolling a Puget Sound ferry lane near Seattle early in the war. Following the attack on Pearl Harbor by the Japanese and the resulting fear of invasion of the Pacific coast, the Coast Guard quickly supplemented its limited active-duty fleet in Puget Sound with many types of civilian craft. (Courtesy Coast Guard Museum Northwest.)

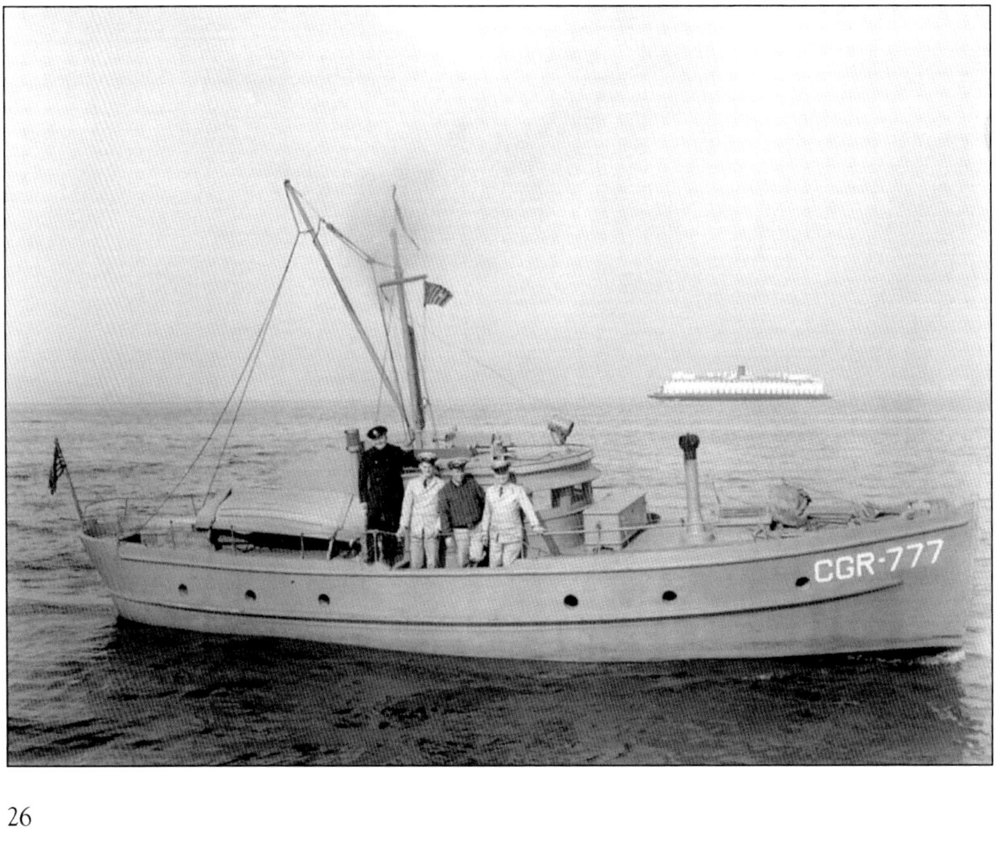

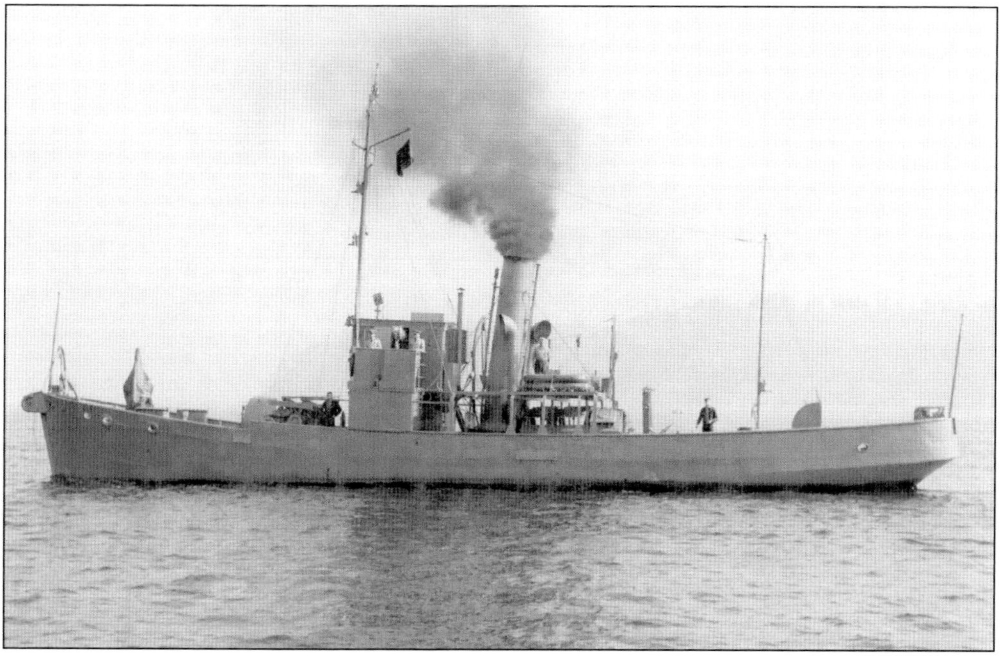

Converted Whaling Boat. One of the most unusual conversions of a commercial vessel to a Coast Guard patrol boat was the charter and refitting of the 103-foot, steam-powered whale-chaser *Caddo*, originally named *Tyee Junior*. Built in 1907 by Seattle's Moran Brothers shipyard, the fast, maneuverable whaler is shown in Puget Sound in March 1943 before her reassignment to patrol duties in Alaska. (Courtesy US Coast Guard Historian's Office.)

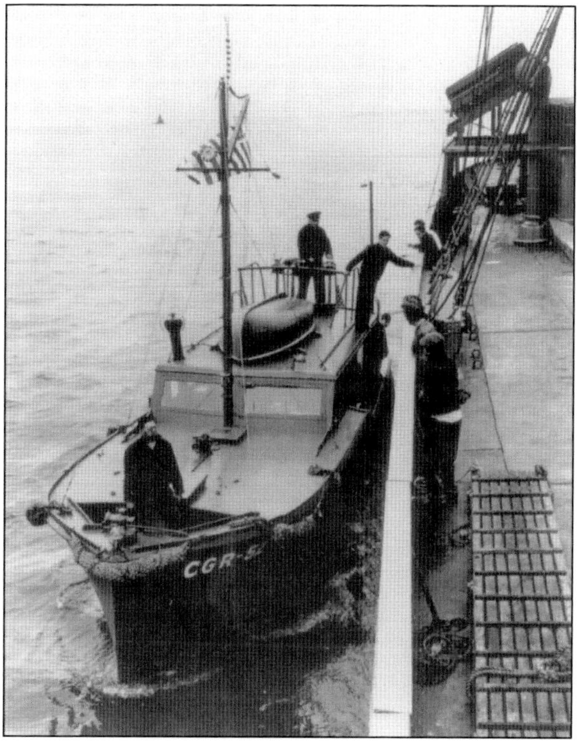

Wartime Boarding. A key responsibility of Coast Guard Reserve crews and vessels during World War II was boarding any recreational or commercial vessel suspected of illegal activity. Here a reserve-duty motor yacht comes alongside a commercial ship in Puget Sound to inspect her manifest and cargo. As boatyards supplied more purpose-built patrol boats to the Coast Guard by mid-1943, most of the emergency-acquired Coast Guard Reserve and Auxiliary craft were returned to their owners. (Courtesy Coast Guard Museum Northwest.)

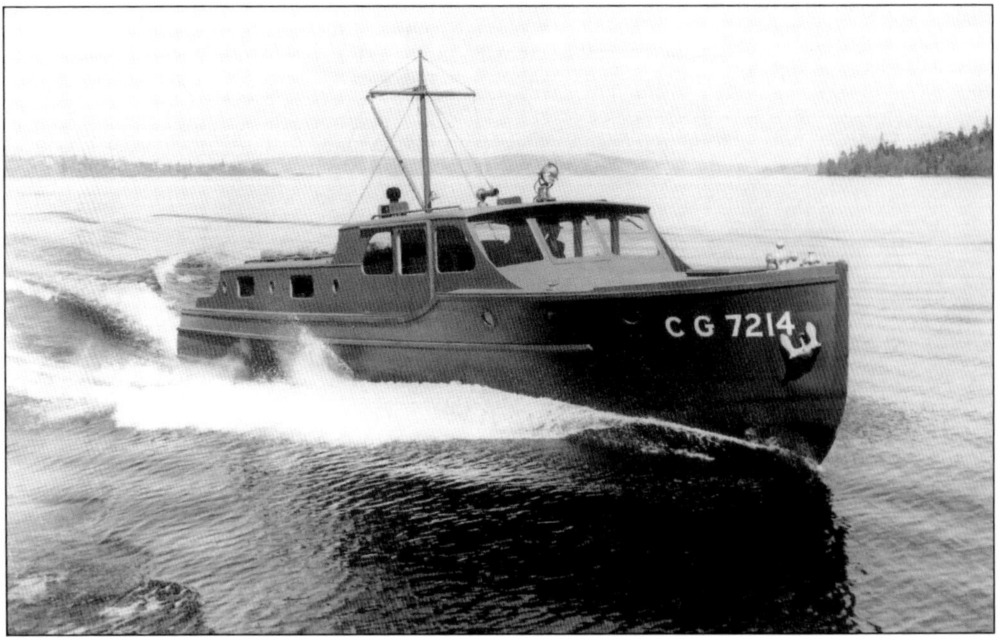

SEATTLE-BUILT BOATS. The World War II 50-foot Coast Guard harbor patrol boats were a Pacific Northwest phenomenon; all 54 were built by different Seattle yards. Above, CG-7214, built by Olsen & Winge Marine Works, demonstrates the 17-knot (20 miles per hour) capability of these craft, while the two boats below show the power of their twin 140-horsepower Chrysler Royal gasoline marine engines. Constructed of wood, the boats used durable red cedar above the waterline and white cedar below. In addition to Olsen & Winge, five other companies received federal contracts to build the boats beginning in 1943: Shain Manufacturing, Washington Boat Works, Barbee Marine Yard, Jensen Motorboat Company, and Grandy Boat Works. (Above, courtesy MOHAI, No. 1972.5503.69; below, No. 1972.5503.68.)

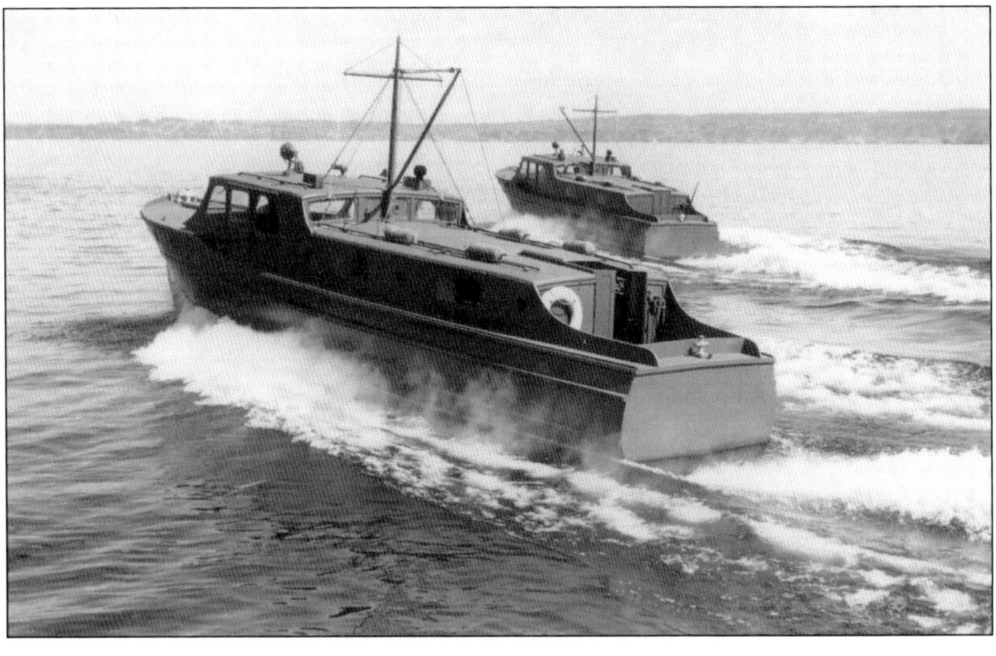

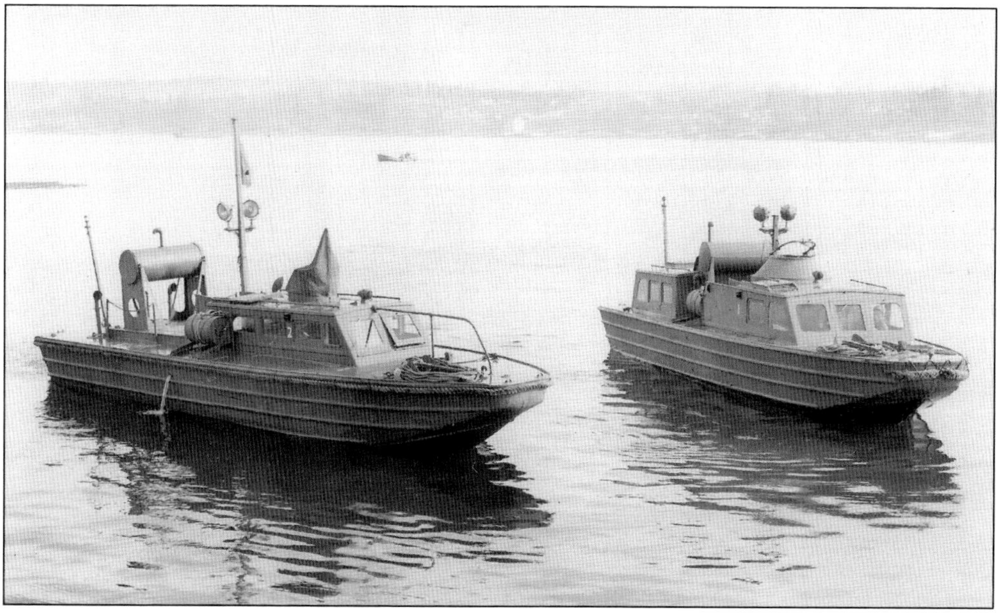

Shipyard Sisters. Two types of craft patrolled the water perimeter of the Puget Sound Navy Yard during World War II. The smaller of the two types, shown above, were the machinegun-armed 36-foot utility patrol boats built by Higgins Industries, Inc., which also produced the well-known LCVP landing craft and PT boats. Called "J" boats, they were used for near-shore patrol duties on Bremerton's Sinclair Inlet. In addition PSNS converted a venerable, 1920s–1930s 75-foot Coast Guard boat to YP-7, which guarded battleships and other major Navy vessels under repair or construction at the shipyard. (Both courtesy Puget Sound Navy Museum.)

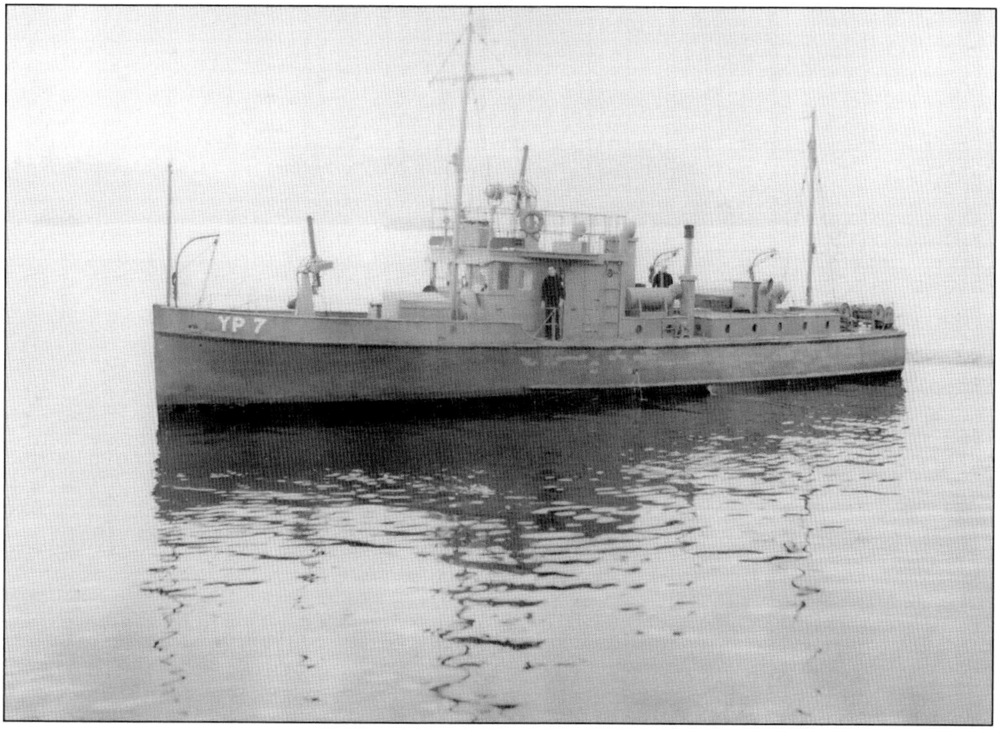

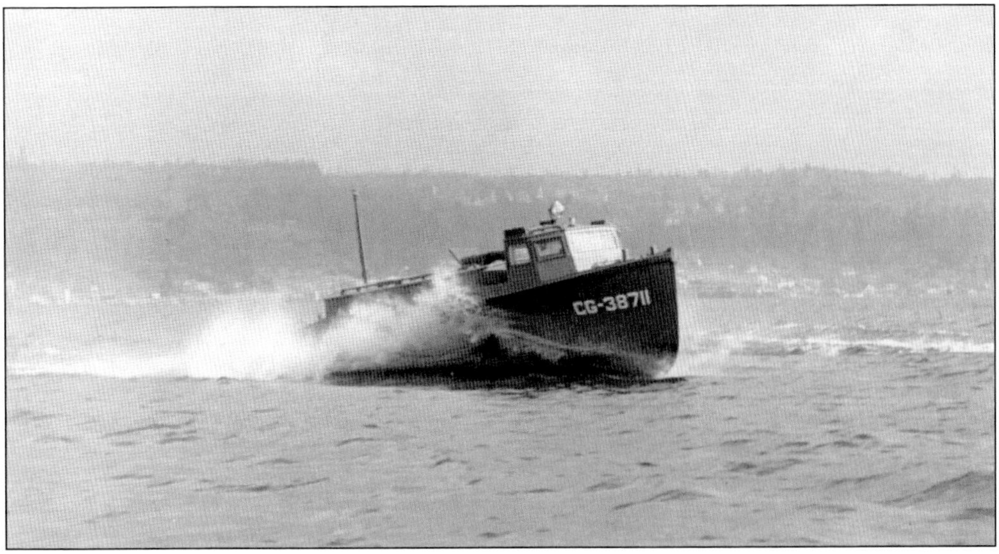

Picket Boat Production. The Ballinger Boat Works of Kirkland, near Seattle, also known as Kirkland Marine Construction, was the third largest producer of 38-foot Coast Guard cabin picket boats during World War II. Shown above on sea trials in Lake Washington is CG-38711, the 14th boat off the production line, pictured below. The Ballinger-built boats were powered by 225-horsepower Kermath gasoline engines, which produced speeds from 15 to 20 knots (17 to 23 miles per hour). The reliable 38-footers performed harbor patrol duties on waterways throughout the nation, and many Ballinger-built craft were assigned to Coast Guard bases throughout the Puget Sound region. (Courtesy Kirkland Heritage Society, Philip F. Toman Collection.)

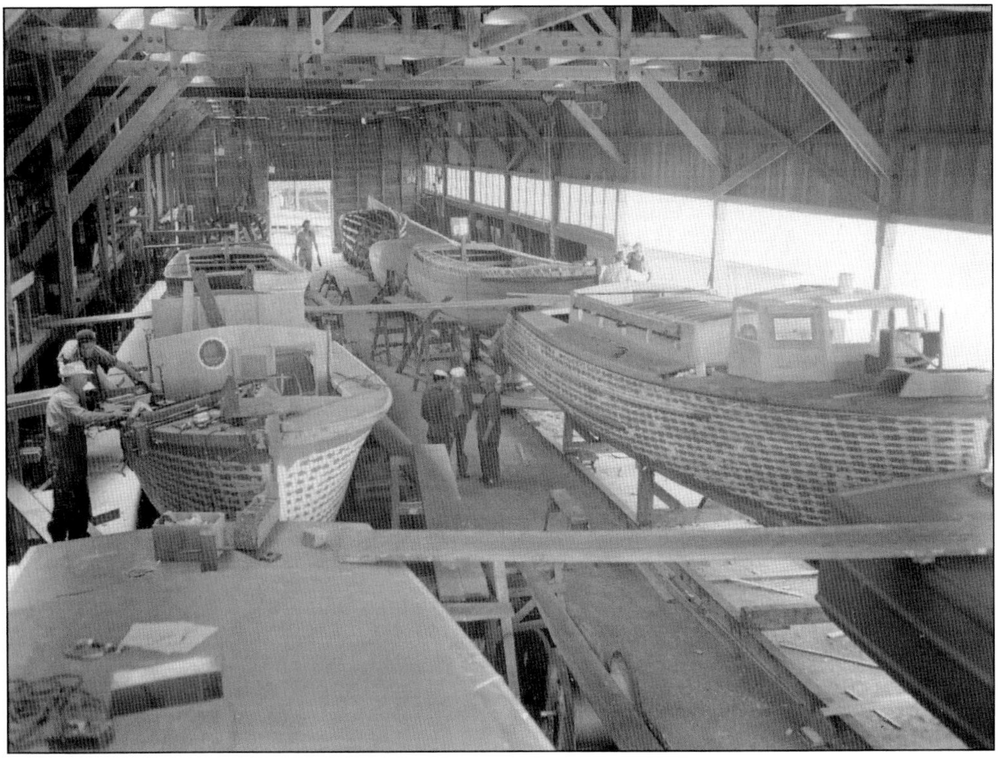

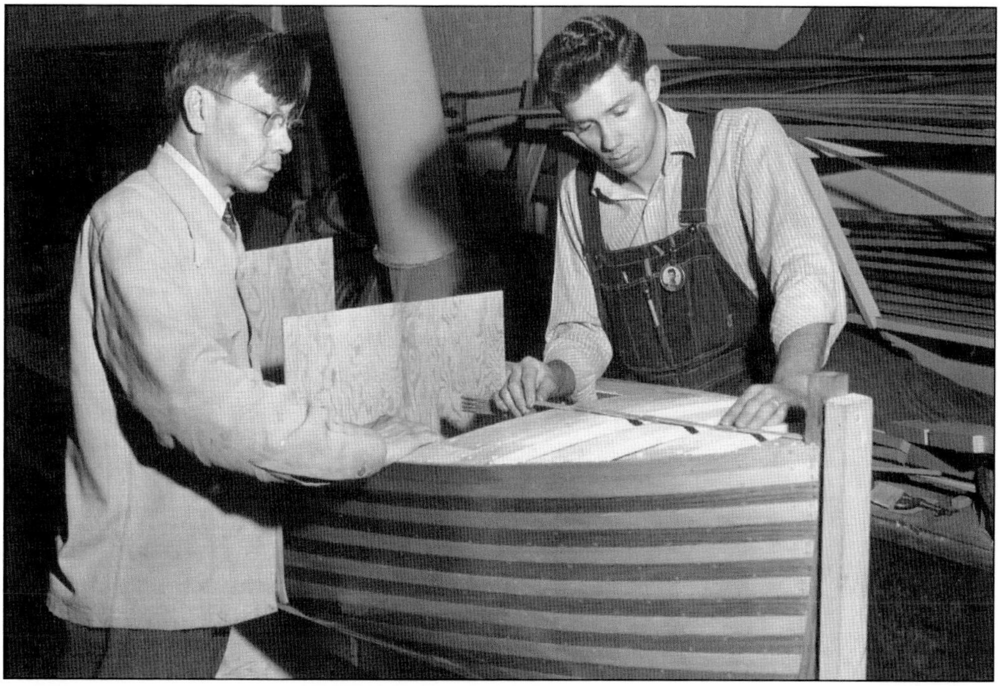

SHIPYARD MODEL PROGRAM. To demonstrate traditional boat building techniques to Puget Sound Navy Yard apprentices, an eight-foot-long model of a 38-foot Coast Guard picket boat was constructed in the yard's boat shop between 1946 and 1948. In the photograph above, instructor Louis Barrazona (left) supervises apprentice Charlie Rennick as he takes measurements on the model's foredeck. During the late 2000s, the impressive model, shown below with Puget Sound Navy Museum curator Danelle Feddes, was on exhibit at the museum in Bremerton. The model is historically significant because it marked the transition of small craft construction from wood to plastics and laminates. (Above, courtesy Puget Sound Navy Museum; below, photograph by Dan Withers.)

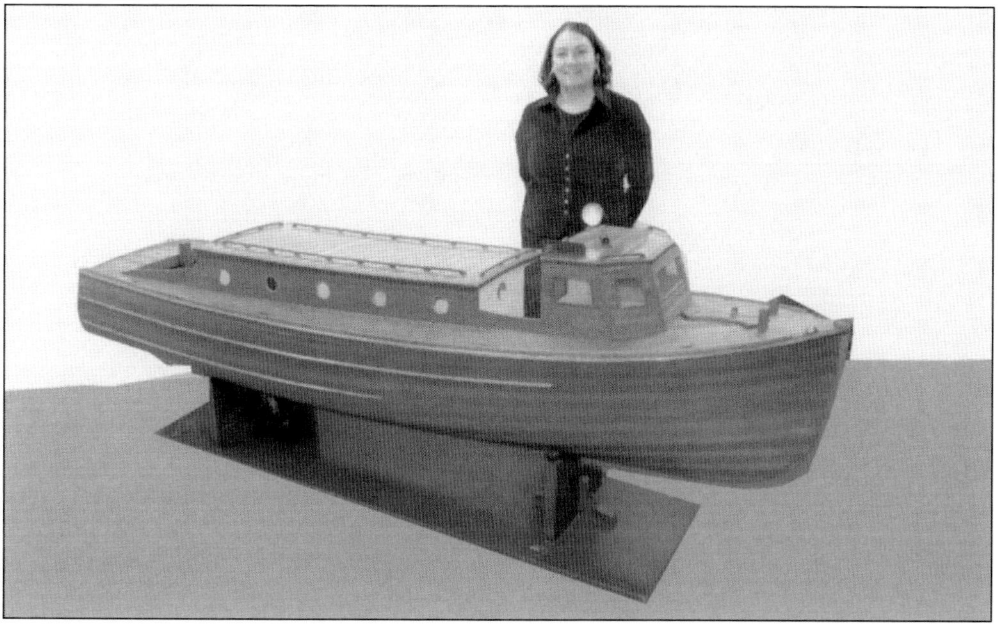

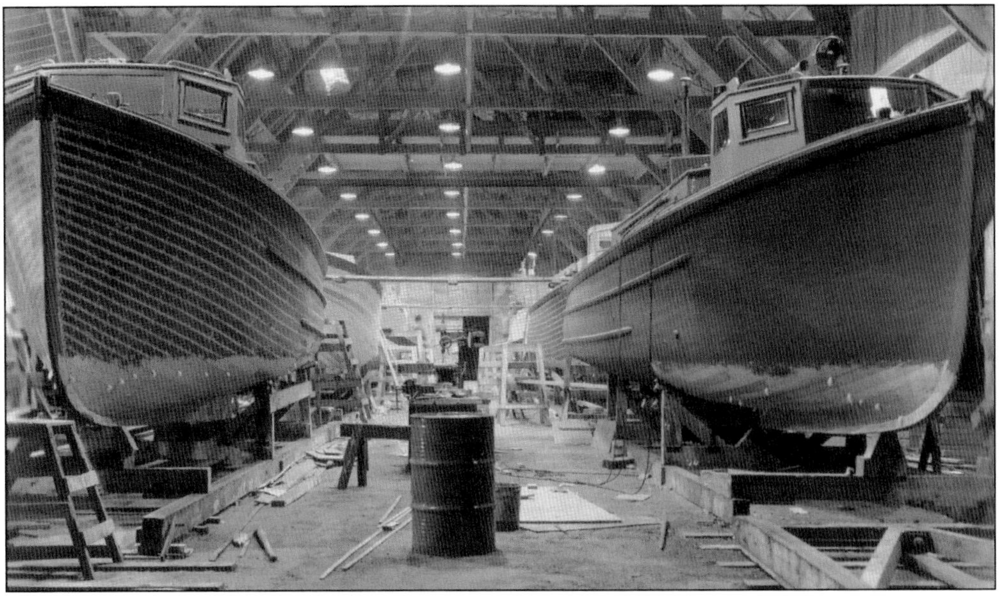

Proceeding down the Line. In the photograph above, two planked and caulked 38-foot picket boat hulls proceed down the production line at Kirkland Marine Construction, as Ballinger Boat Works was known during World War II. The company, which employed about 50 workers, was located on the northeast shore of Lake Washington north of the Houghton Shipyard, which built larger military and commercial vessels during the war. Production was checked continually by Coast Guard officer inspectors, one of whom is depicted below talking to a worker near CG-38745, a boat built during the latter part of the entire Kirkland Marine Construction production run. (Both courtesy KHS, Philip F. Toman Collection.)

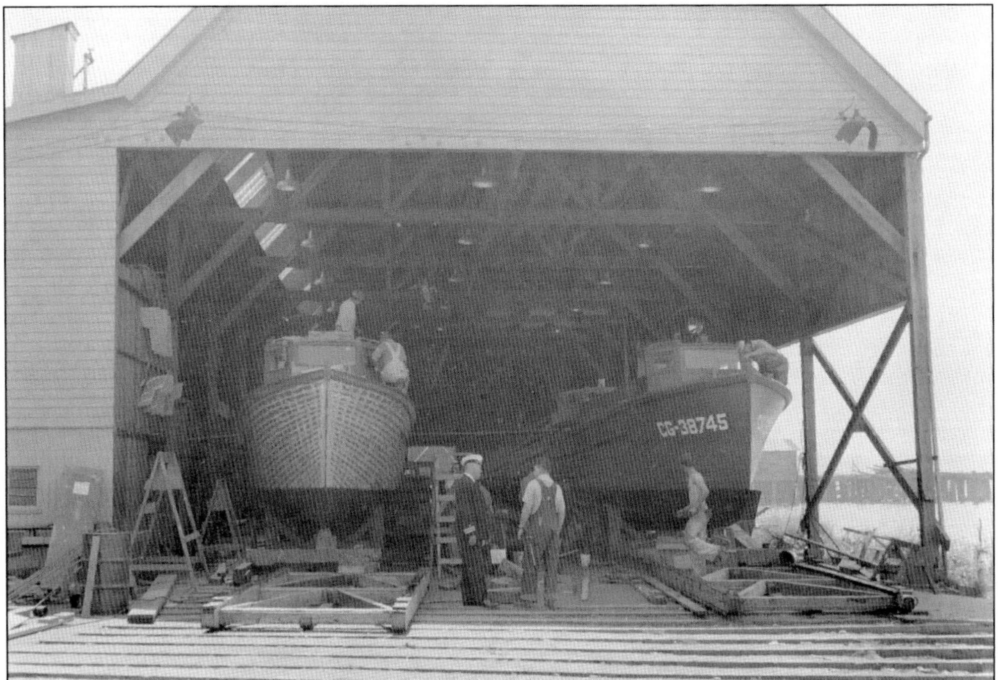

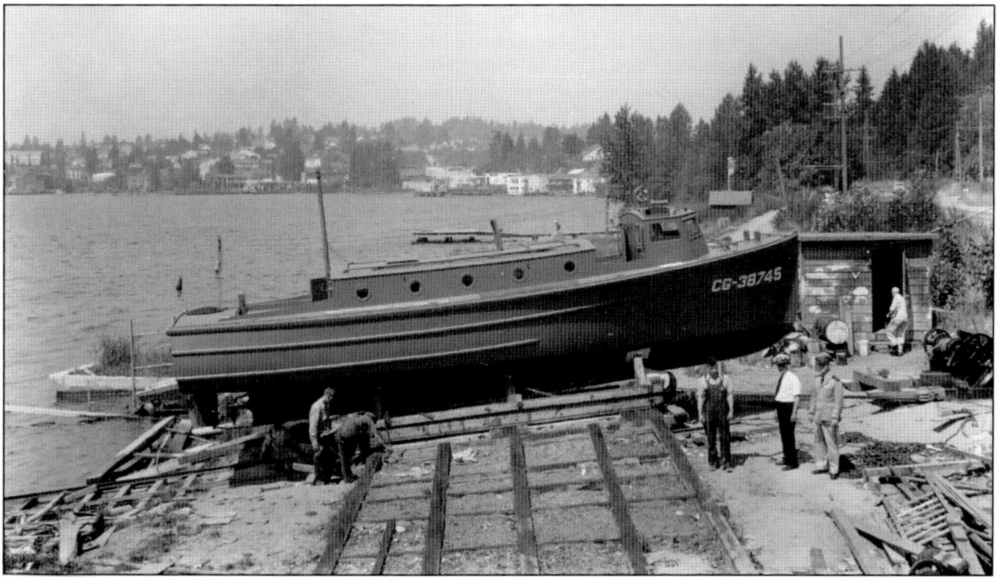

Ready for Action. CG-38745 is shown above completed on the ways prior to launch on the shores of Lake Washington and sea trials. In total, all shipyards in the nation built 538 of the 38-foot picket boats, 470 after the Japanese attack on Pearl Harbor on December 7, 1941. As part of the Pacific Northwest response to the attack, as shown in the photograph below, the Coast Guard positioned picket boats and a 63-foot aircraft crash rescue boat at locations near the Pacific Ocean, such as Neah Bay at the northernmost tip of Washington State. (Above, courtesy KHS, Philip F. Toman Collection; below, courtesy Coast Guard Museum Northwest.)

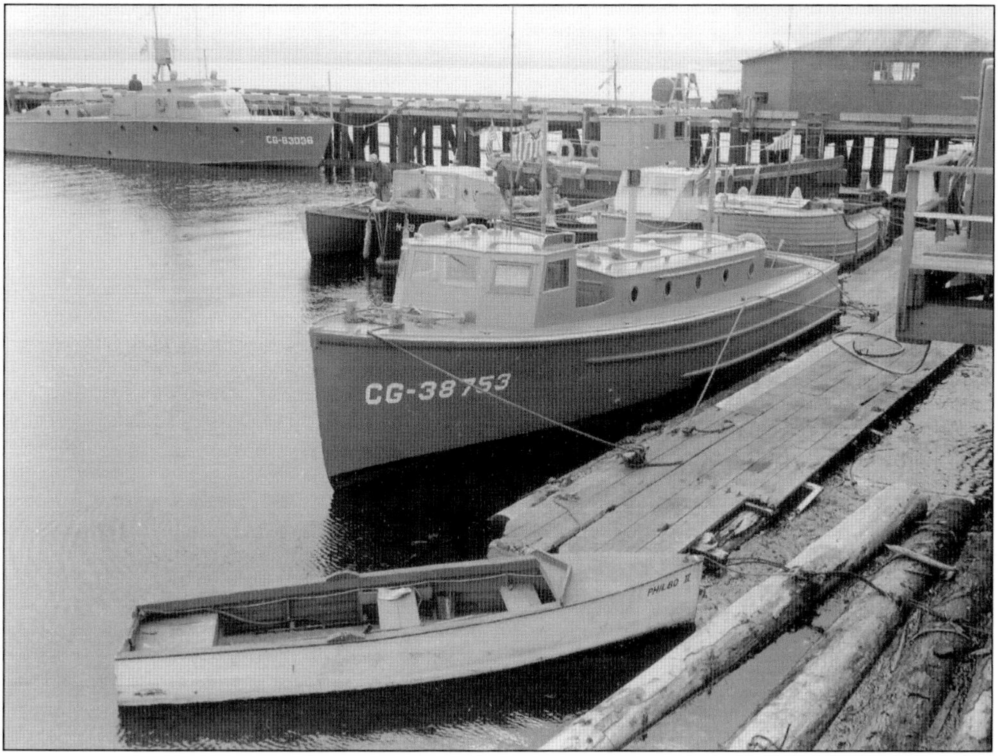

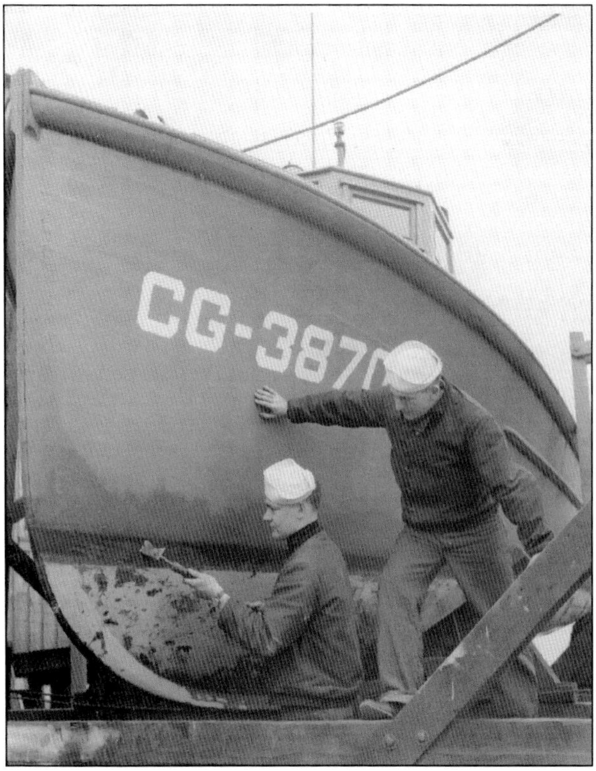

Shore and Sea Duty. Two Coast Guardsmen are pictured at left during World War II performing a traditional vessel maintenance duty, scraping paint. Known for being relatively easy to maintain, the 38-foot picket boats were well liked by their crews. Three Kirkland-produced craft, which each cost about $10,000 to build during the war, are seen below in formation while on sea trials in early 1943. They are among the first 10 boats to come off the production line. This type of picket boat was used extensively for patrol and boarding duty, customs inspection, and harbor emergency assignments. (Both courtesy Coast Guard Museum Northwest.)

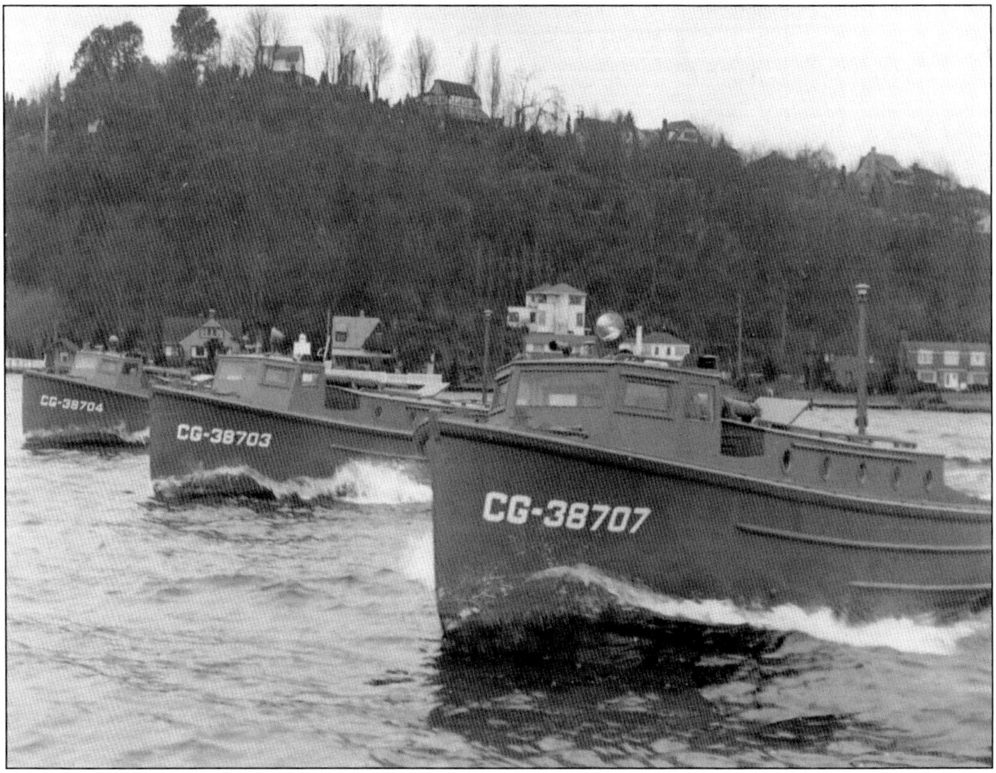

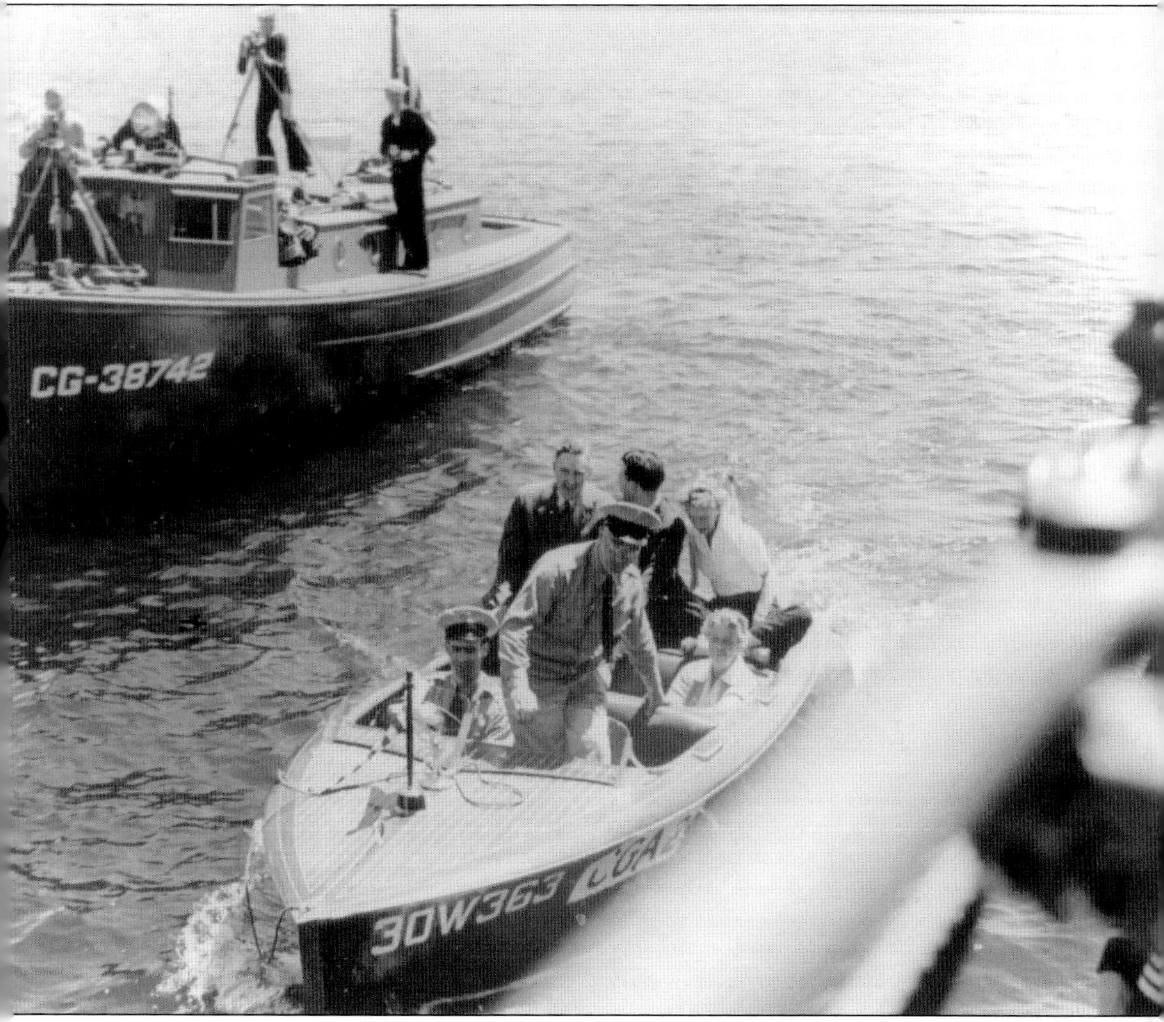

First Lady in Focus. The 38-foot picket boat pictured above was used as a photographer's platform when First Lady Eleanor Roosevelt visited Seattle in 1942. She is shown sitting at far right in the front of a Coast Guard Auxiliary speedboat as it reaches its mooring dock. The president and first lady made several trips to the Puget Sound area before and during World War II. Their daughter, Anna Roosevelt Boettiger, was married to *Seattle Post Intelligencer* newspaper publisher John Boettiger, and the Roosevelts visited Seattle in 1937 and later in 1942 and 1943. During his 1942 visit, President Roosevelt toured and greeted employees at the Puget Sound Navy Yard in Bremerton and the Boeing B-17 bomber plant in Seattle. At the same time, Eleanor Roosevelt visited hospitals and servicemen and -women's centers. (Courtesy Coast Guard Museum Northwest.)

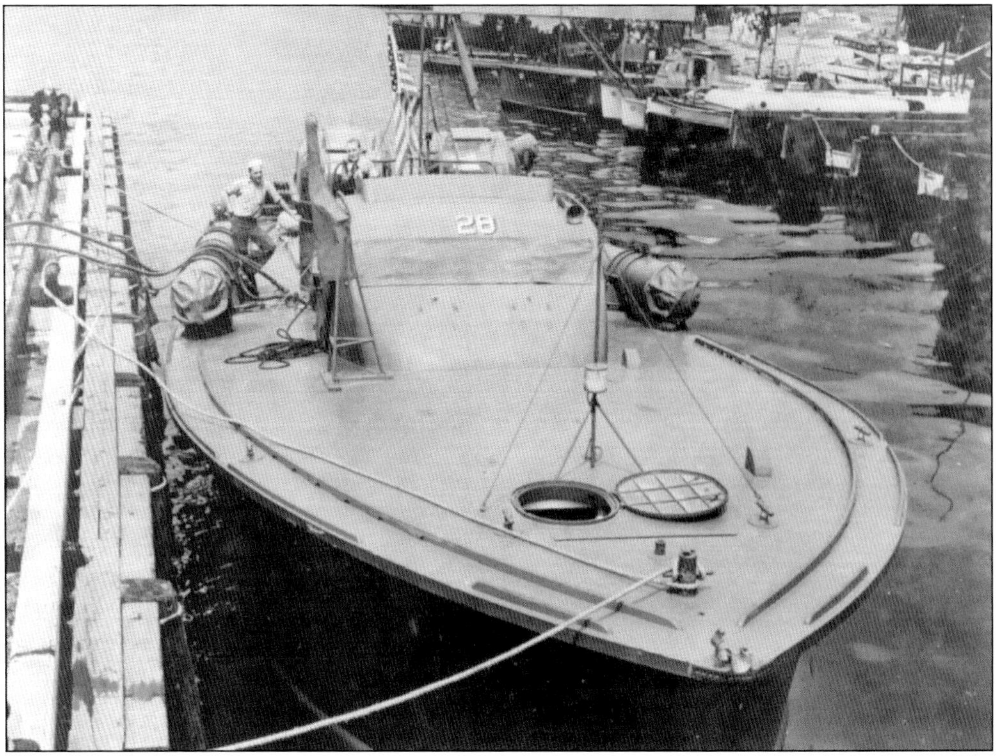

Sound PT Connections. When the Japanese attacked Pearl Harbor, 12 PT boats were present, including PT-28, shown dockside above. One of the early Elco 77-foot boats, this patrol torpedo craft was destined for service in the South Pacific. But the likelihood of another Japanese attack on the Aleutian Islands in Alaska in early 1942 caused the reassignment and loading of PT-22, -24, -27, and -28 aboard the cargo ship *Irvin MacDowell* for transport from Hawaii to Puget Sound. Once in the sound, they were off-loaded and traveled under their own power 2,500 miles to Alaska. The photograph below features the aft section of a 77-footer in Hawaii before the attack and shows the turrets and bubble canopies over the twin .50-caliber machine guns, a torpedo launching tube, and depth charges on the stern. Visible across the water in the background is a four-engine Pan American Clipper seaplane. (Both courtesy National Archives, Washington, DC.)

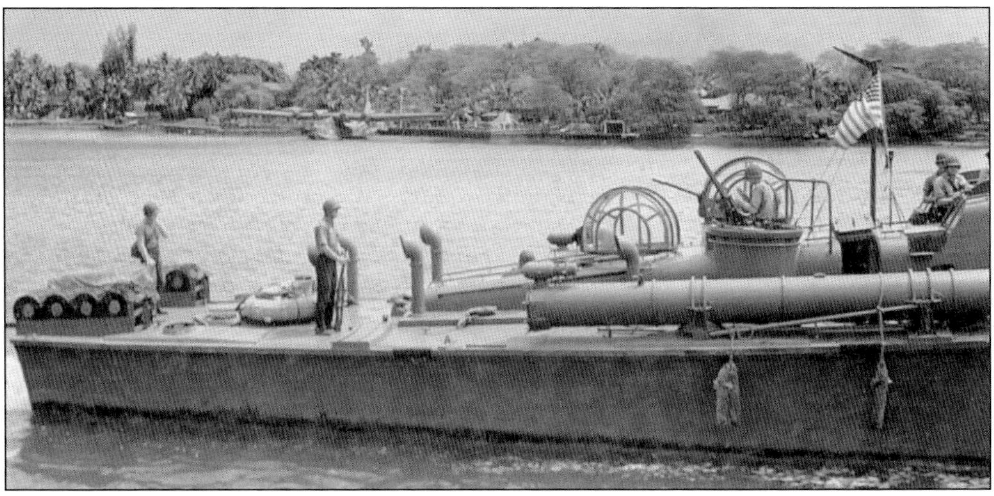

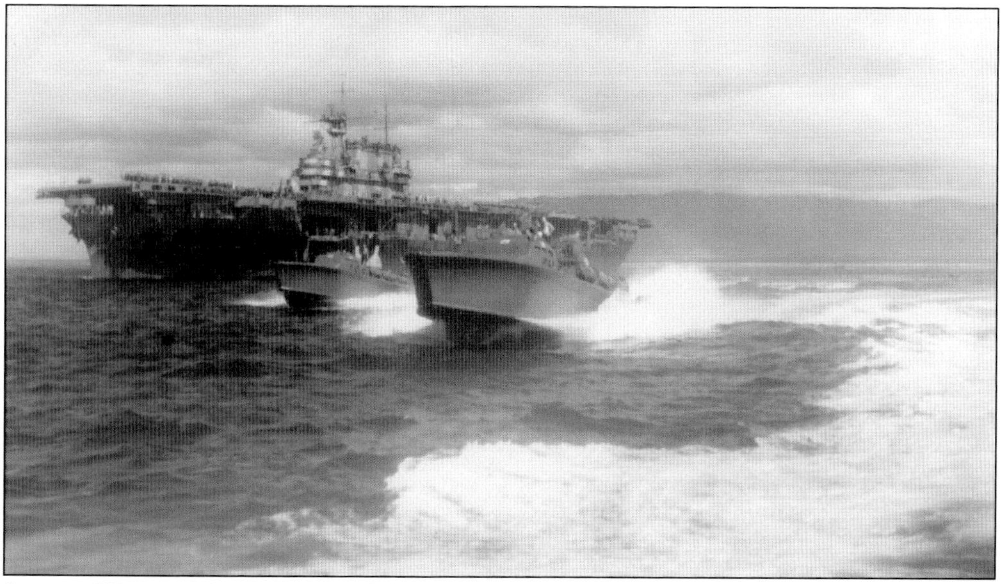

Special Wartime Scenes. One of the earliest US military victories was the bombing of the Japanese homeland on April 18, 1942, by B-25 medium bombers led by legendary Army Air Force major James (Jimmy) Doolittle. Launched from the deck of the aircraft carrier USS *Hornet*, the Doolittle Raid was a psychological victory that energized the war effort and the civilian population. Pictured above are PT-28, which was later sent through Puget Sound (at right in the foreground), and PT-20 proudly escorting the *Hornet* back to Pearl Harbor after participating in the successful raid. The rare photograph below shows PT-27 at full speed during her stopover in Puget Sound before reassignment to Alaska in the summer of 1942. Taken by a newspaper photographer, such images were usually censored and not released publically because of security restrictions. (Above, courtesy PT Boats, Inc.; below, courtesy John Akin, US Navy, World War II PT Boat Squadron 1)

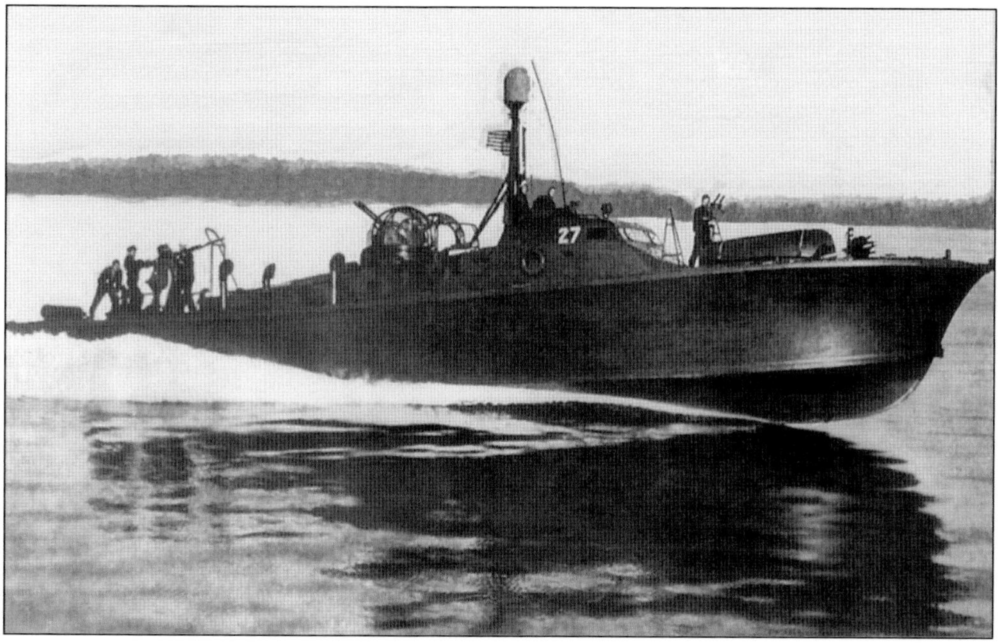

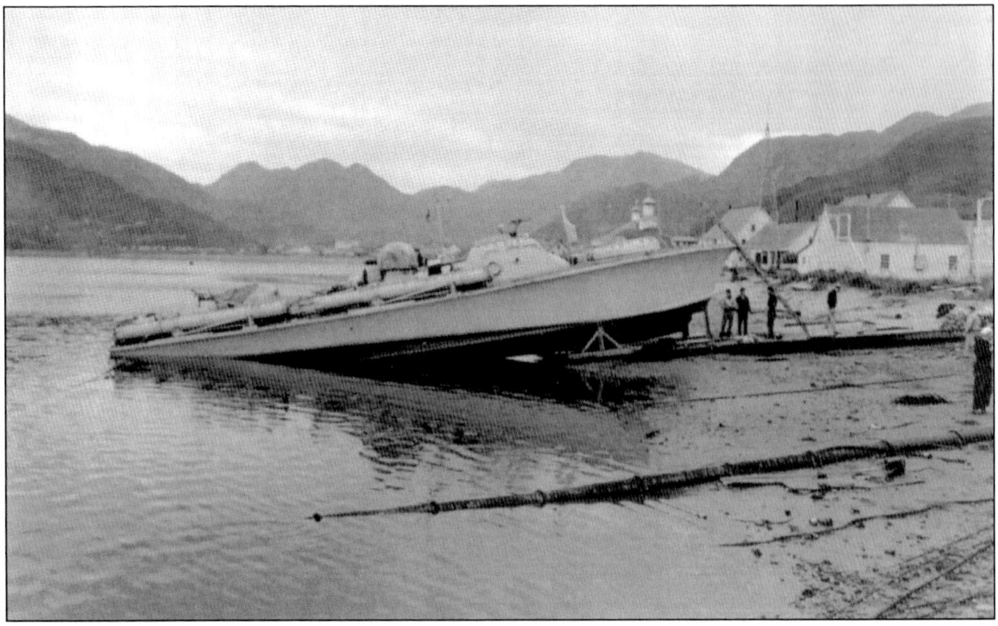

ON-SCENE IN ALASKA. PT-28 is shown above hauled out on the marine railway at Naval Air Station Dutch Harbor for bow repair in October 1942. The harsh Alaskan conditions caused major damage to the lightly built PT boats, and they soon required extensive overhaul maintenance. Among the improvements made to the boat while undergoing repair was the installation on the wheelhouse of an early radar system and aircraft antennas, as shown below. However, after she was back in action, PT-28 was disabled in heavy seas in January 1943 and washed up on the rocks at King Cove on the northwest side of the harbor. According to the book *At Close Quarters*, despite repeated salvage efforts, all attempts to refloat PT-28 failed, and she was abandoned and broke up on the rocks. (Both courtesy National Archives, Washington, DC.)

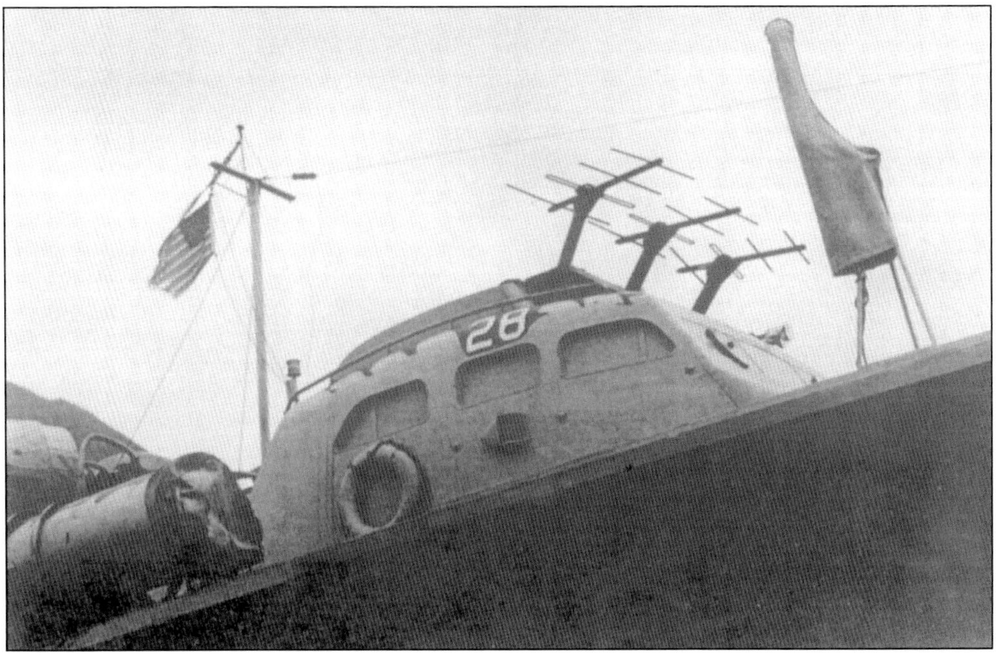

SEATTLE RETURN AND REPAIR. The primary shipyard in Seattle capable of major military wooden boat repairs and outfitting was Olsen & Winge Marine Works on the ship canal in Ballard. With the loss of PT-28 and PT-22 in Alaska, PT-24 and -27 returned to Seattle under their own power for major repair. While photos of PT boats were normally not allowed during World War II, the image at right of PT-24 in the foreground and PT-27 in the background was taken at the shipyard in the summer of 1943 for government documentation purposes. The extensive damage to the boats in Alaska is shown dramatically in the photograph below of PT-27. Both boats were almost totally reconstructed at Olsen & Winge and subsequently shipped back to Hawaii for coastal patrol service and experimental mine-laying testing. (Both courtesy MOHAI; above, No. 72.5503.75; below, No. 72.5503.73.)

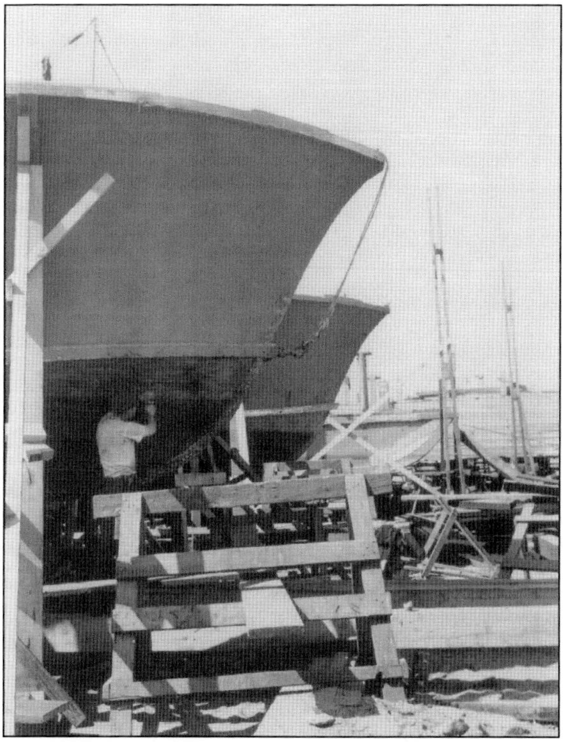

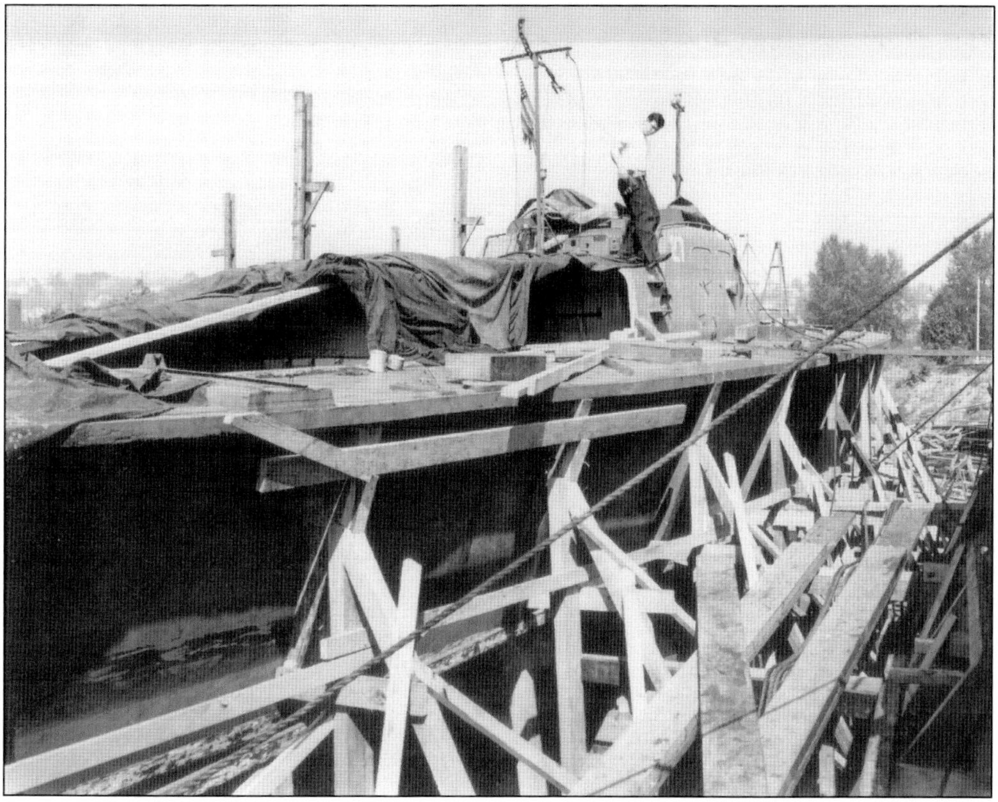

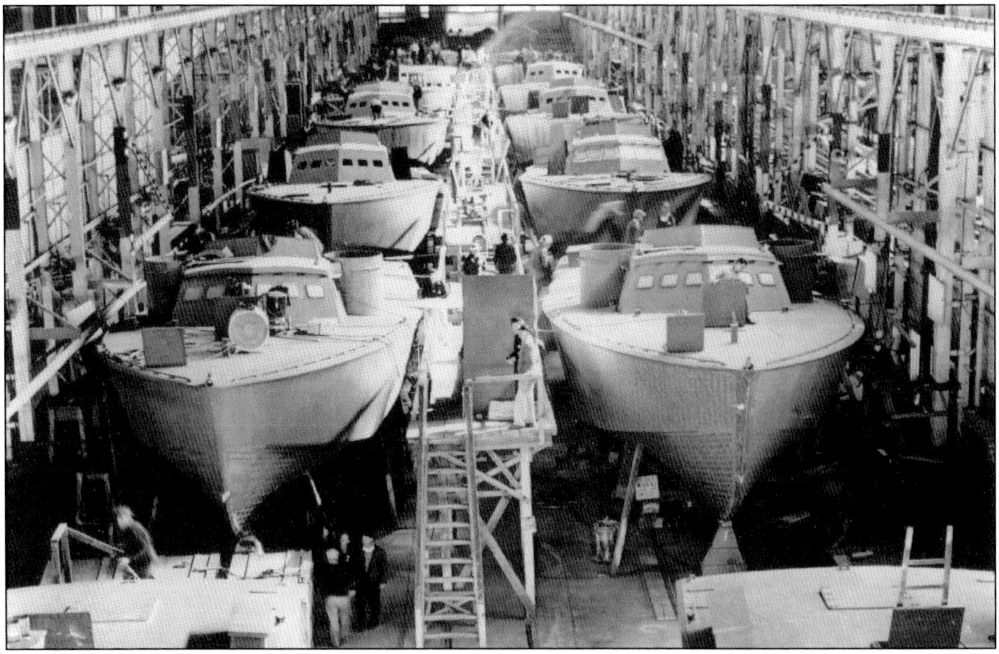

In Production, In Action. Higgins Industries of New Orleans, Louisiana, was one of two major producers of PT boats during World War II. Shown above is the production line at the company's City Park manufacturing plant around 1943. The boat hulls proceeded from back to front during the production process, with the boat builders adding the wheelhouse and other components along the way. A dramatic bow-on view of a completed boat underway, PT-84, is depicted below. PT-84 was the last of 12 boats built for Squadron 13 (RON 13) that passed through Puget Sound, and was commissioned coincidentally on the first anniversary of the Pearl Harbor attack, December 7, 1942. (Both courtesy National Archives, Washington, DC.)

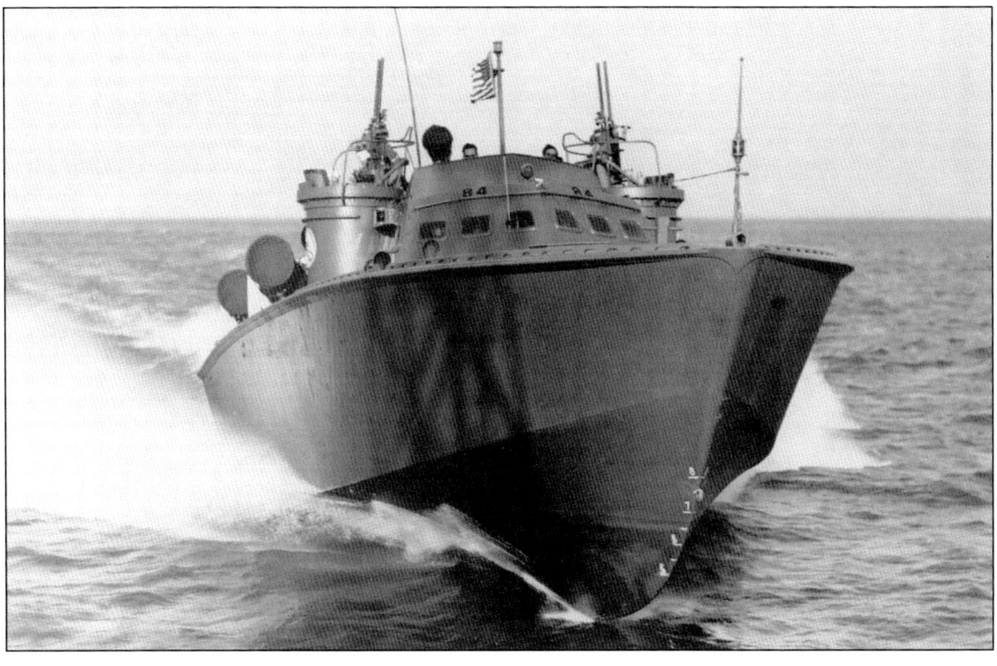

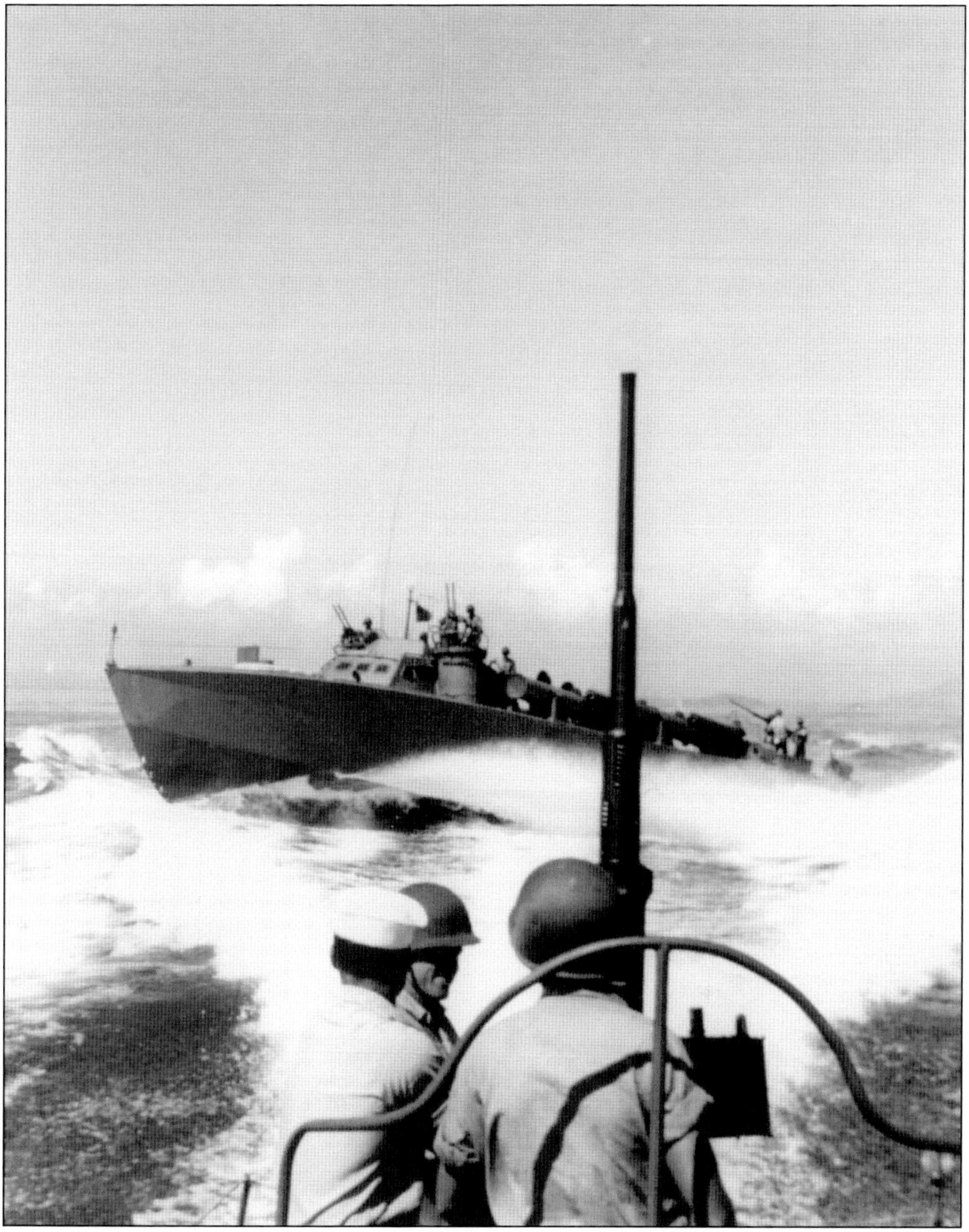

Wake Crossing. Another Squadron 13 boat, PT-77, is shown crossing the wake of a sister PT while en route in the Caribbean to the Pacific coast. The unit and Squadron 16 were the only two sent to Alaska to help remove Japanese forces from their occupation of Attu Island, beginning with an Army invasion in May 1943. Together, both squadrons had a total of 29 boats. Each of the boats was powered by three 1,250-horsepower Packard V-12 marine engines connected to three shafts and propellers and were capable of an operational speed of more than 35 knots (40 miles per hour). Initially, their basic armament consisted of four Mark 8 steam-launched torpedoes in tubes on-deck, two twin-.50 machineguns in turrets on the sides of the wheelhouse, and a 20-millimeter cannon on the stern. (Courtesy National Archives, Washington, DC.)

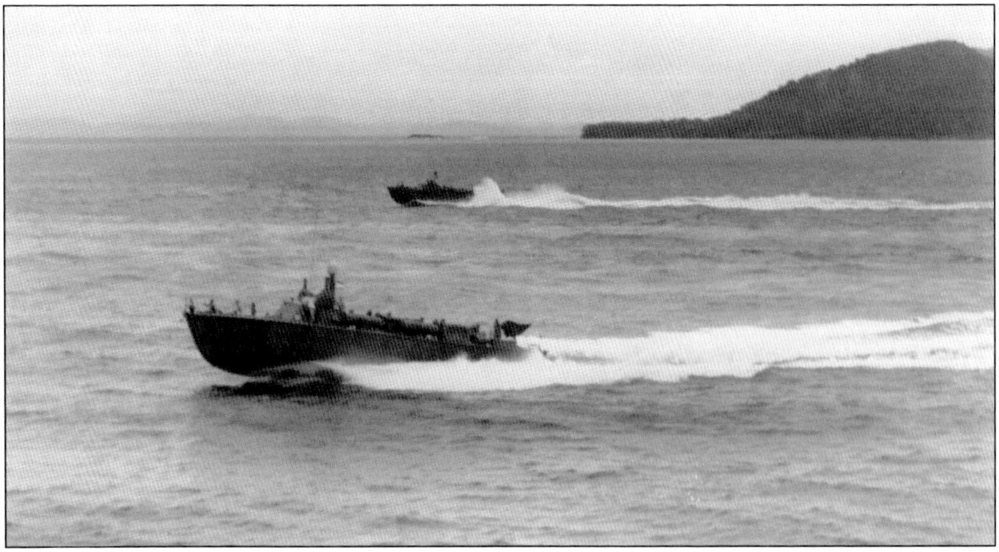

Pacific Coast Passage. Before arriving at Taboga on the western side of the Panama Canal Zone, two of the Squadron 13 PT boats are shown above in early 1943. There, they were loaded aboard Liberty ships to be transported to the Puget Sound Navy Yard in Bremerton. Each cargo ship carried two PTs on the aft deck, as shown in the dockside photograph below taken at the shipyard. This transport process was repeated until all 12 boats of the squadron had been shipped up the coast to Bremerton. Visible in the background is a Black Ball Line ferryboat loading passengers and vehicles destined for Seattle at the terminal adjacent to the shipyard. (Above, courtesy National Archives, Washington, DC; below, National Archives, Seattle.)

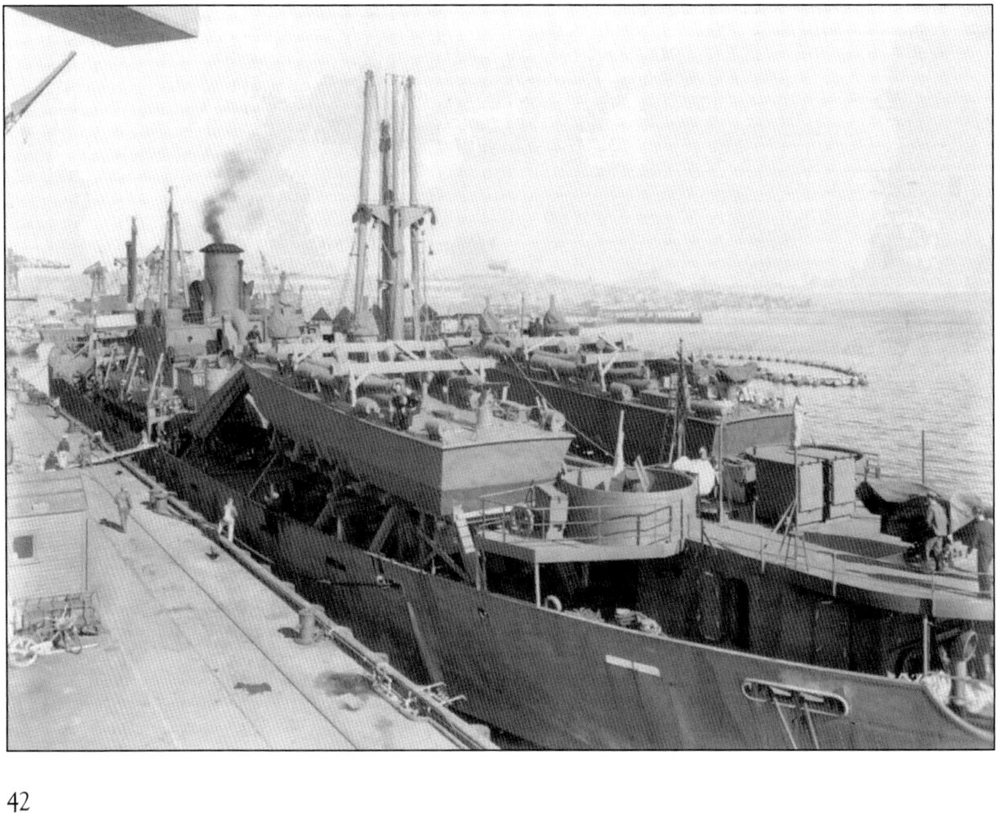

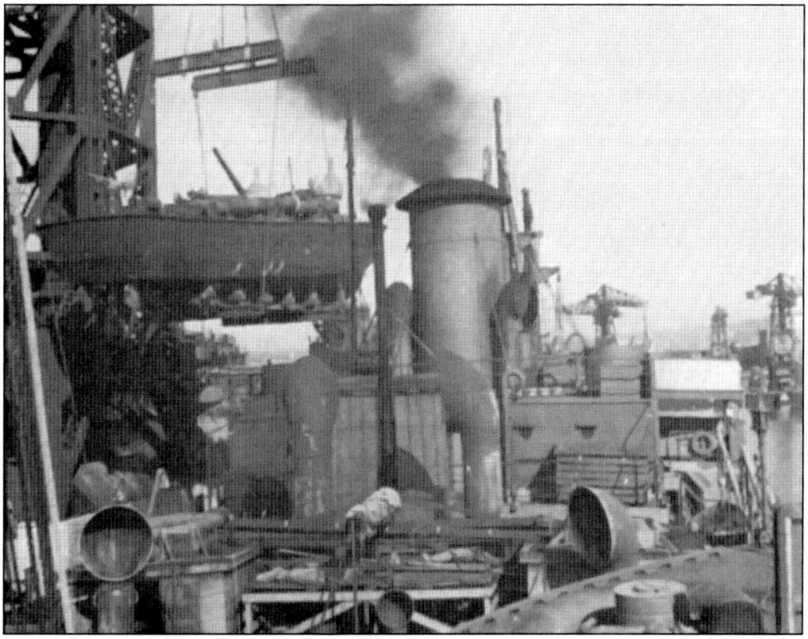

EN ROUTE TO ALASKA. In Bremerton at the Puget Sound Navy Yard, as shown above, the 78-foot Higgins PT boats of Squadron 13 in their shipping cradles were offloaded by dockside cranes into Sinclair Inlet and outfitted for the arduous trip to Alaska's Aleutian Islands. Although official Navy photographs like these could be taken for documentation, images taken by the public were strictly forbidden during World War II for security purposes. This included photographs of PT operations, like the scenic Navy image below of the boats traveling north through the Inside Passage of British Columbia, Canada. Although travelling in secrecy, there were some complaints from port communities along the way that the wakes of the fast PTs were causing damage to fishing boats and docks. (Above, courtesy National Archives, Seattle; below, courtesy National Archives, Washington, D.C.)

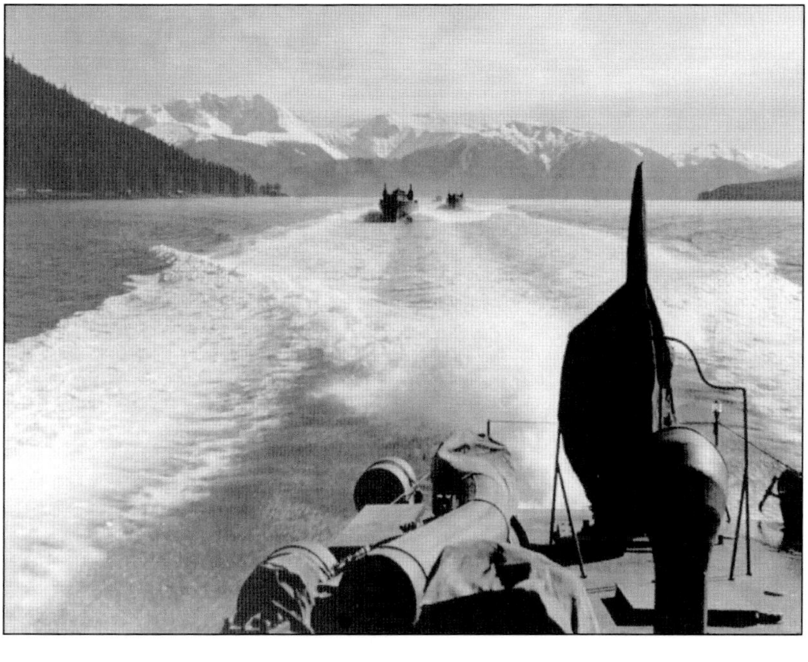

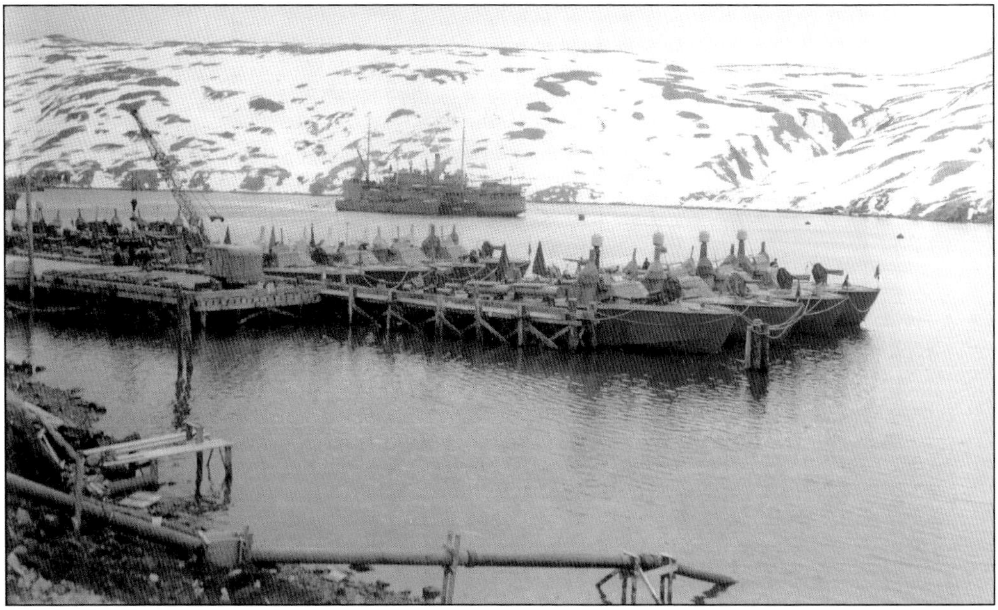

PT Journey's End. Once at Attu Island, at the western end of the Aleutian chain near Russia, PT boats of Squadron 13 faced varied weather and sea conditions. The photograph above shows almost all 12 of the unit's boats rafted together, with the tender *Tatoosh* anchored in the background. Sometimes, calmer and relatively warmer weather allowed crewmembers to gather on the foredecks of their boats, as pictured below in Massacre Bay on Attu Island. Originally in color, this image is believed to have been taken by Howard Bristol, a *Life* magazine cameraman who during the war was a member of famed photographer Edward Steichen's Navy photographic unit, which documented the service's activities worldwide. (Both courtesy National Archives, Washington DC.)

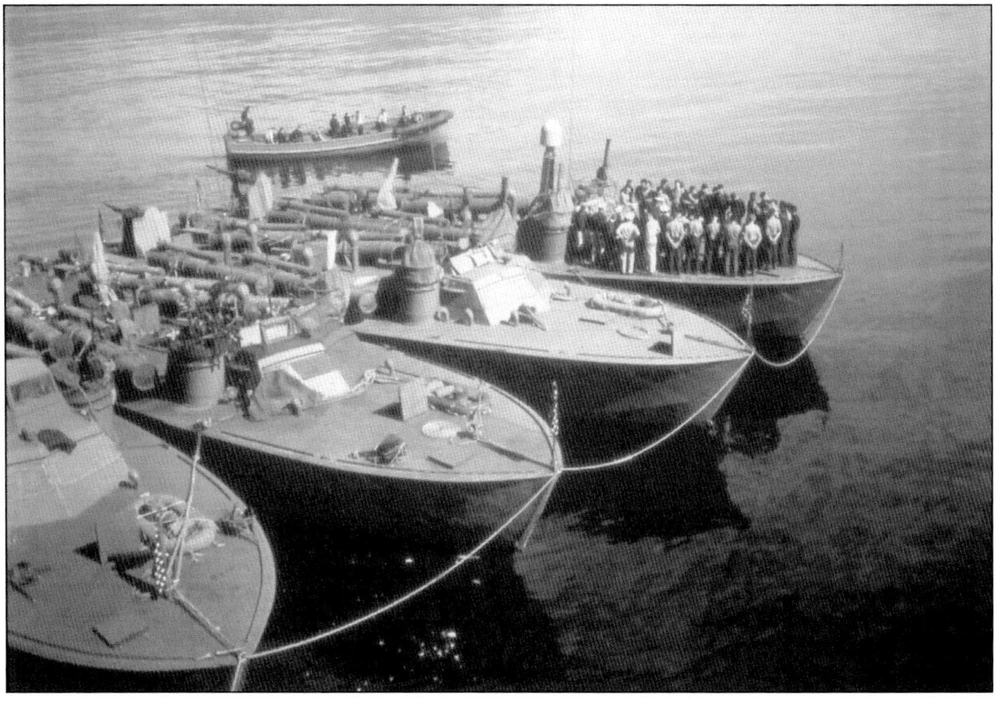

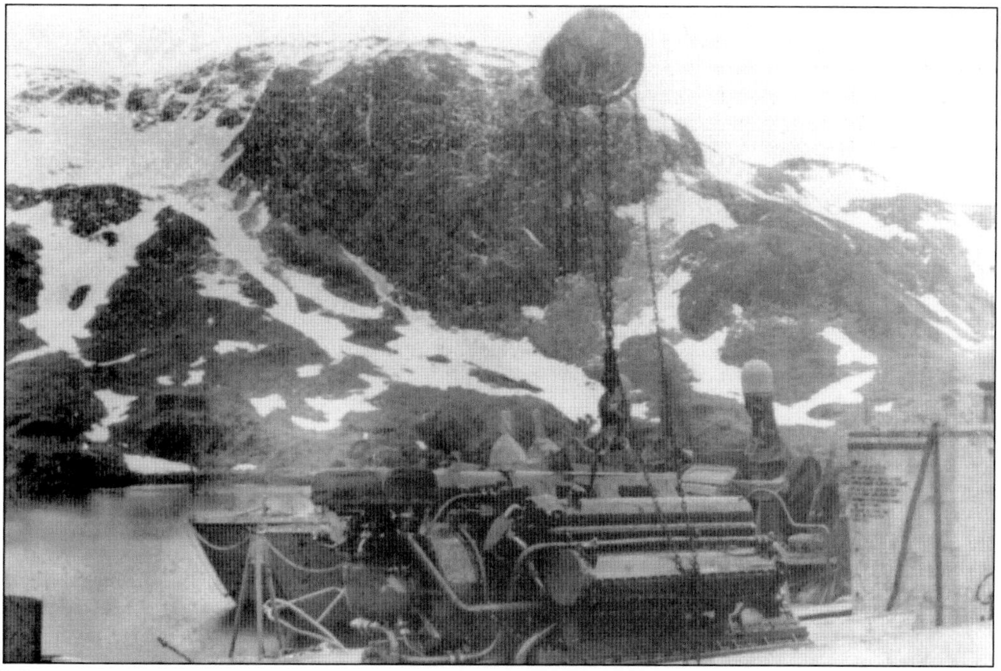

Mountainous Maintenance. Because of the harsh Alaska weather, the PT boats of Squadron 13 and later Squadron 16 required constant repair and maintenance. As shown above, engine changes were a way of life for crewmembers as they battled the elements and tough operating conditions to keep each boat's three V-12 Packard marine engines running consistently. As pictured below, tractors were used to haul out the 50-ton, 78-foot PT boats in their wheeled mobile cradles. Continually foggy conditions, as well as hidden rocks and other obstacles, required ongoing hull, shaft, and propeller repairs to the relatively lightly built wooden boats. (Both courtesy National Archives, Washington, DC.)

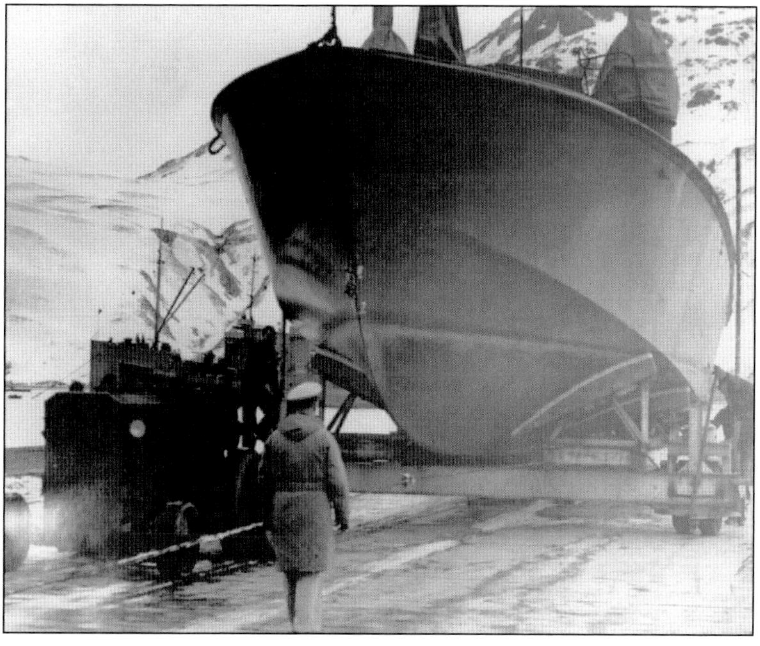

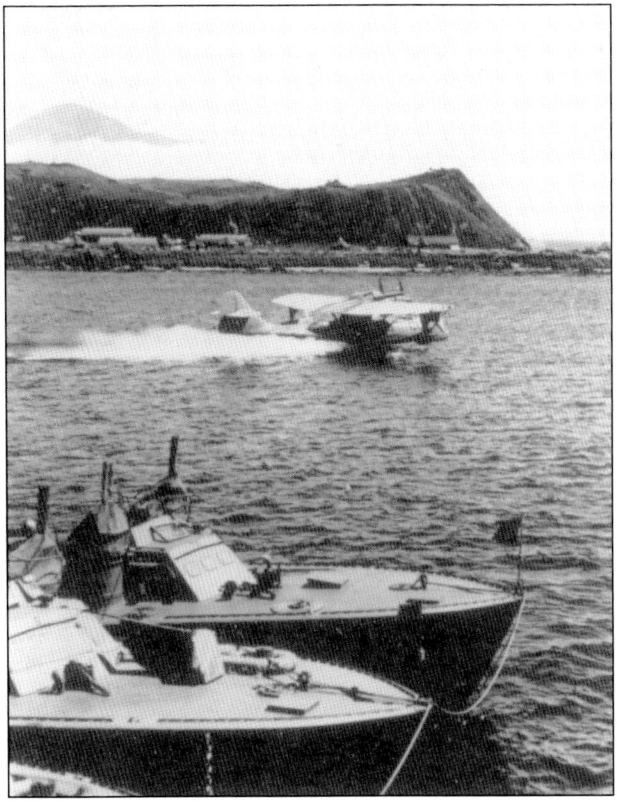

Squadron Sightings. These photographs are also believed to have been taken by Howard Bristol. At left, a PBY Catalina flying boat is landing behind two rafted Squadron 13 PT boats (foreground) at Casco Cove on Massacre Bay, Attu Island. PBYs were used for reconnaissance missions to prepare for the US Army invasion to retake Attu Island from the Japanese in May 1943 and also to rescue crewmen of downed aircraft in icy Alaskan waters. Although the mountainous rock in the background looks a little like Diamond Head in the Hawaiian Islands, Oahu Island is about 2,800 miles to the south. The photograph below shows three PT boats rafted to the tender USS *Gillis*, which is also providing support for another PBY astern. (Both courtesy National Archives, Washington, DC.)

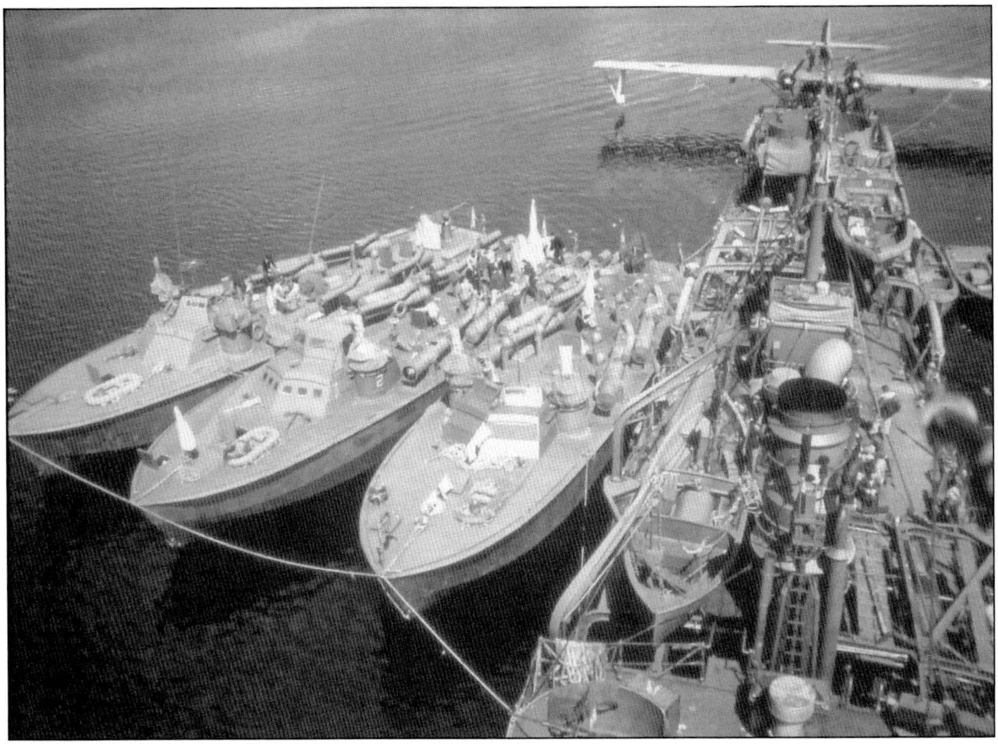

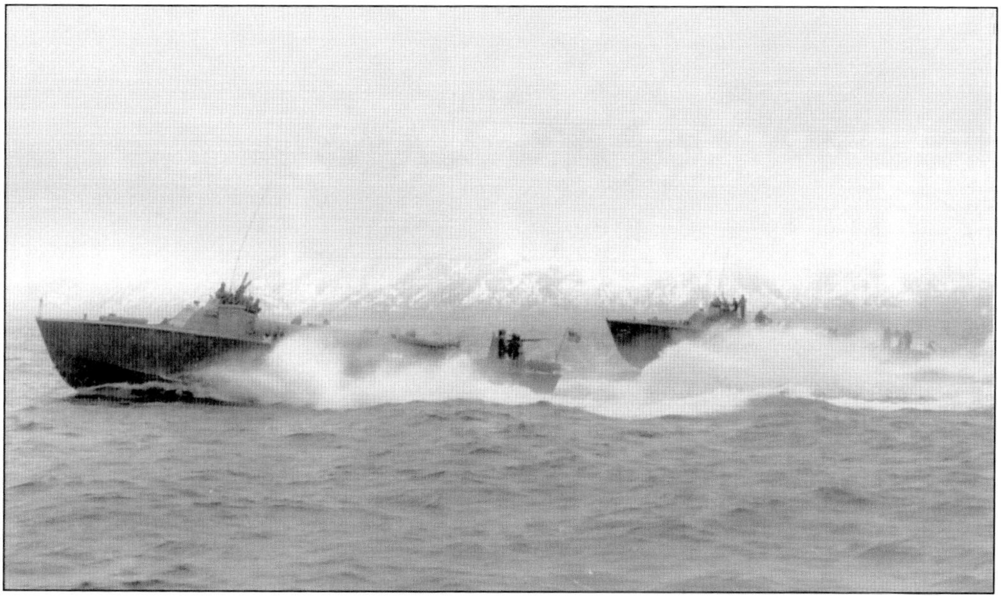

PTs in Heavy Seas. PT boat operations in Alaska in mid-1943 were a far cry from those in Puget Sound, which the Squadron 13 boats had passed through only a few months earlier. As depicted above, the craft had to reduce speeds in usually rough open seas while on both tactical and training missions. However, crews developed innovative ways to protect themselves from wind, rain, snow, and below-freezing temperatures. Impromptu canvas bridge enclosures were built on the PTs, and salvaged Plexiglas fighter plane canopies were used on some Army Air Force crash rescue boats to shield crew members from the harsh weather conditions. (Both courtesy National Archives, Washington, DC.)

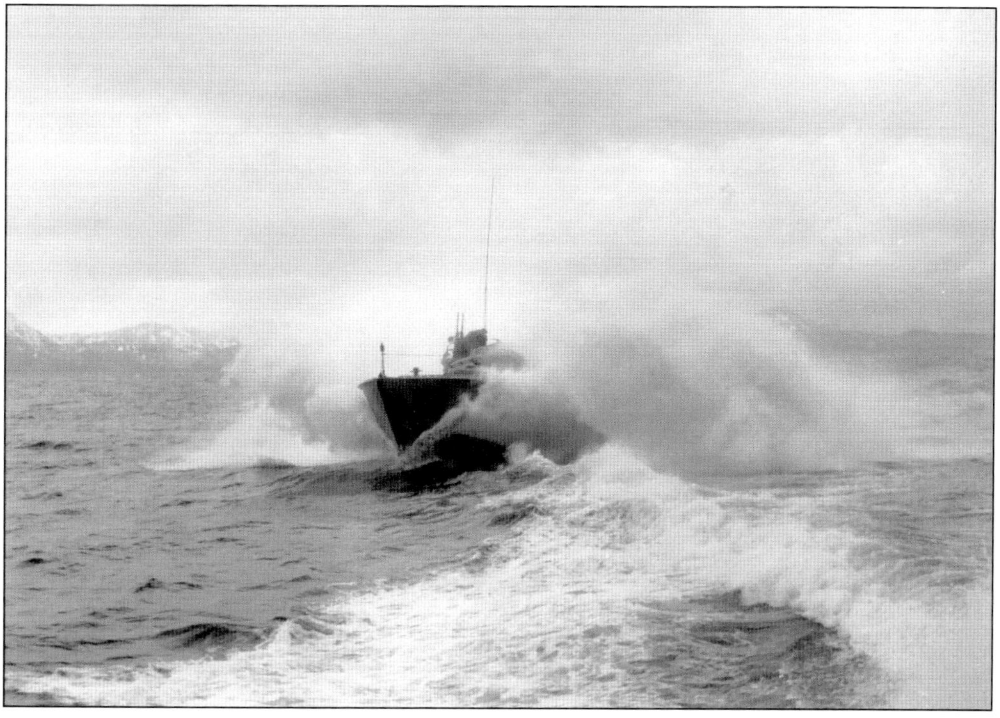

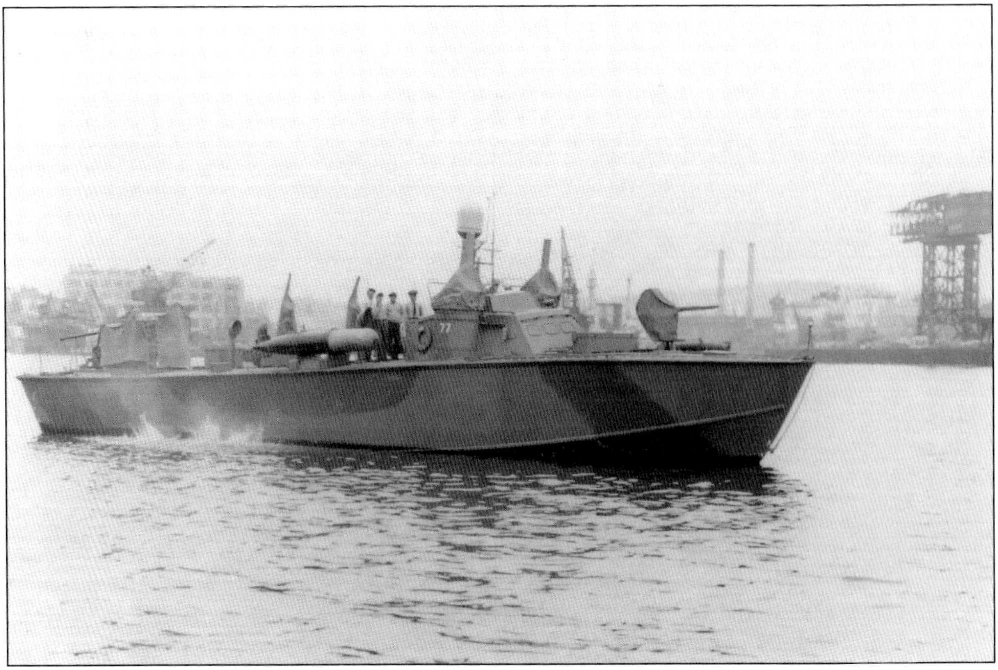

Back in Bremerton. PT-77, one of the most photographed boats in Squadron 13, is shown above with engines idling on Sinclair Inlet in Bremerton in July 1944. The distinctive hammerhead crane at the Puget Sound Navy Yard is seen at right. Two of the then-new Mark 13 torpedoes, developed to be dropped from aircraft, are visible amidships on the boat. While at the yard, all boats had new radar systems installed, and the old torpedo tubes were removed and new roll-off racks added to accommodate the new torpedoes. The squadron and its boats were then reassigned to combat areas in the South Pacific. Unfortunately, because of faulty identification, PT-77 was destroyed during a friendly fire incident on February 1, 1945, off Talin Point, Luzon, in the Philippine Islands. (Both courtesy US Navy, Puget Sound Navy Yard.)

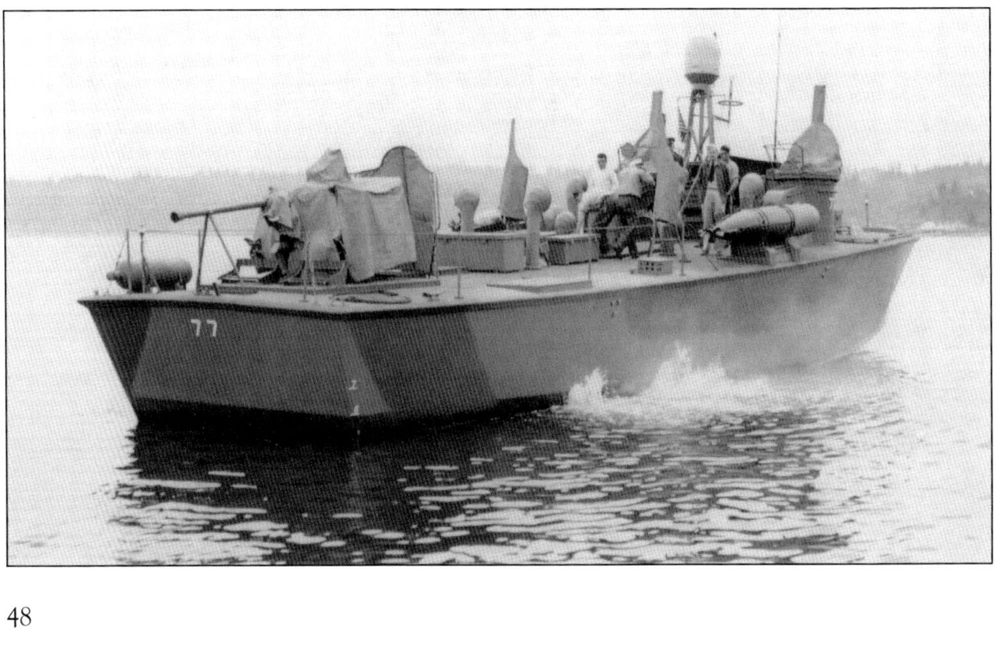

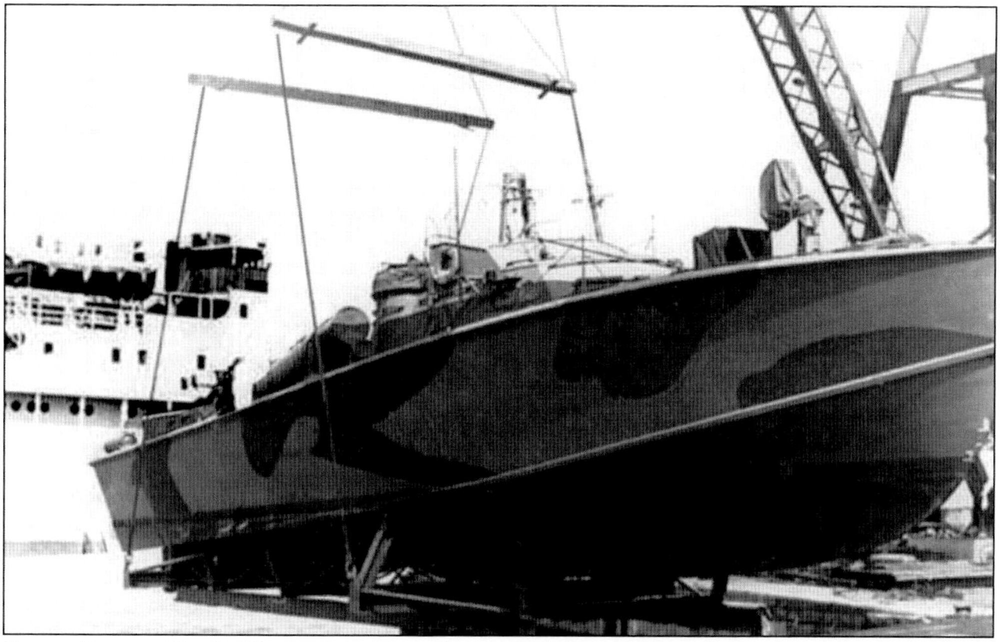

Off to Russia. The PT Ferrying Command was a little-known Navy operation at the end of World War II in the summer of 1945. As part of the US federal government's Lend-Lease armaments sharing program with allied nations, Higgins PT boats produced in New Orleans during the closing days of the war with Japan were run under their own power and also transported on ships to Bremerton for handover to the Russians. Above, PT-657 is offloaded from a barge used to transport the PT boats from the manufacturing plant to awaiting LSTs (Landing Ship Tank) for reshipping. The photograph below of two boats may also include PT-658, which more than 40 years later would be discovered in California, saved, and restored to operation by dedicated World War II PT crew veterans and volunteers in Portland, Oregon. (Both courtesy PT Boats, Inc.)

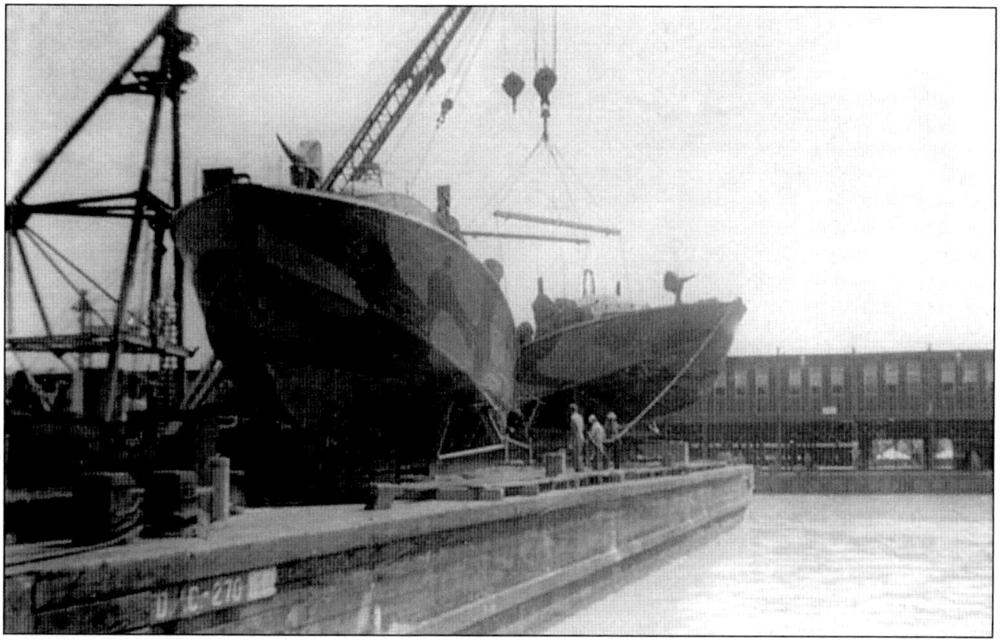

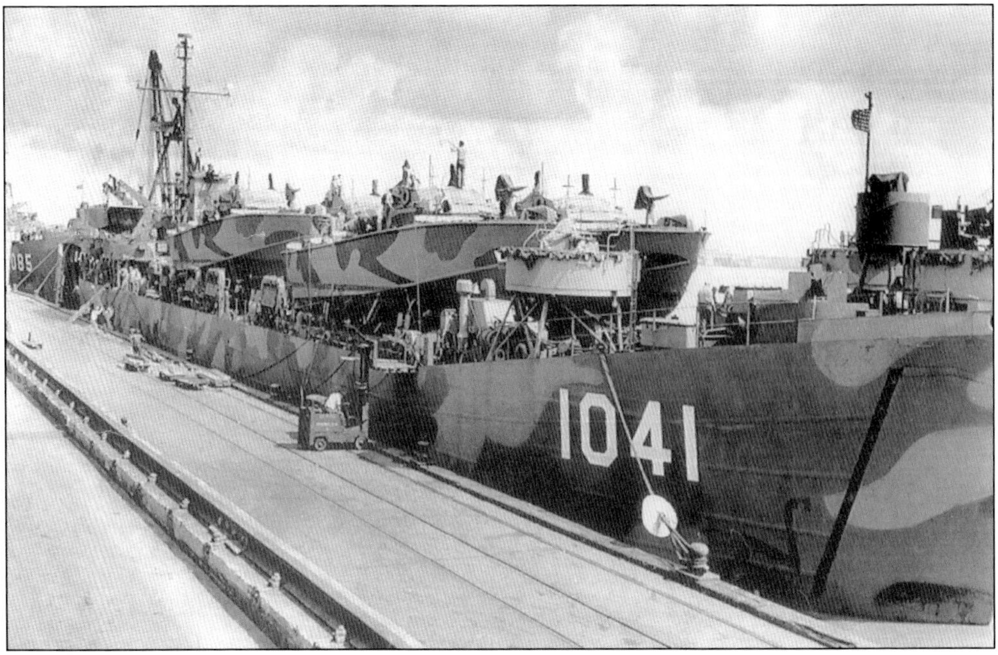

Puget Sound Arrival. LST-1041 is pictured dockside at the Puget Sound Navy Yard in early summer 1945 after her arrival with PT Ferrying Command boats destined for turnover to Russia. Each 330-foot landing craft carried four Higgins PT boats during the long voyage from New Orleans. Once offloaded into Sinclair Inlet, the crewmen tested, prepared, and ran the boats north in Puget Sound for transfer to an awaiting Russian freighter, which would then transport them to Vladivostok in the North Pacific Ocean. The rare photograph below from a Ferrying Command crewman shows his boat, PT-646, at idle while undergoing post-shipping testing on Puget Sound. (Above, courtesy PT Boats, Inc.; below, courtesy Fred Gilmartin, US Navy PT Ferrying Command.)

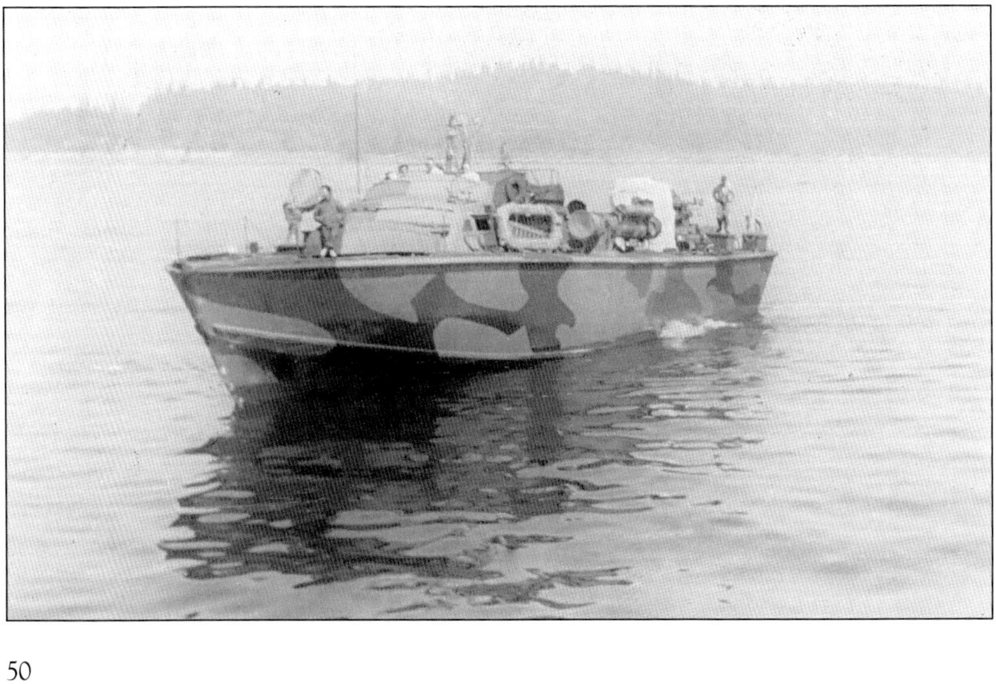

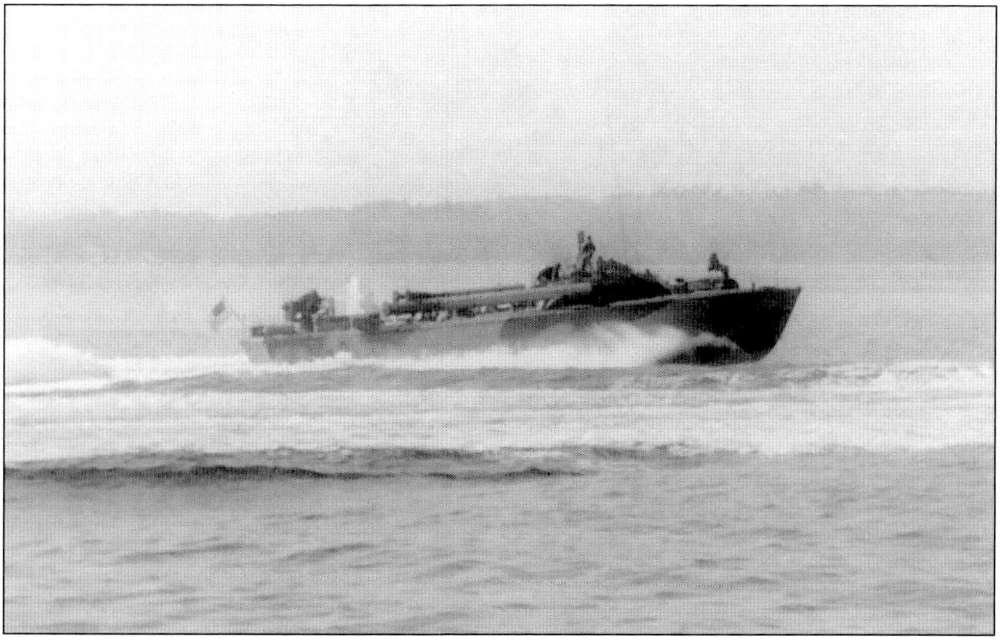

PT AT SPEED ON THE SOUND. As part of her testing on Puget Sound, PT-646 is shown above underway in June 1945 at more than 30 knots (35 miles per hour) between Bremerton and Seattle. Some minor damage to the bow of the boat during shipping caused the PT to go briefly to Seattle's Lake Union Dry Dock for repair. After checkout and any necessary maintenance, four boats at a time were run north in Puget Sound to their Russian freighter destination. In the image below, taken from PT-646, the boats thread their way through what is likely Agate Pass on their way to the Russian Liberty cargo ship. (Both courtesy Fred Gilmartin, US Navy PT Ferrying Command.)

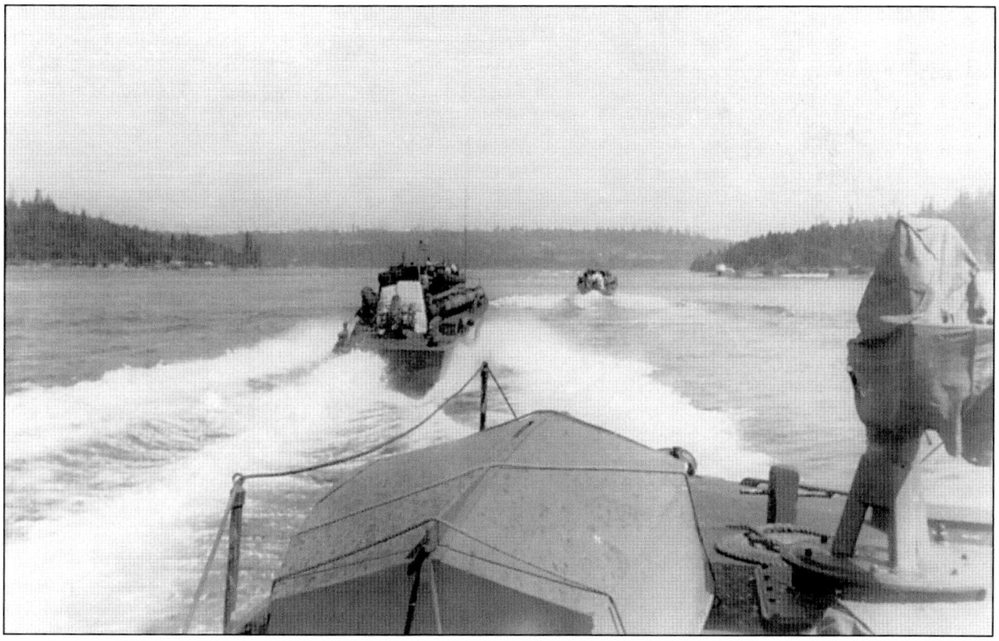

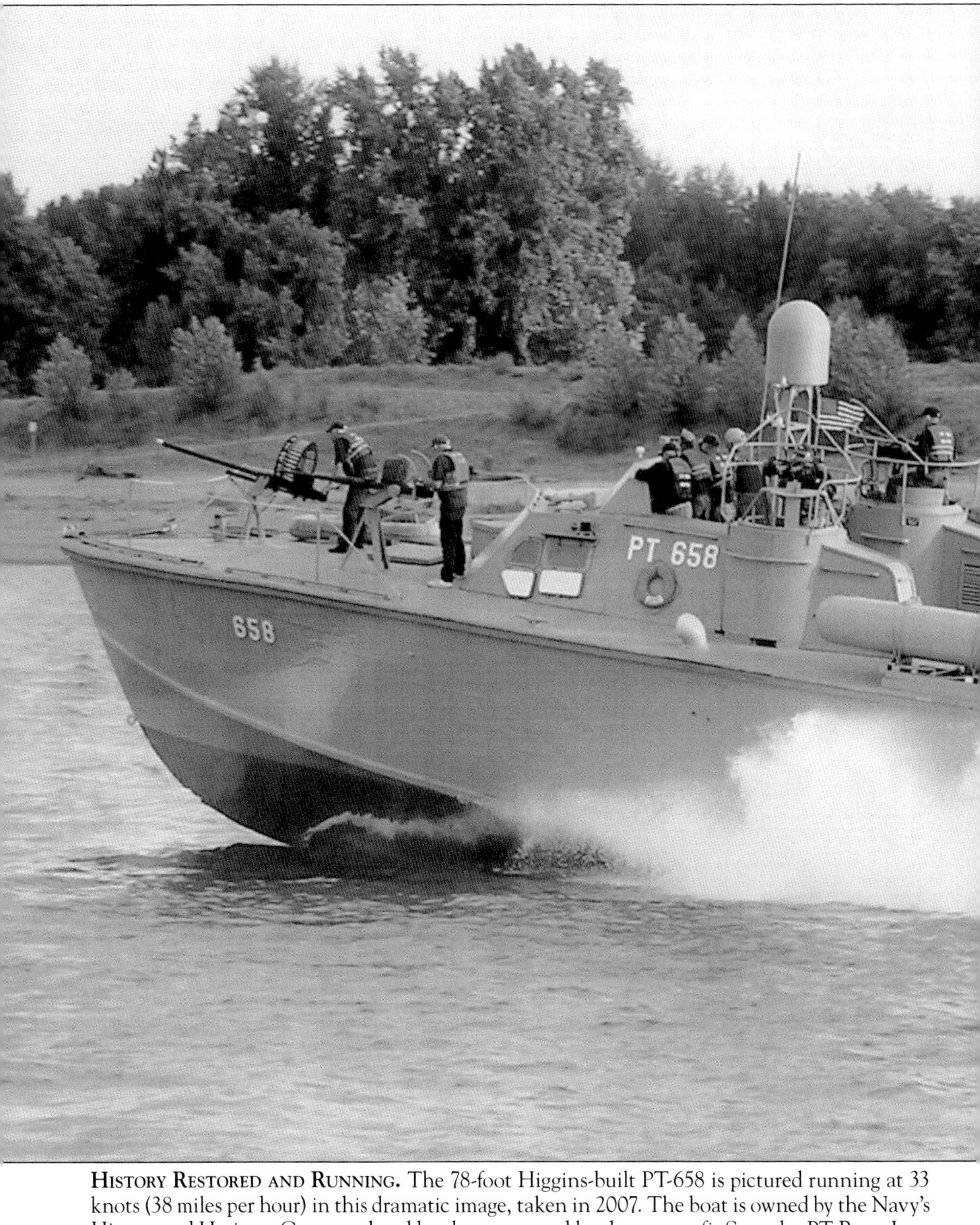

History Restored and Running. The 78-foot Higgins-built PT-658 is pictured running at 33 knots (38 miles per hour) in this dramatic image, taken in 2007. The boat is owned by the Navy's History and Heritage Command and has been restored by the nonprofit Save the PT Boat, Inc., in Portland, Oregon. In 2004, after an eight-year-long restoration process, the 50-ton wooden craft became the only fully restored, equipped, and operating World War II patrol torpedo boat in the world. One of the last of her type built before the war ended, she was destined for transfer

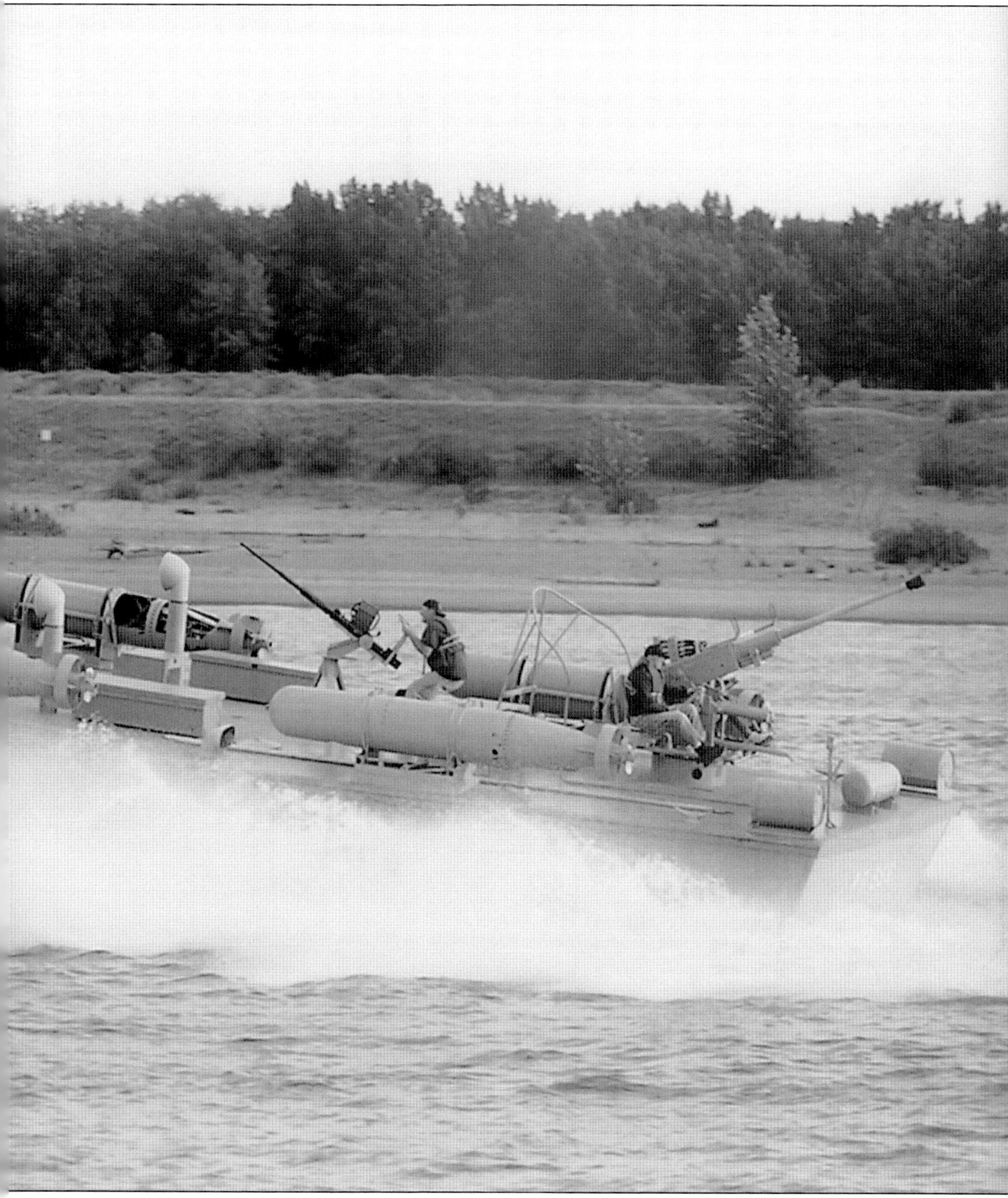

to Russia under the Lend-Lease program. However, the boat escaped this fate when the program was cancelled while she was in Bremerton awaiting turnover to Russia. Subsequently, PT-658 was sent south to California, where during the 1950s and 1960s, she became a missile range patrol boat at Port Hueneme, assigned to the Navy testing unit at the air station at Point Mugu. (Photograph from *Classic Boat* magazine, courtesy Save the PT Boat, Inc.)

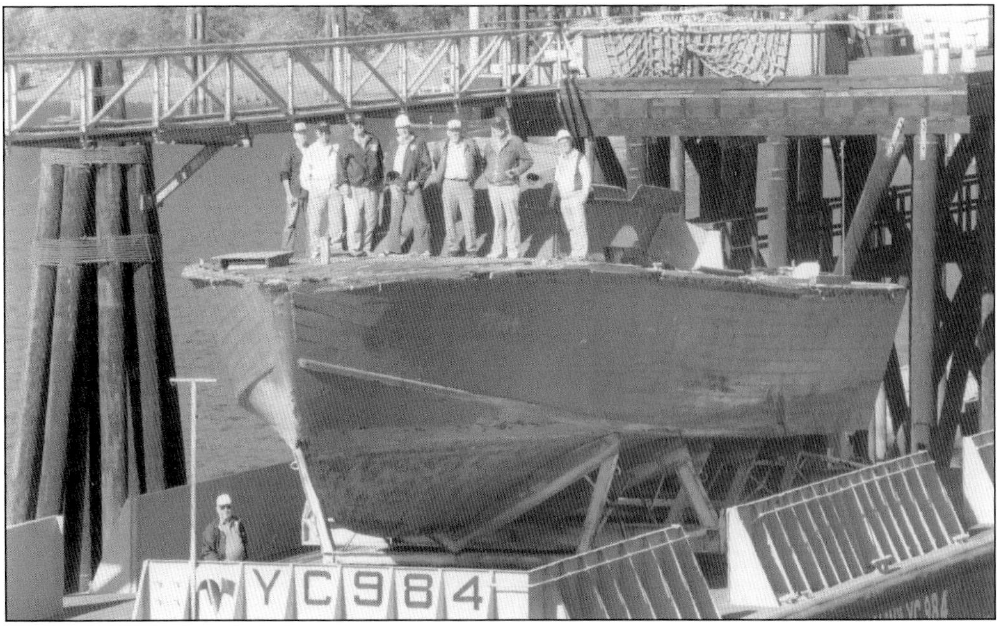

PT in the Rough. PT-658 is shown in 1994 as she arrived on a Navy barge at the Navy and Marine Reserve Center in Portland. She was shipped up the Pacific coast from California aboard a Washington State Army National Guard ship as part of a cargo repositioning training mission. On the foredeck are World War II Navy PT boat veterans who were part of the original crew that acquired the seriously dilapidated wooden boat from its private owner in the San Francisco Bay area. (Courtesy Save the PT Boat, Inc.)

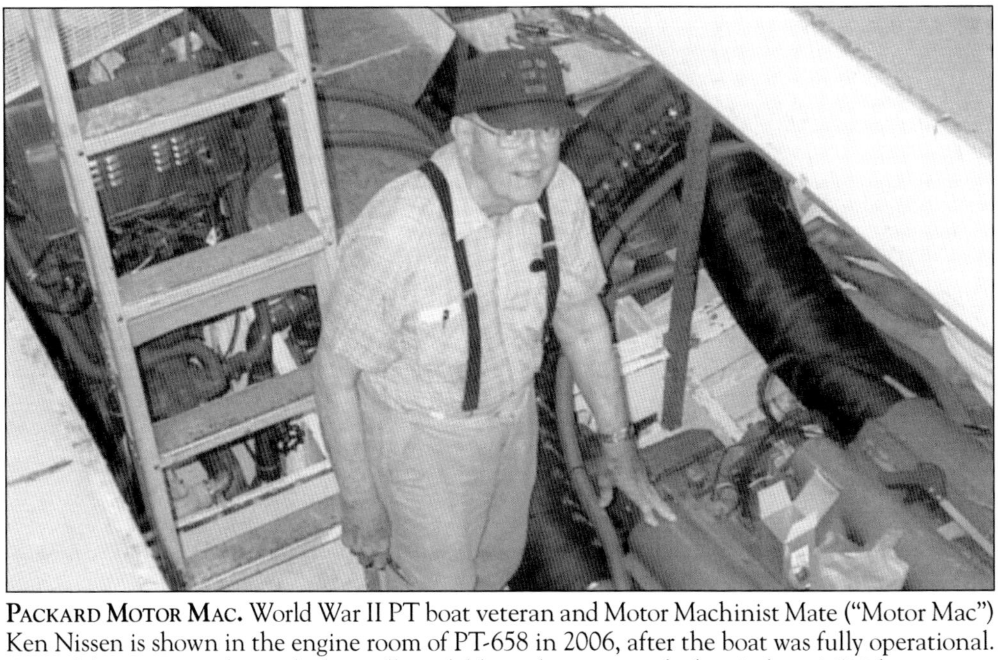

Packard Motor Mac. World War II PT boat veteran and Motor Machinist Mate ("Motor Mac") Ken Nissen is shown in the engine room of PT-658 in 2006, after the boat was fully operational. One of the veterans who worked proudly and diligently to return the boat's three 1,500-horsepower engines to working condition, Nissen served in Squadron 20 aboard the Higgins-built PT-245 in the South Pacific during the war. (Photograph by Chuck Fowler.)

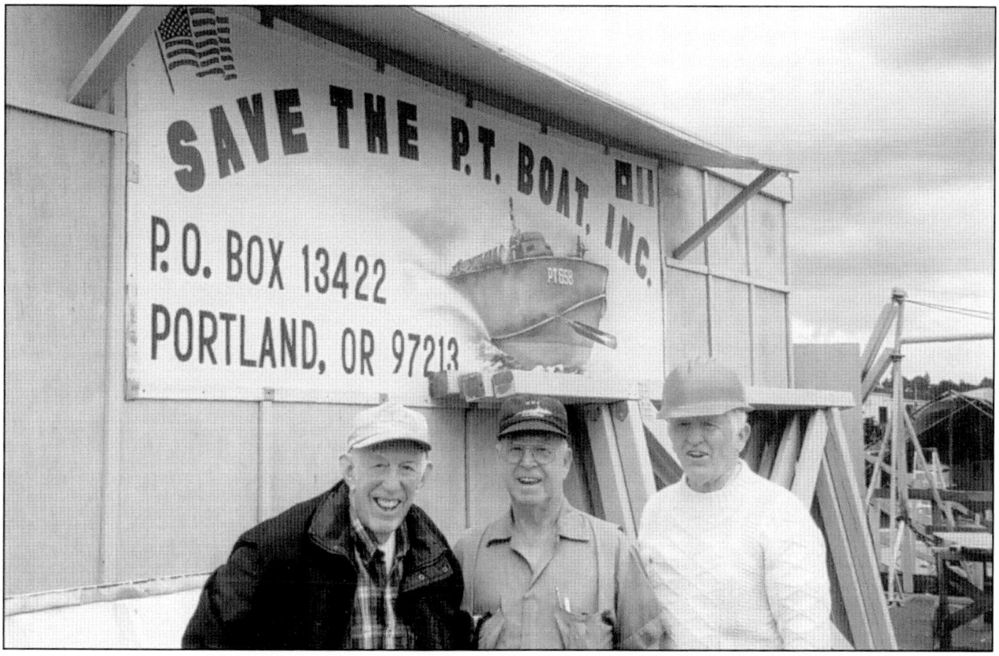

Save the PT Boat Stewards. Three of the Navy veterans who were part of the original Save the PT Boat, Inc. (STPTB) restoration crew and stewards of the boat are, from left to right, Richard (Dick) Lowe, James (Jim) Brunette, and Harry Wiedmaier. Wiedmaier was instrumental in acquiring and transporting PT-658 to Portland and before his passing in 2009 was the respected longtime president of the organization. (Photograph by Chuck Fowler.)

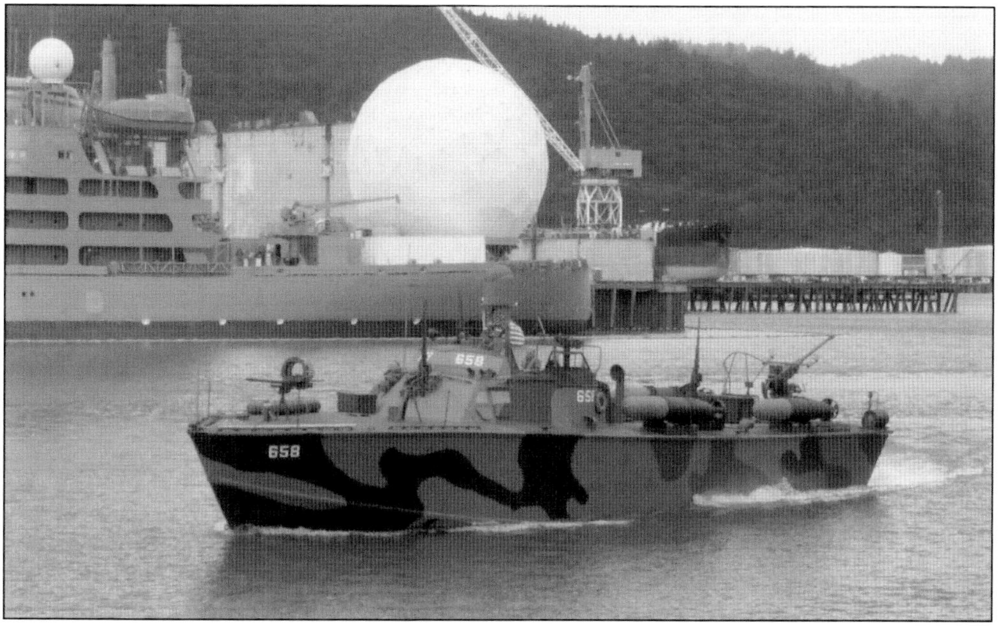

Original World War II Paint. In early 2011, STPTB volunteers restored PT-658's original camouflage paint scheme from when she was launched in April 1945. For more than 15 years after the boat's arrival in Portland for restoration and through her initial years of operation, she had been painted Navy gray. (Photograph by Wally Boerger.)

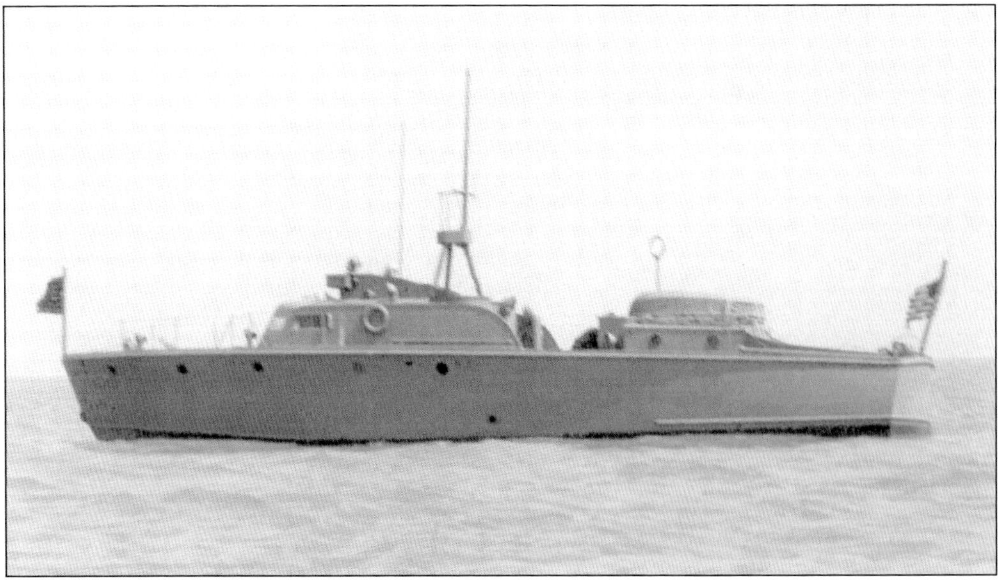

Point Defiance Crash Boat. P-615, pictured here, was one of two 63-foot Army Air Force crash rescue boats (CRBs) brought to Puget Sound and Tacoma under the command of Warrant Officer Charles W. (Bill) Somers in the early summer of 1945. Her purpose was to support air operations at McChord Field, and she was stationed with a small unit at the Point Defiance boathouse to rescue crew members whose disabled aircraft ditched in the sound. (Courtesy Bill Somers.)

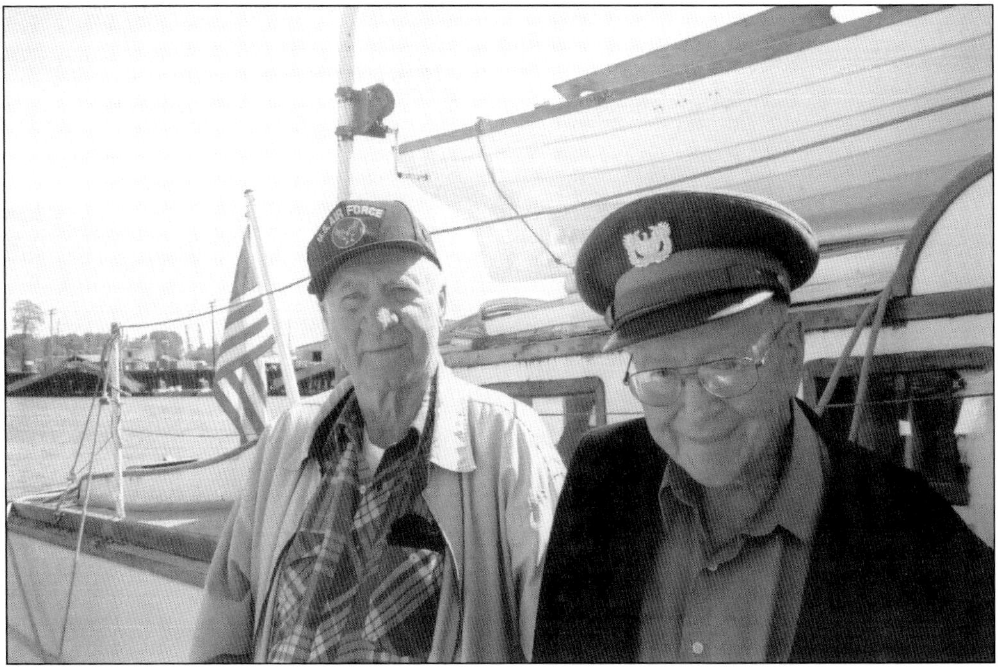

Crash Boat Crewmates. World War II veteran and Army Air Force warrant officer Bill Somers (right) was the skipper of 63-, 85-, and 104-foot crash boats in northern California during the war. He and his wartime first mate, S.Sgt. Clarence "Bunny" Bundrock, who became the skipper of P-615 and, following discharge from active duty, the longtime manager at the boathouse, were reunited in 2004. (Photograph by Chuck Fowler.)

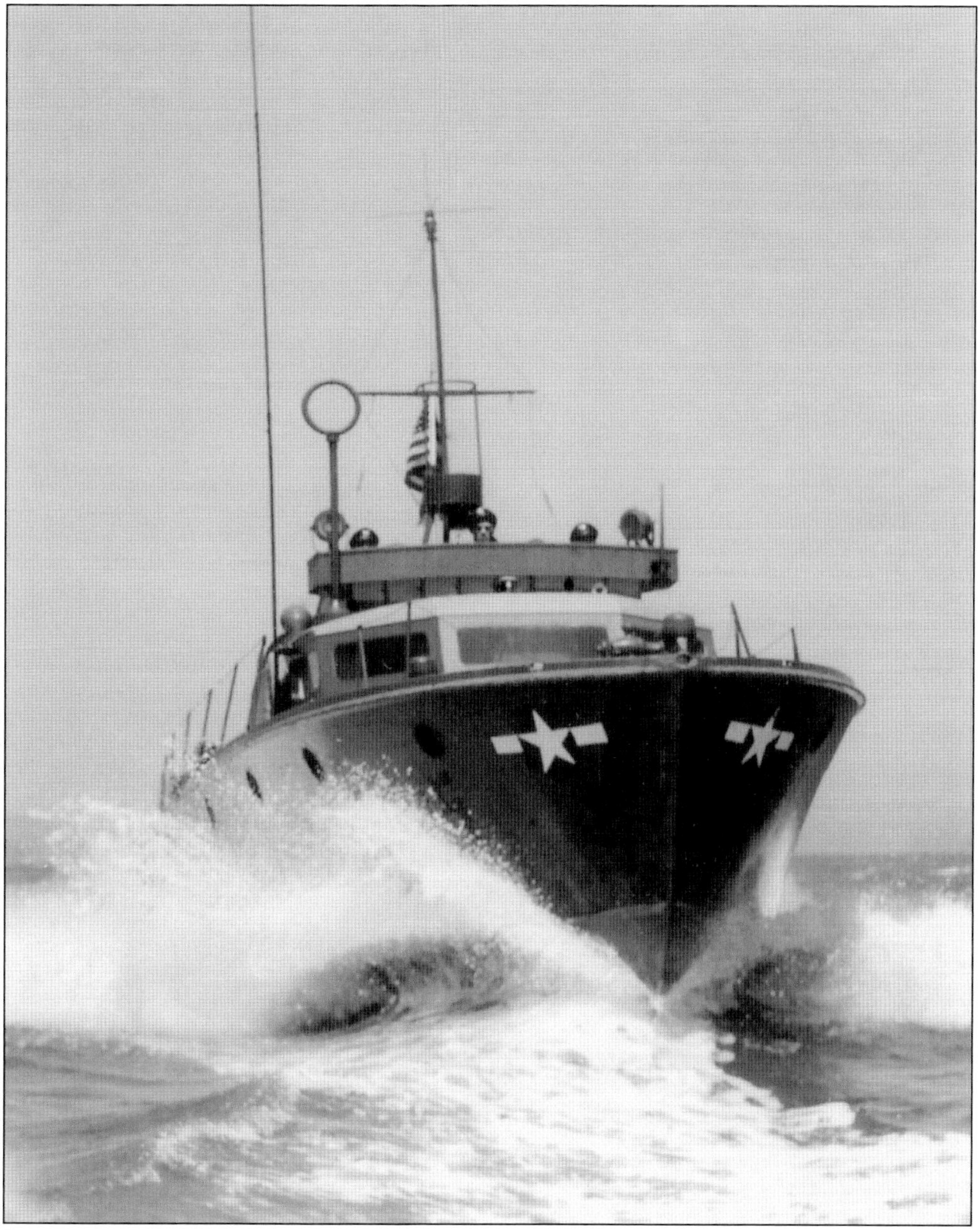

Powering Through. A 63-foot Army Air Force CRB similar to P-615 is depicted here powering through the surf during a training mission. Twin 630-horsepower Hall-Scott V-12 engines, which burned high octane aviation gasoline, drove these 20 ton boats at speeds up to 35 knots (40 miles per hour). Designed by Dair Long during the war, the 63- and 85-foot CRBs were constructed by many builders on the Pacific coast and served in the Navy and Coast Guard as well as the Army Air Force. In addition to the boat stationed in Tacoma, P-614 was assigned to Mukilteo, north of Seattle, to support fighter defense and other air operations at Paine Field in Everett. Carrying a crew that included a medic, the 63-footers featured an infirmary space in the aft cabin designed to provide initial care for rescued crewmembers while en route to shoreside hospital facilities. (Courtesy Bill Somers.)

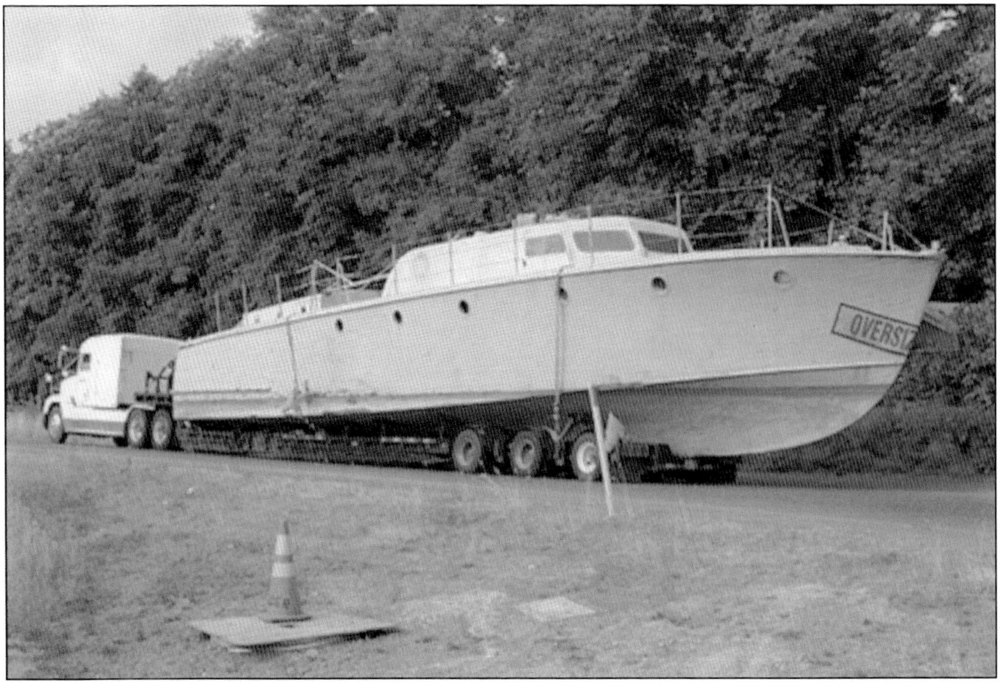

Crash Boat on Wheels. In July 2006, Canadian performance bicycle builder and wooden boat enthusiast Randy Cunningham purchased a 63-foot World War II crash rescue boat in northern California and had her transported to his home in British Columbia. A former Sea Scout training boat in the San Francisco Bay area during the 1960s and 1970s, the ex–Army Air Force P-619 was trailered more than 1,000 miles north on Interstate Highway 5 to her new home in New Westminster. (Photograph by Randy Cunningham.)

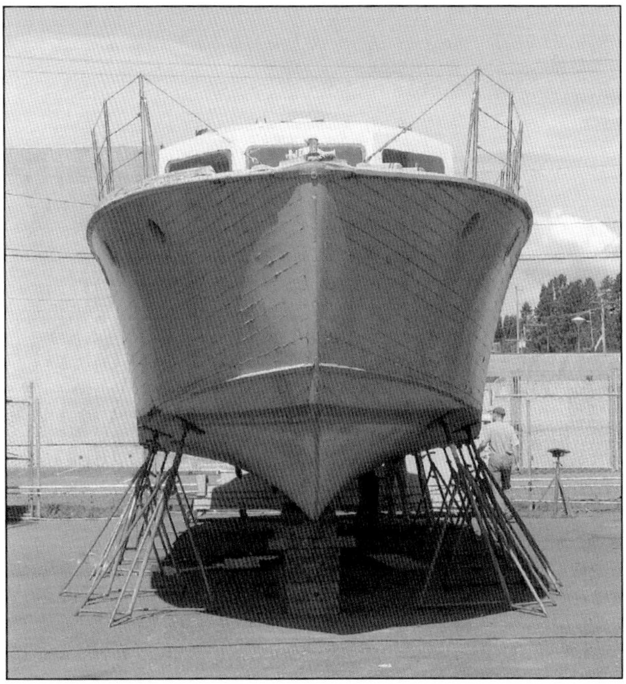

Bow-on Beauty. The sleek, curved lines of a Dair Long–designed 63-foot crash rescue boat are shown in this image taken at the boatyard in Bellingham, Washington. Like PT boats, the fast crash boats' hulls were built of alternating diagonal fir or Oregon pine strips with aircraft cloth glued between and then planked horizontally with Honduras mahogany. P-619 was offloaded and inspected before being placed in the water for her trip across the US-Canadian border under her own power to her new homeport. (Photograph by Chuck Fowler.)

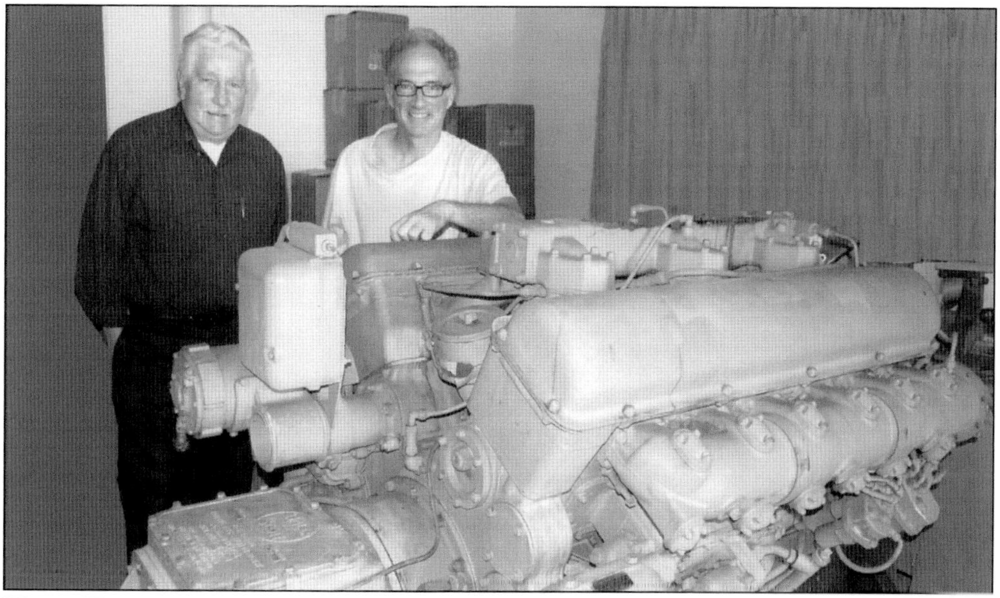

Heavy Horsepower. Korean War US Air Force crash boat veteran Donald (Don) Lashua (left) and Randy Cunningham stand behind one of two 630-horsepower, 3,900-pound Hall Scott Defender V-12 gasoline engines that originally powered 63-foot CRBs during World War II and later in Korea. Cunningham purchased the engines in 2010, both with zero running time since their complete overhaul by the Navy in 1958, to install them in his restored boat, P-619. (Photograph by Chuck Fowler.)

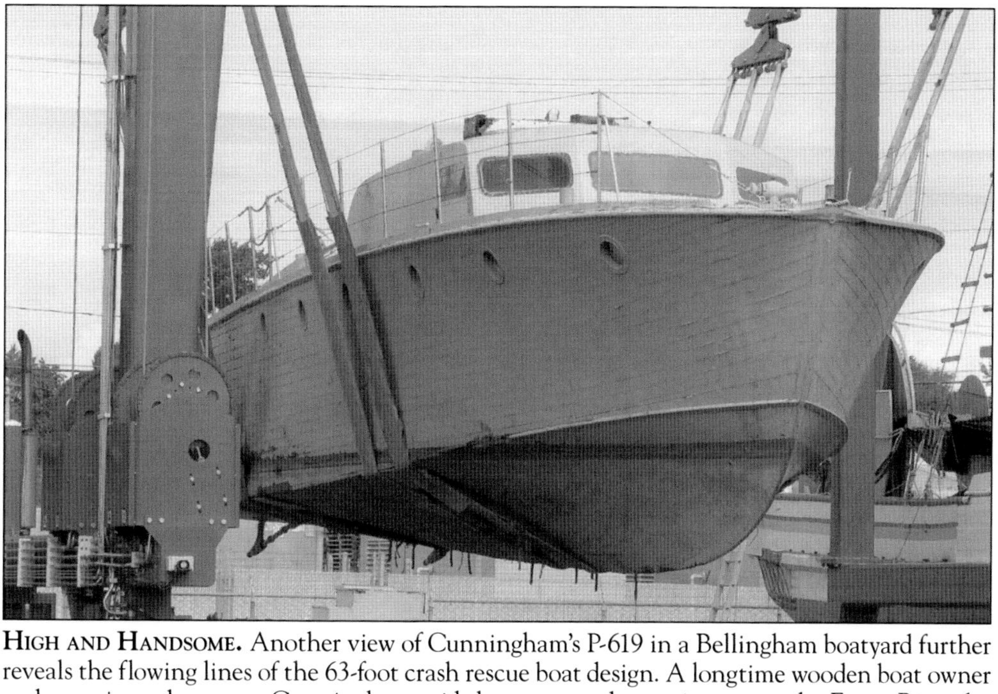

High and Handsome. Another view of Cunningham's P-619 in a Bellingham boatyard further reveals the flowing lines of the 63-foot crash rescue boat design. A longtime wooden boat owner and experienced restorer, Cunningham said that as a youth growing up on the Fraser River, he was attracted to the PT-boat-like appearance of a converted 63-footer operated by the British Columbia Ministry of Forestry as a patrol boat. (Photograph by Chuck Fowler.)

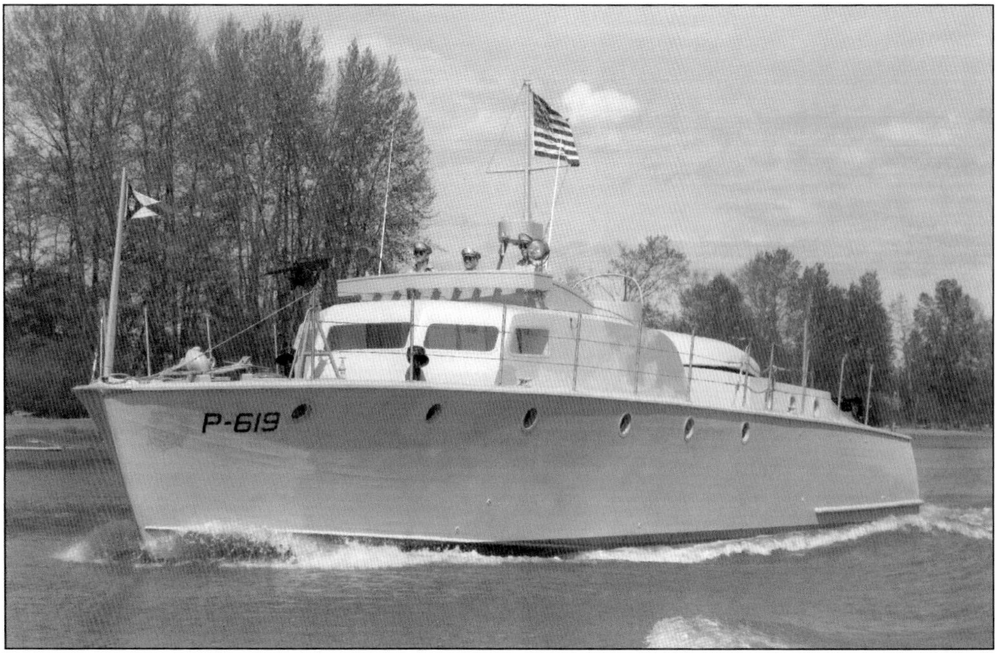

Restored and Underway. Underway on the Fraser River after more than five years of restoration, Randy Cunningham and his volunteer crew are pictured above outfitted in World War II US Army Air Force uniforms to recreate his crash boat's wartime history. With the installation of .50-caliber machineguns in twin turrets and original Hall-Scott Defender engines, the boat will be the most authentically restored 63-foot CRB in the world. The image below shows the beamy transom of P-619 and the aft cabin under the skiff stored on top. This cabin was originally equipped and used to provide initial medical care for crewmembers whose aircraft ditched at sea after accidents or were shot down. (Both photographs by James Milligan.)

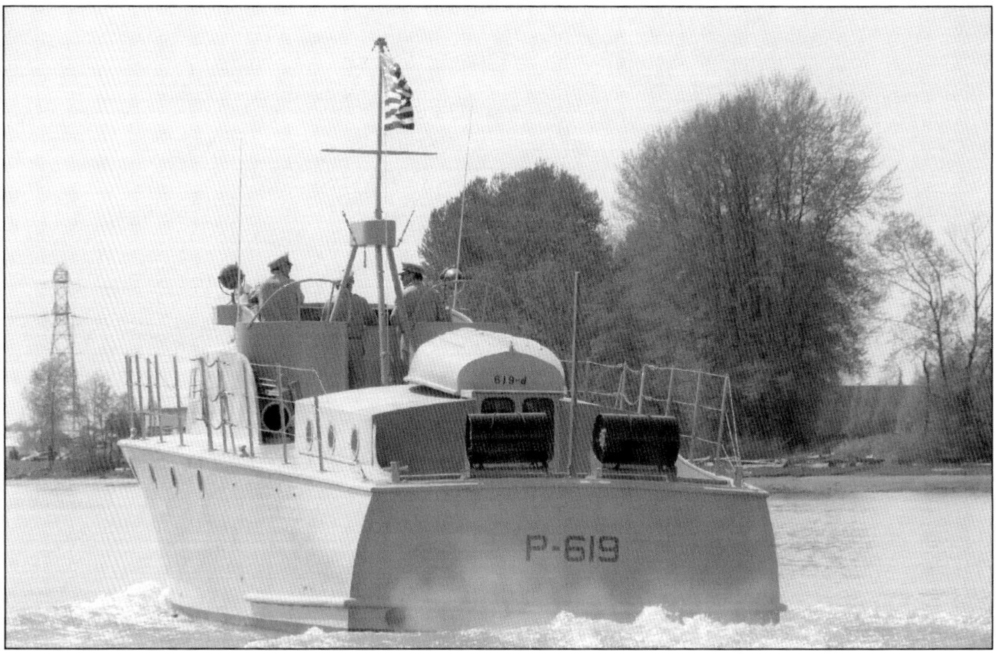

Canadian Connections. During World War II, crash boat service extended across the US-Canada border into British Columbia. Historically, crash rescue boat activity began in Britain in the late 1930s, when the Royal Air Force established fast boat units to rescue air crews downed in the English Channel and elsewhere during initial hostilities with Germany. Using Canadian versions of the early Scott Paine–designed patrol torpedo boats, the Royal Canadian Air Force stationed a crash boat unit at Patricia Bay Air Base near Sidney on Vancouver Island. The image below shows the M-232 *Takuli* being eased into the water on its mobile cradle during the war. George Maude, who served as a crewman on a sister crash boat, the M-235 *Huron*, is pictured at right with a personally built model of his wartime craft. (Right, photograph by Chuck Fowler; below, courtesy of George Maude.)

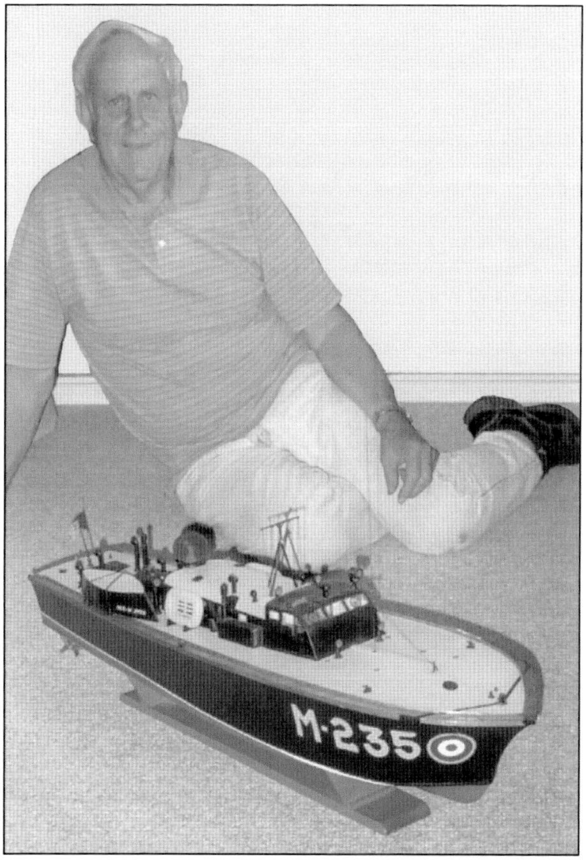

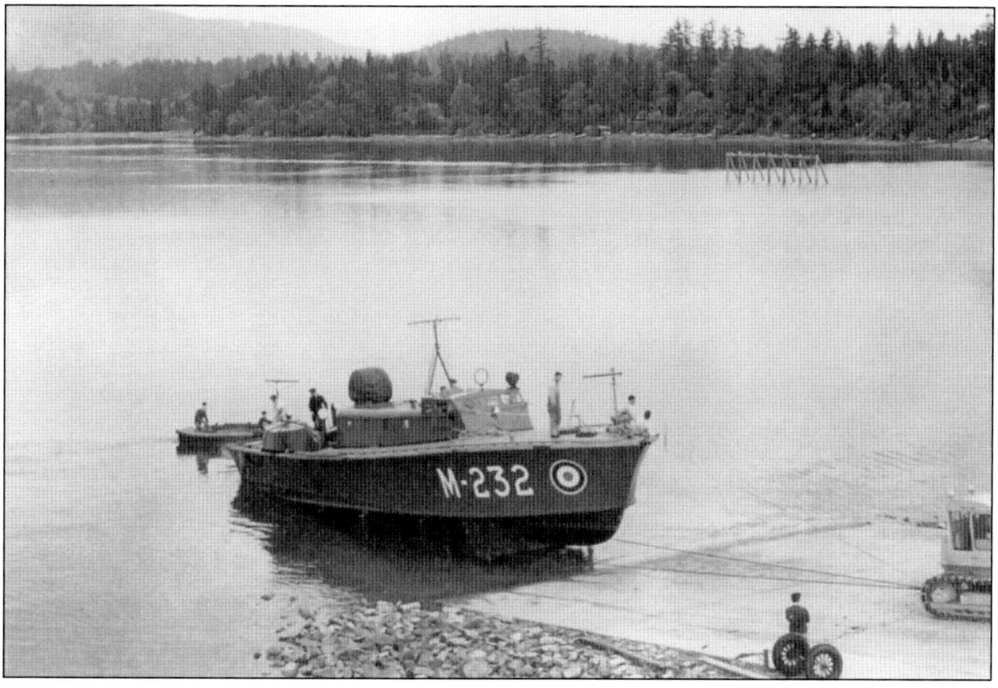

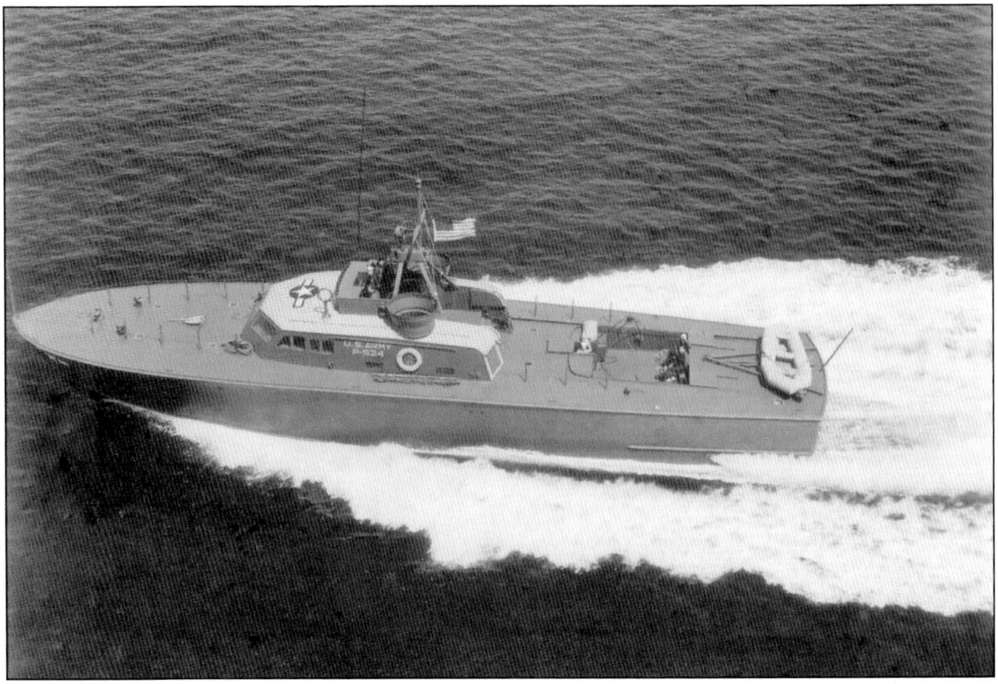

Crash Boat Crewmen, Past and Present. The 85-foot Army Air Force crash rescue boat P-524 is pictured above at full speed in an official photograph taken in 1945, toward the end of the war. Warrant Officer Bill Somers was the skipper of this boat when it was assigned to Hamilton Field on San Francisco Bay and subsequently on the Pacific coast at Bodega Bay. Somers, second from right, is shown holding a model of P-524 during the 2005 visit to his Museum of Puget Sound on Stretch Island by the crew of the restored crash rescue boat P-520. The crewmembers, from left to right, are Tony Wasson, Don Broker, Joe Plesente, Somers, and Jerry Tretter. (Above, courtesy Bill Somers; below, photograph by Kurt Tretter.)

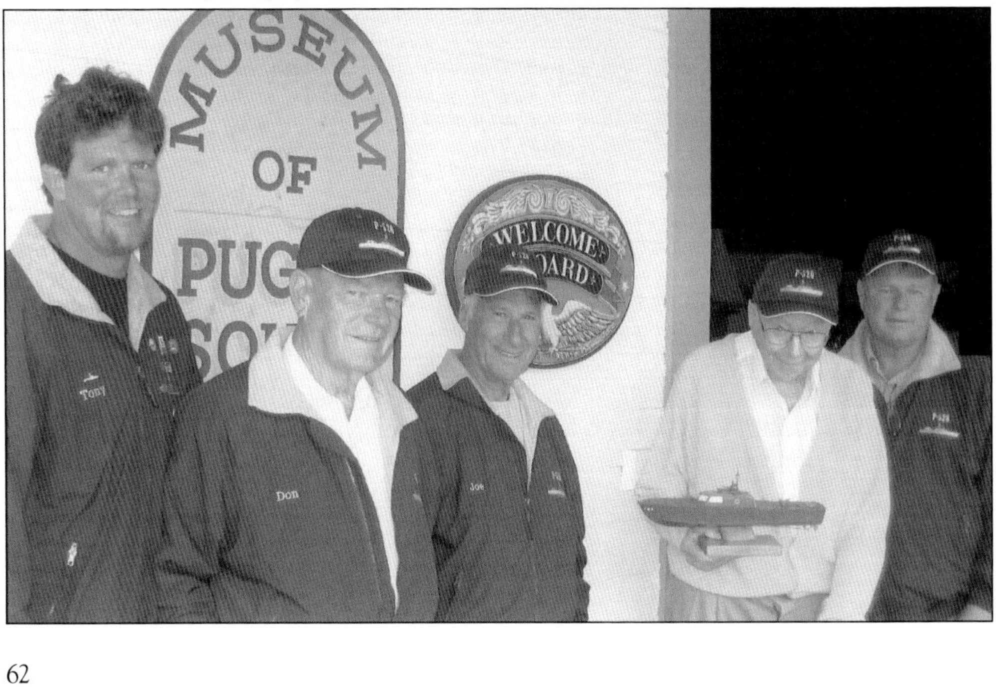

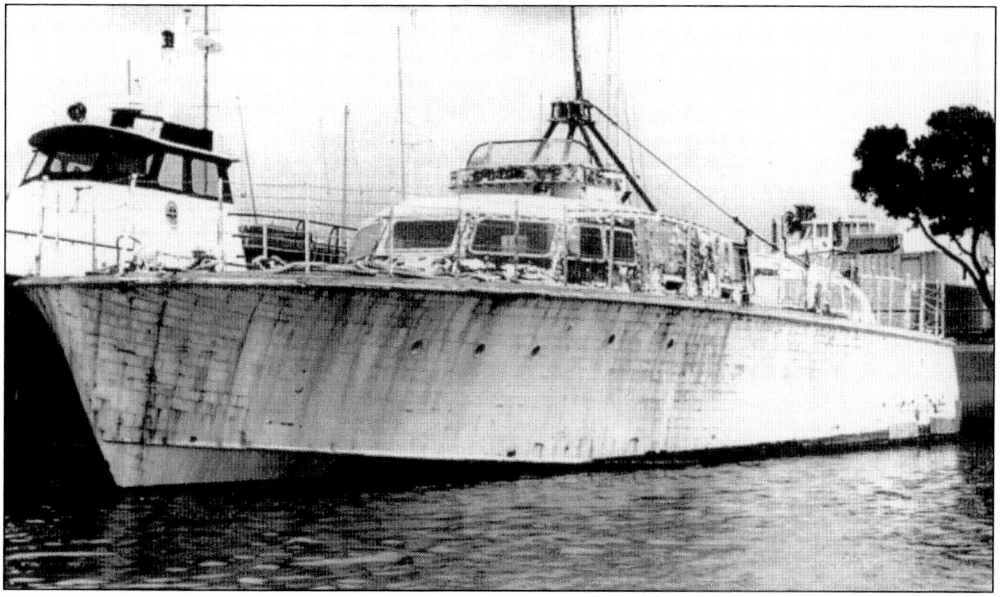

Restoration Revealed. The World War II wooden crash rescue boat P-520 was in very poor condition, as revealed by the 1997 photograph above, taken when she was acquired by US Air Force veteran and Korean War crash boat crewman Delbert "Bud" Tretter. Tretter, the owner of Long Beach Marina Shipyard, worked with his sons, Jerry and Kurt, and their employees, for eight years on P-520's major restoration. With the exception of her original twin 1,500-horsepower engines and basic system upgrades, the boat has been returned to virtually original wartime condition. The quality of the boat's restoration work is shown in the photograph below, taken during her proud participation in the parade of ships at the 2005 Tacoma Tall Ships event, viewed by more than 500,000 spectators. (Above, courtesy Bud Tretter; below, photograph by Christopher J. Yetter Photography.)

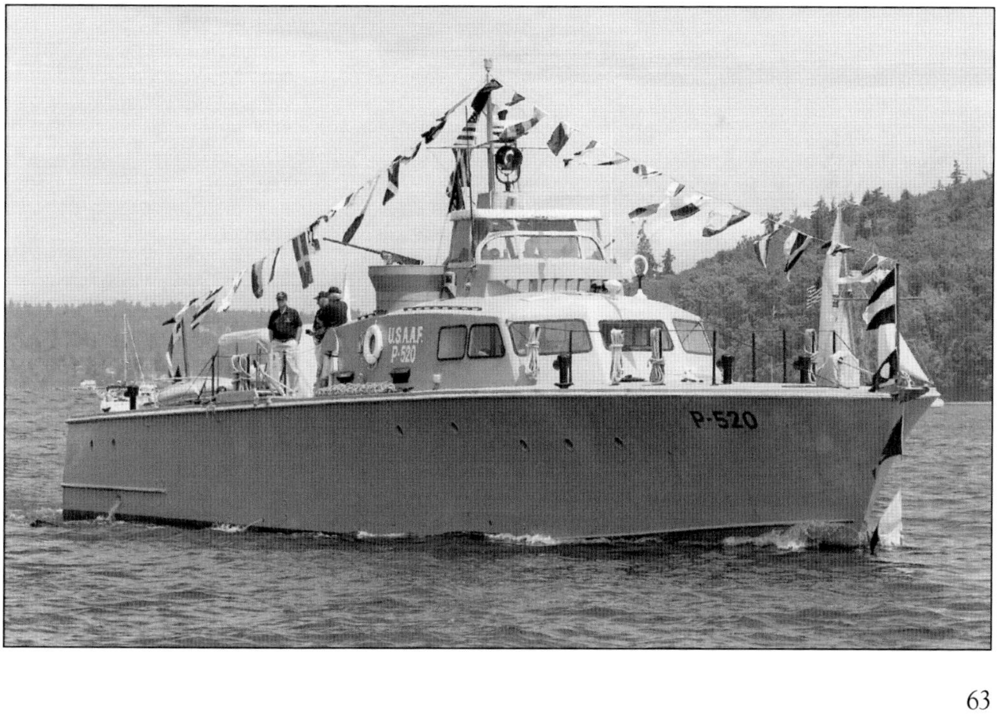

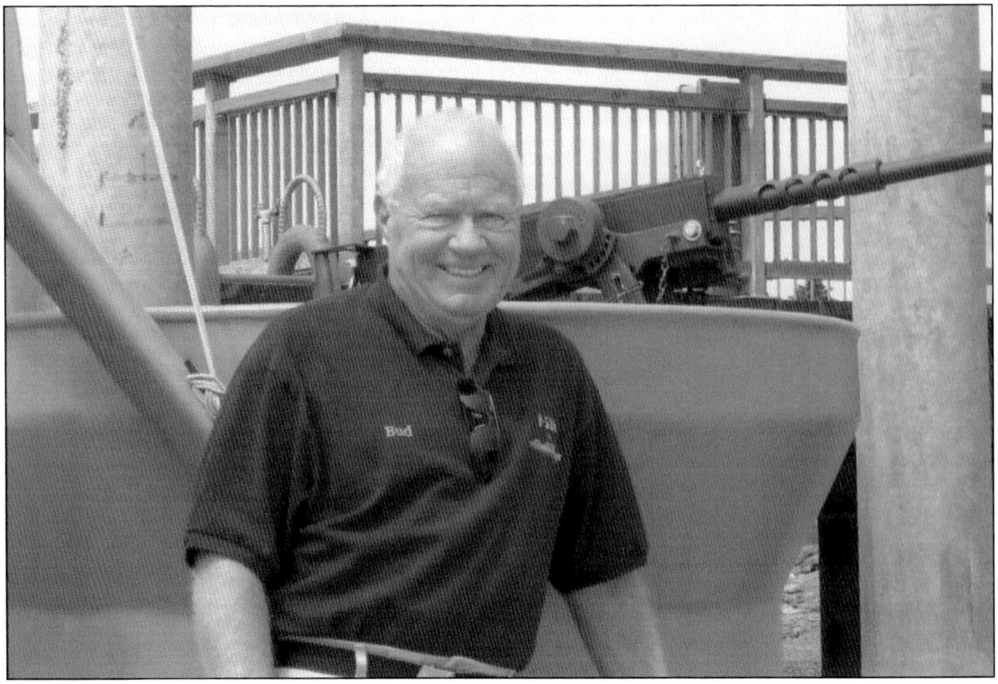

Bud and His Boat. Bud Tretter, shown above aboard P-520 during her visit to Puget Sound in 2005, spent more than $1 million to restore a crash boat similar to the one he served on as a crewmember during the Korean War in the early 1950s. In addition to aircraft crew rescue duties, his boat ran CIA spies in and out of North Korea on covert missions. The image below shows P-520 in Bremerton approaching the museum ship USS *Turner Joy*, one of two Navy destroyers involved in the Tonkin Gulf incident in August 1964, which led to active US involvement in the Vietnam War. The crash boat crew toured the historic ship, which was launched in Seattle in 1958 and hauled out for maintenance several times at the Puget Sound Navy Yard during its 23 years of active Navy service. (Above, photograph by Tony Wasson; below, photograph by Chuck Fowler.)

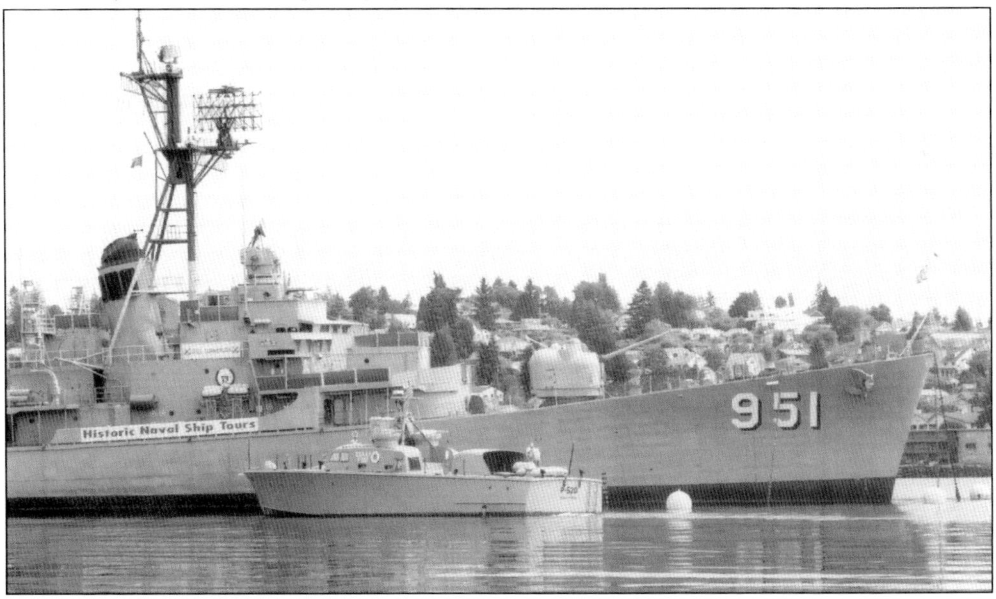

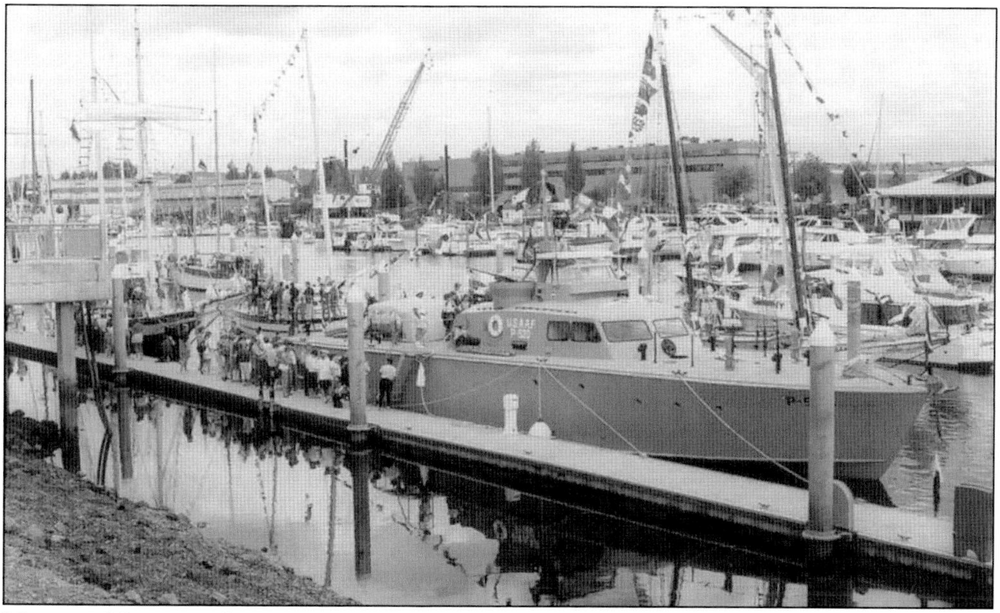

Military Maritime Attraction. P-520 is pictured above dockside during the Tacoma Tall Ships event in 2005 as visitors line up to go aboard. The historic World War II crash boat attracted more than 1,300 people in her three and a half days in Tacoma before moving on to Seattle for an exhibit over the Independence Day weekend at the Wooden Boat Festival at Lake Union Park. In total, more than 3,000 people toured the boat during its month-long visit to Washington State and Puget Sound. Often mistaken for a PT boat, which is slightly smaller, the sleek, beamy, 85-foot-long P-520 is seen below approaching the Hiram Chittenden Locks in Seattle's Ballard neighborhood on her way to the Wooden Boat Festival. (Above, photograph by Chuck Fowler; below, photograph by Brad Lashua.)

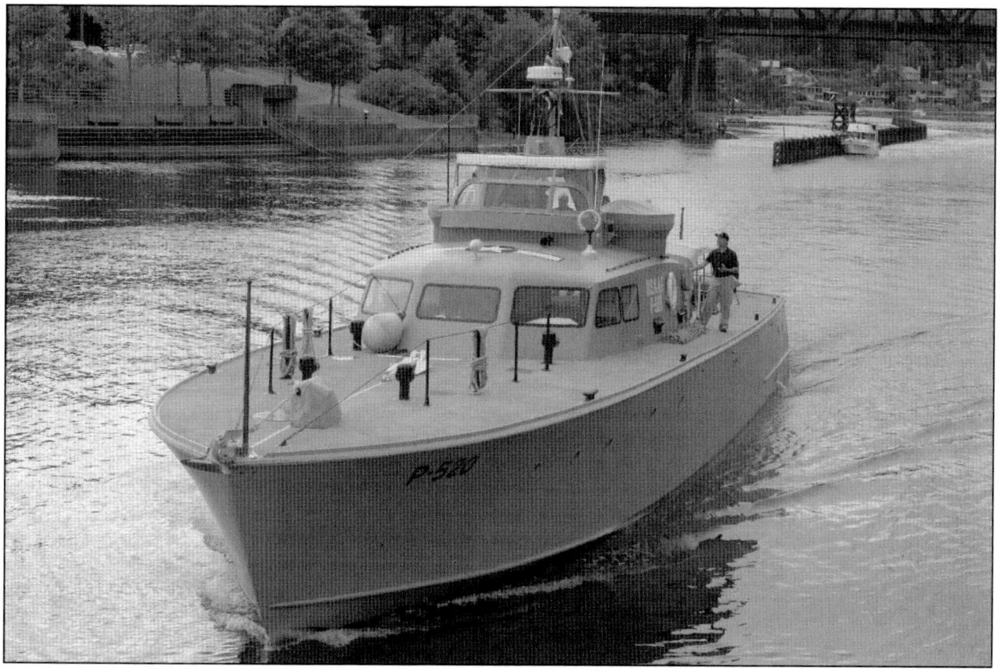

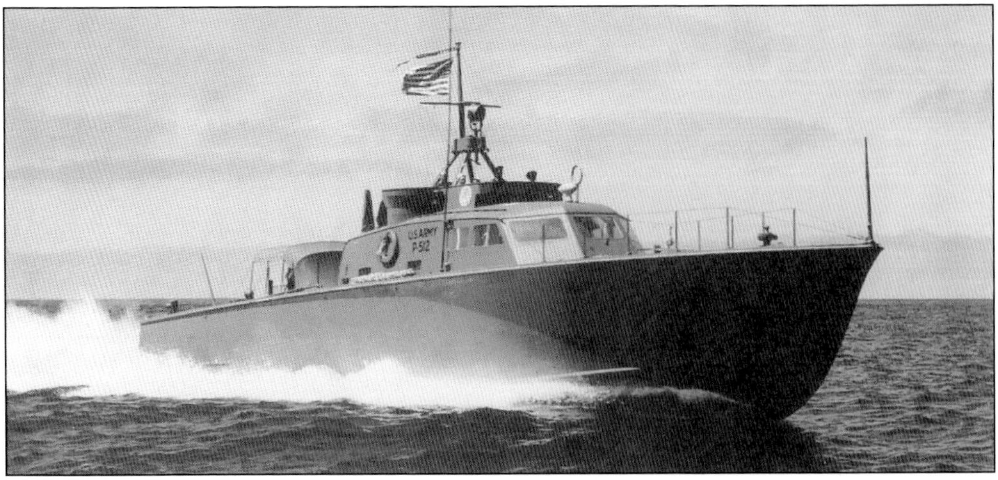

Crash Boats in Puget Sound. Although no 85-foot crash rescue boats were built in Seattle during World War II, many constructed in California were outfitted in June 1944 at the Olsen & Winge Marine Works in Ballard before leaving under their own power for assignment in Alaska. The photograph above shows P-512, one of five boats brought up the Pacific coast from the Wilmington Boat Works in the Los Angeles area, entering Puget Sound. Aboard was Army Air Force technical sergeant Harold (Hal) Turner, second from the right in the first row of the image below, who served as the boat's executive officer. Called "Big Stoop" by his crewmates because of his six-foot, four-inch height, Turner became a naval architect in Seattle after the war and later worked on commercial and military hydrofoil projects for the Boeing Company in the 1970s. (Both courtesy Hal Turner.)

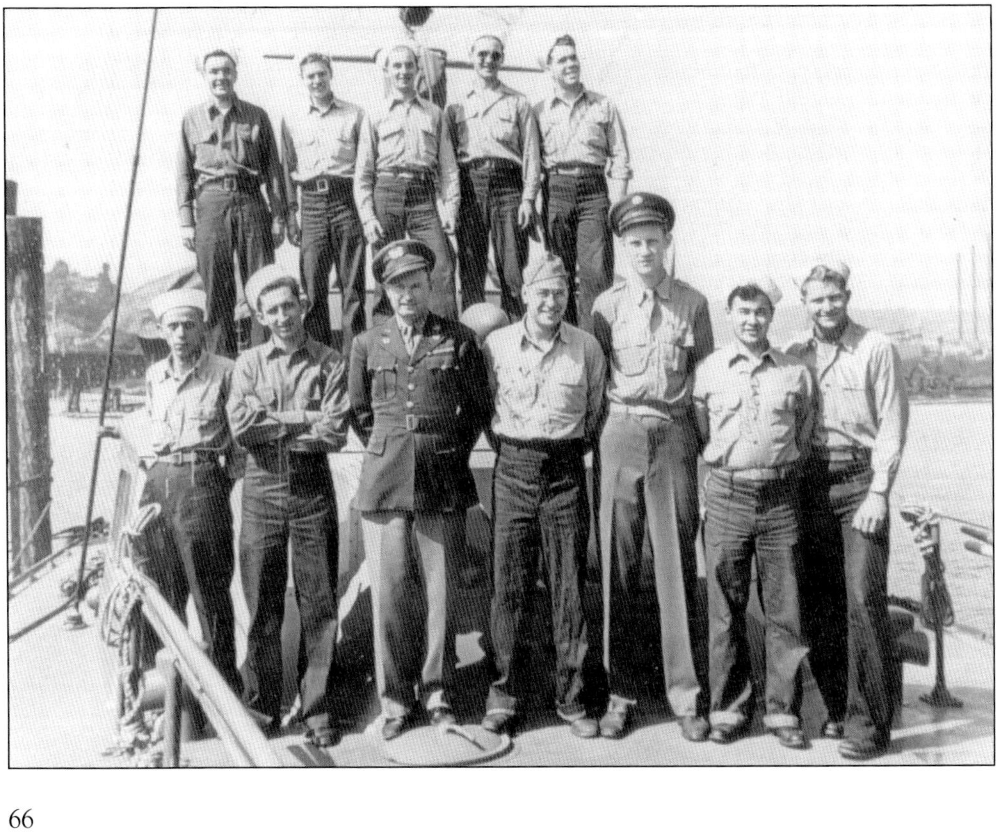

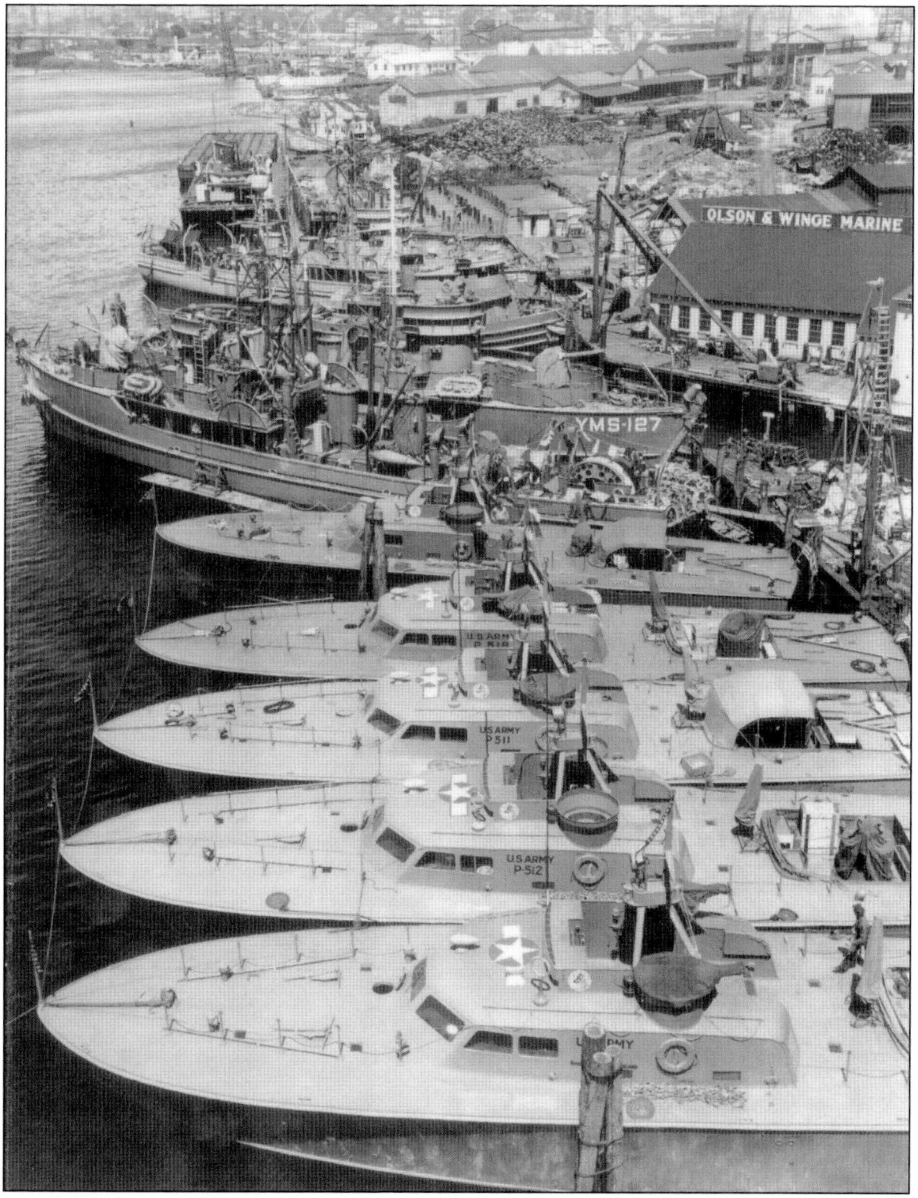

SHIPYARD SCENE. Seattle's Olsen & Winge Marine Works gained an excellent reputation during World War II for its ability to build quality smaller vessels and solve challenging outfitting and repair problems. Known by some as the "Swede Shipyard," the business was located on the Lake Washington Ship Canal and worked on hundreds of projects throughout the war. The documentation photograph featured here depicts five crash rescue boats, yard minesweepers, and other vessels being outfitted before leaving for various assignments, including Alaska's Aleutian Islands. According to a collections guide prepared for the Museum of History and Industry (MOHAI), from about 1941 to 1944, Olsen & Winge "devoted its production facilities completely to the war effort." The description continued that the business was "the first shipyard in the Northwest to begin a full program of Army-Navy repair and refitting work" and specifically mentioned that the yard "performed extensive outfitting of uncompleted high-powered aircraft rescue boats" and repaired others. (Courtesy MOHAI, No. 72.5503.103.)

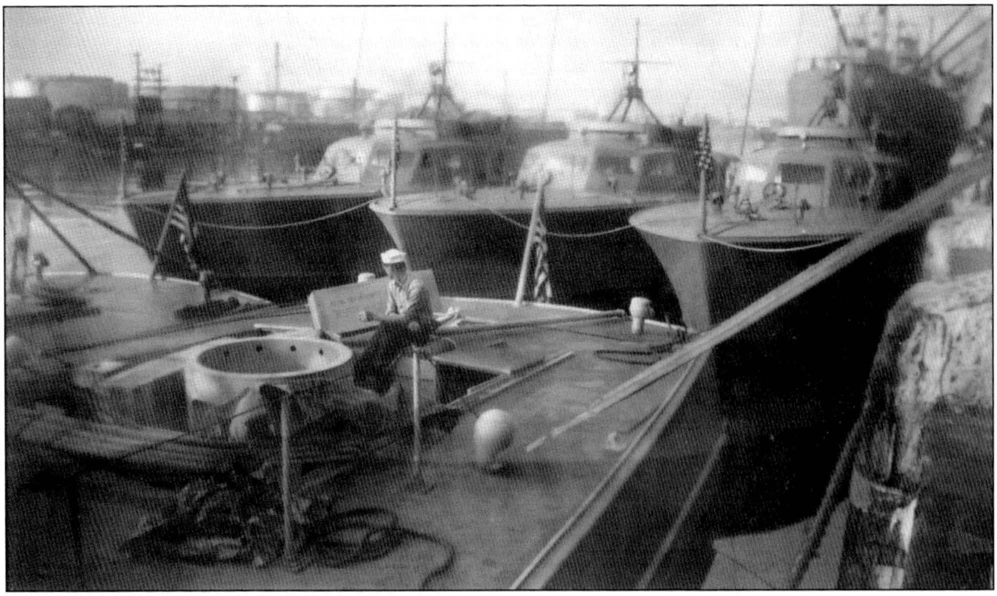

From Seattle to Alaska. A lone Army Air Force sailor is seen above in June 1944 looking over a package on the stern of one of five 85-foot crash boats moored at Piers 90–91 in Seattle. The boats had arrived from California and were on their way to the Olsen & Winge shipyard for outfitting. The round base for a 20-millimeter cannon is visible at left, while a cargo freighter is seen moored at the pier in the background. After her 2,500-mile trip north through British Columbia's Inside Passage and then west in the open Pacific Ocean, the P-512 is pictured below tied to a dock at Attu Island in Alaska. (Both courtesy Hal Turner, US Army Air Force.)

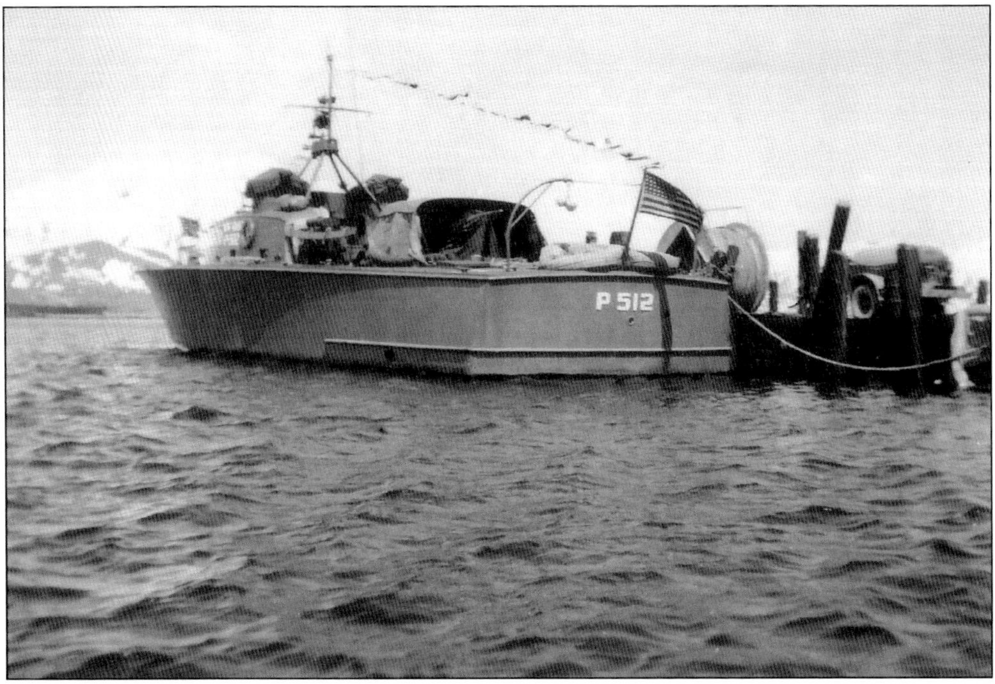

Insignia and Instruction. Like 1,200 other military units during World War II, the Army Air Forces's 10th Emergency Rescue Boat Squadron, based in Alaska, had its own Walt Disney Studios–designed insignia provided at no charge. As seen at right, the artwork featured a determined Donald Duck in a raincoat driving a small fast boat to the scene of a rescue. This embroidered version was presented to former squadron members at an Army Air Force/US Air Force Crash Rescue Boat Association reunion in Newport Beach, California, in 2004. The photograph below shows young T.Sgt. Hal Turner in training, firing a twin .50-caliber machinegun aboard an 85-foot CRB in Alaska in 1944. While CRBs stationed stateside carried no machineguns or cannons, those in combat zones like Alaska were fully armed. (Both courtesy Hal Turner, US Army Air Force.)

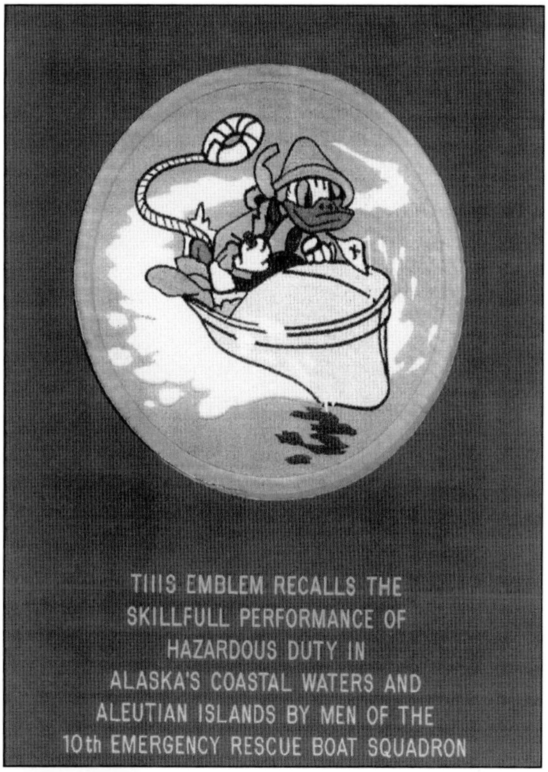

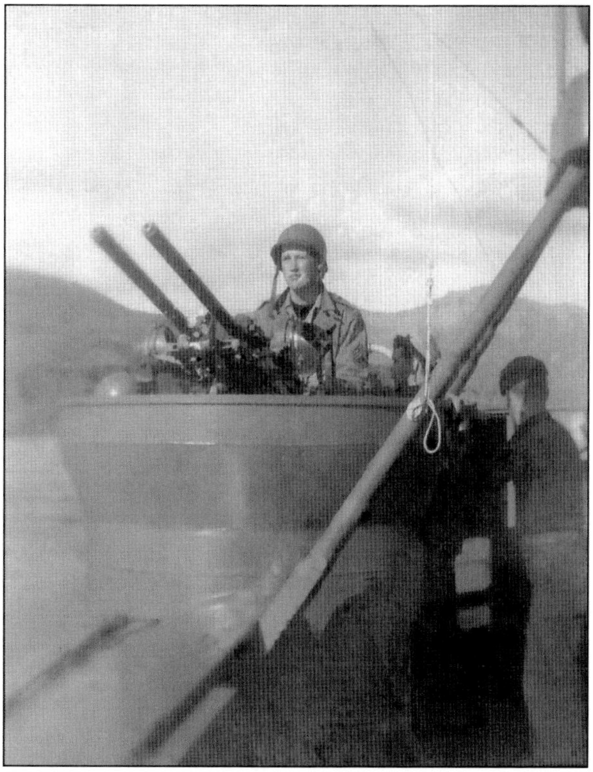

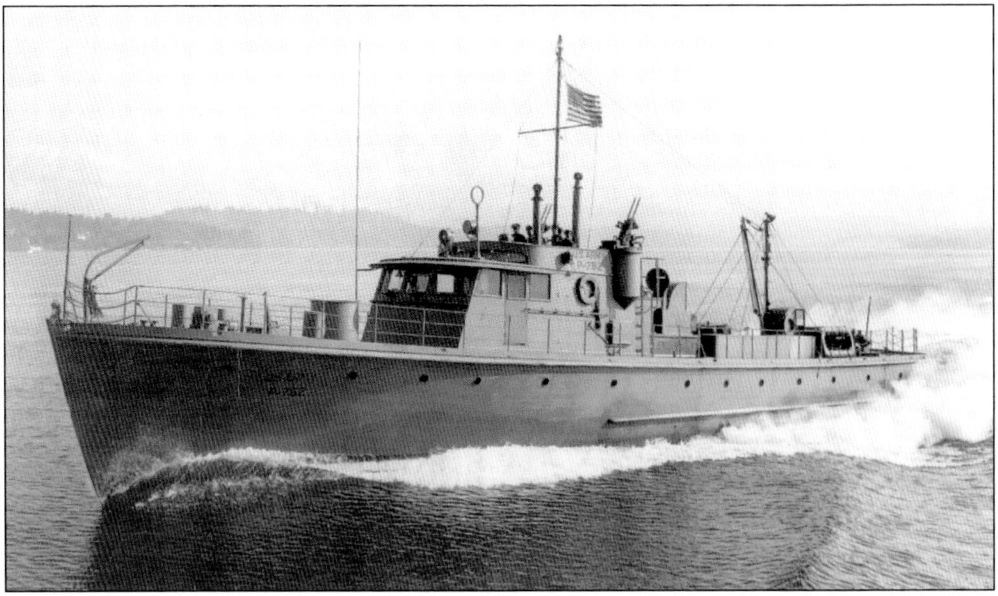

Sea Trial on Lake Washington. While Seattle shipyards like Sagstad in Ballard built 104-foot crash rescue boats during World War II for Alaska operations, Olsen & Winge was given the difficult assignment of redoing the faulty construction work of some Atlantic coast shipyards. The initial 104-foot CRBs assigned to Alaskan service, P-114 and P-115, were built in 1943 by Stephens Brothers Boat Builders in Stockton, California. However, the later boat shown above, P-752, was built on the East Coast and after extensive retrofit work at Olsen & Winge was tested during a sea trial in Lake Washington in 1944. While crash boat skippers were normally warrant officers or noncommissioned officers, an unidentified Army Air Force captain is seen below at the helm during a sea trial. (Above, courtesy MOHAI No. 72.5503.122; below, No. 72.5503.123.)

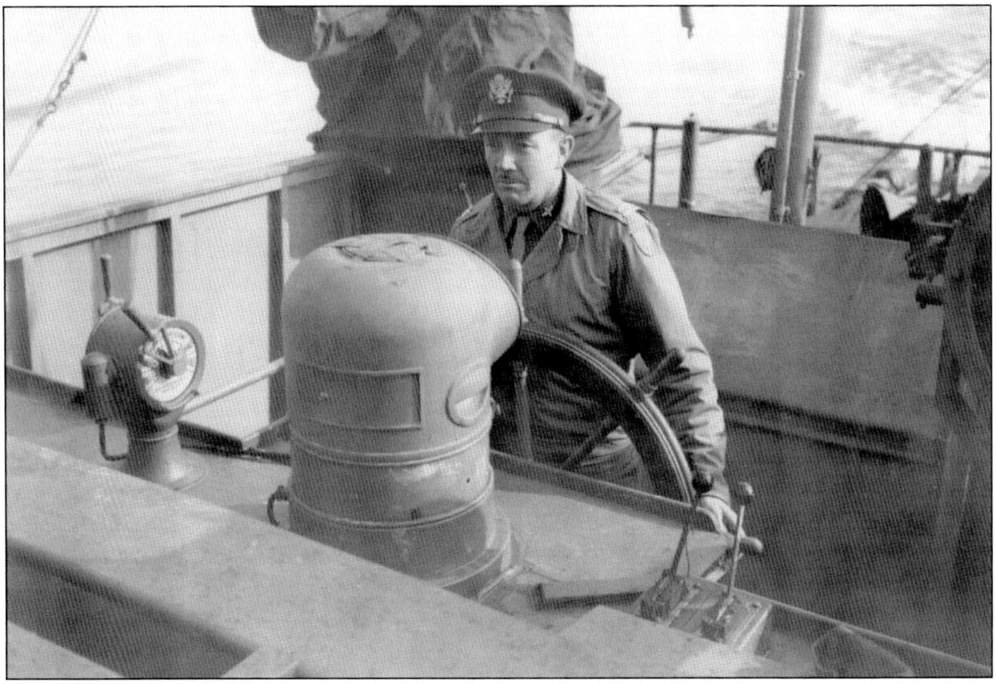

Three

The Cold War Era 1946–1991

The Cold War years, from the end of World War II until the collapse of Communism and the Soviet Union in 1991, also included two regional "hot" wars with international implications for the United States. The Korean War from 1950 to 1953 and the Vietnam War from 1964 to 1975 restarted the industrial armament buildup at home, which included the maritime industry. As they had during World War II, Puget Sound boat builders responded impressively to this new need.

While many mothballed vessels built and operated during World War II were recommissioned for the Korean War, some new boats were constructed—US Air Force crash rescue boats built in Seattle, for example. In addition, the Coast Guard 83-foot patrol boats introduced during World War II became the service's primary security, law enforcement, marine safety, and sometimes firefighting vessels during the first 15 years of this period. In Puget Sound, they were assigned to Coast Guard stations in Bellingham, Friday Harbor, Port Angeles, Port Townsend, and Tacoma.

Little more than a decade after the armistice between South and North Korea, another perceived international threat to US security developed in Vietnam. As part of the balanced naval response of capital ships, specifically aircraft carriers, the Navy also ordered new smaller vessels such as offshore patrol gunboats and fast, highly maneuverable 32-foot PBRs (patrol boat river) capable of operating in the confined rivers and estuaries common in Vietnam. In addition, Boeing began experimenting and adapting its civilian hydrofoil designs for use as high-speed offshore patrol boats.

During the Cold War and regional "hot" war eras, Seattle shipbuilders built destroyers and other major ships, and they and the Puget Sound Naval Shipyard repaired and maintained other major vessels. But Puget Sound builders of smaller patrol and rescue craft also thrived. By being flexible and adapting their production methods, they met rapidly evolving military needs both abroad and at home.

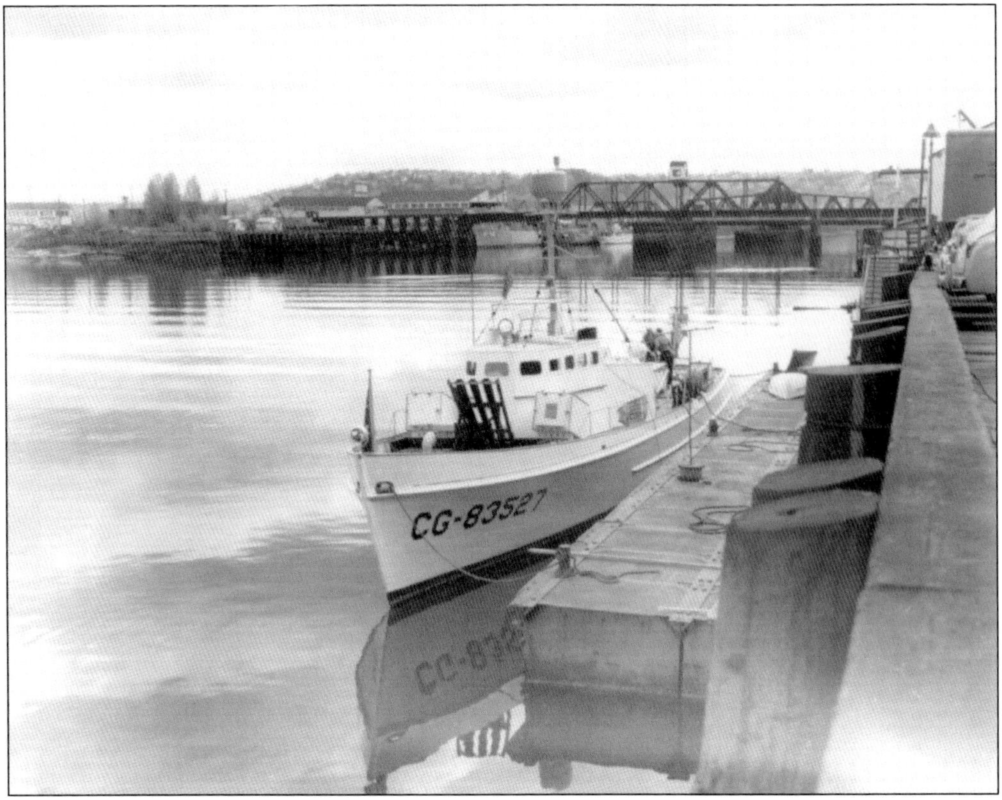

TACOMA HOMEPORT. Pictured above, from 1945 through the Korean War era to her decommissioning in 1962, CG-83527 was based in downtown Tacoma at the Municipal Dock building, near the Eleventh Street Bridge over City Waterway. The 83-foot patrol boat was responsible for marine law enforcement, search and rescue, water safety, and navigation aids monitoring in south Puget Sound from Des Moines in the north to Olympia in the south. The photograph below, taken in the late 1950s, shows the boat underway on Commencement Bay at near full speed, about 20 knots (23 miles per hour). (Above, courtesy Tacoma Public Library; below, PSMHS.)

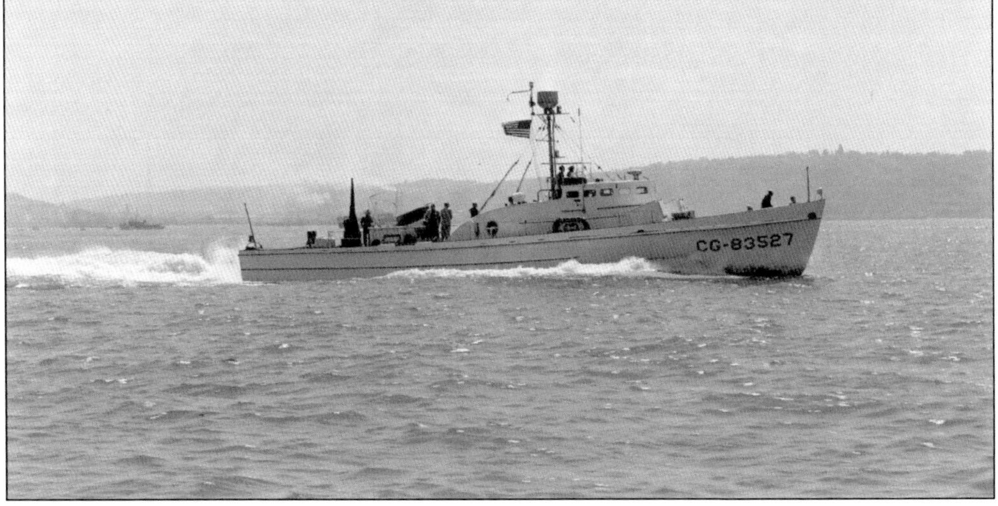

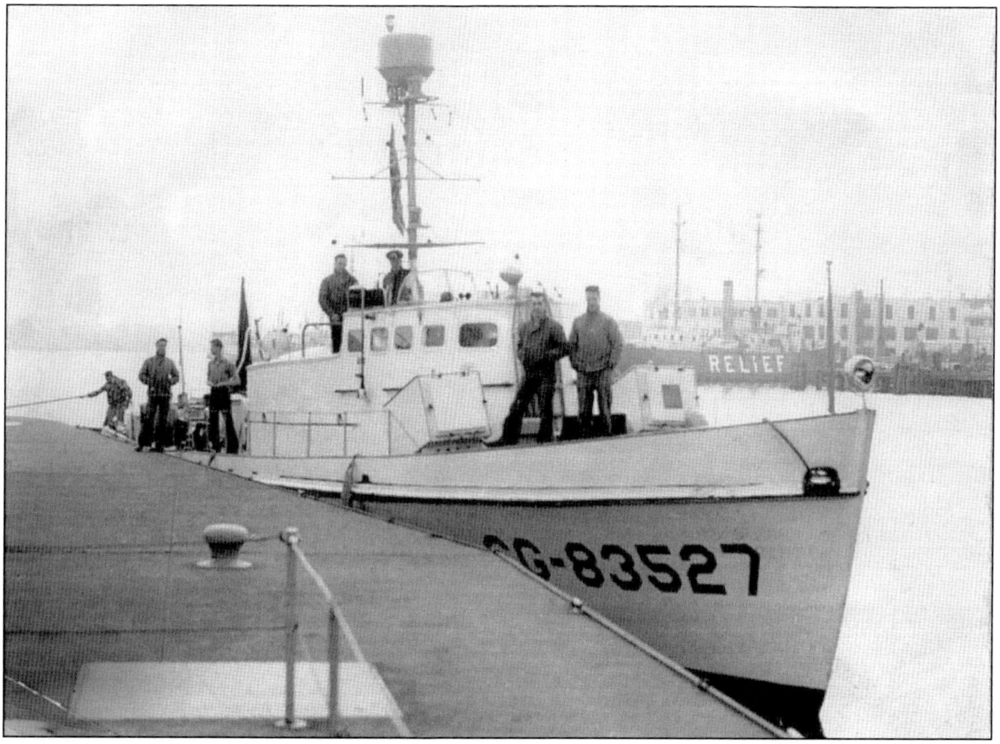

Tie Up and Trestle Action. During her 17 years of active service, CG-83527 passed in and out of the government locks in Seattle countless times. The cutter and her crew are shown above moored at the Ballard Locks with the Coast Guard support base, including the lightship *Relief*, in the background. Among the crewmembers on board are Ed Young (at left on the bow), who was reunited with his patrol boat and other shipmates in 2004 at a crew reunion. CG-83527 responded to many emergencies during her years in the south sound, including fighting the mainline railroad trestle fire (below) that caused a train wreck in Steilacoom in March 1954. (Above, courtesy Myron "Tike" Hillman; below, Jim Frederickson, Northern Pacific Railroad Historical Society.)

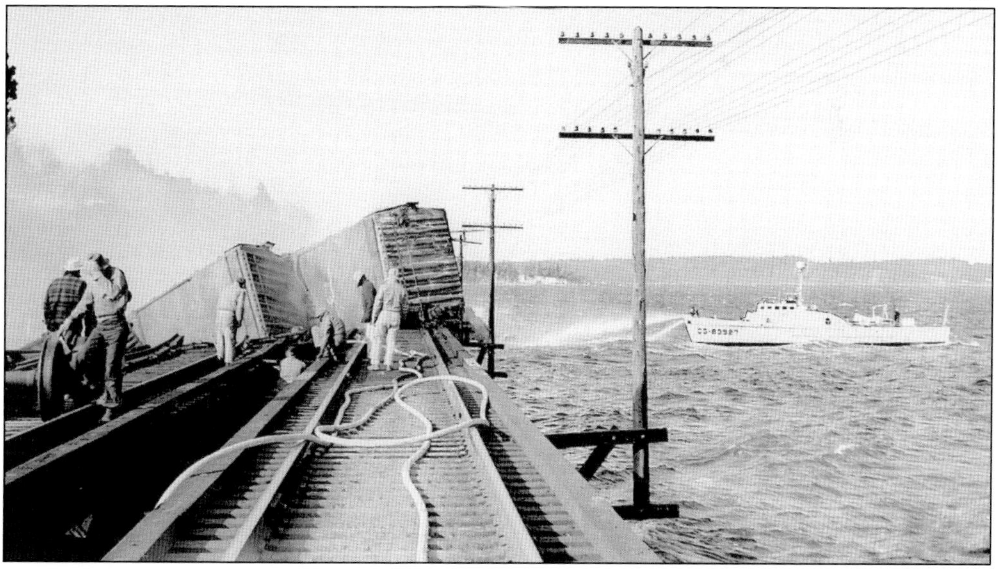

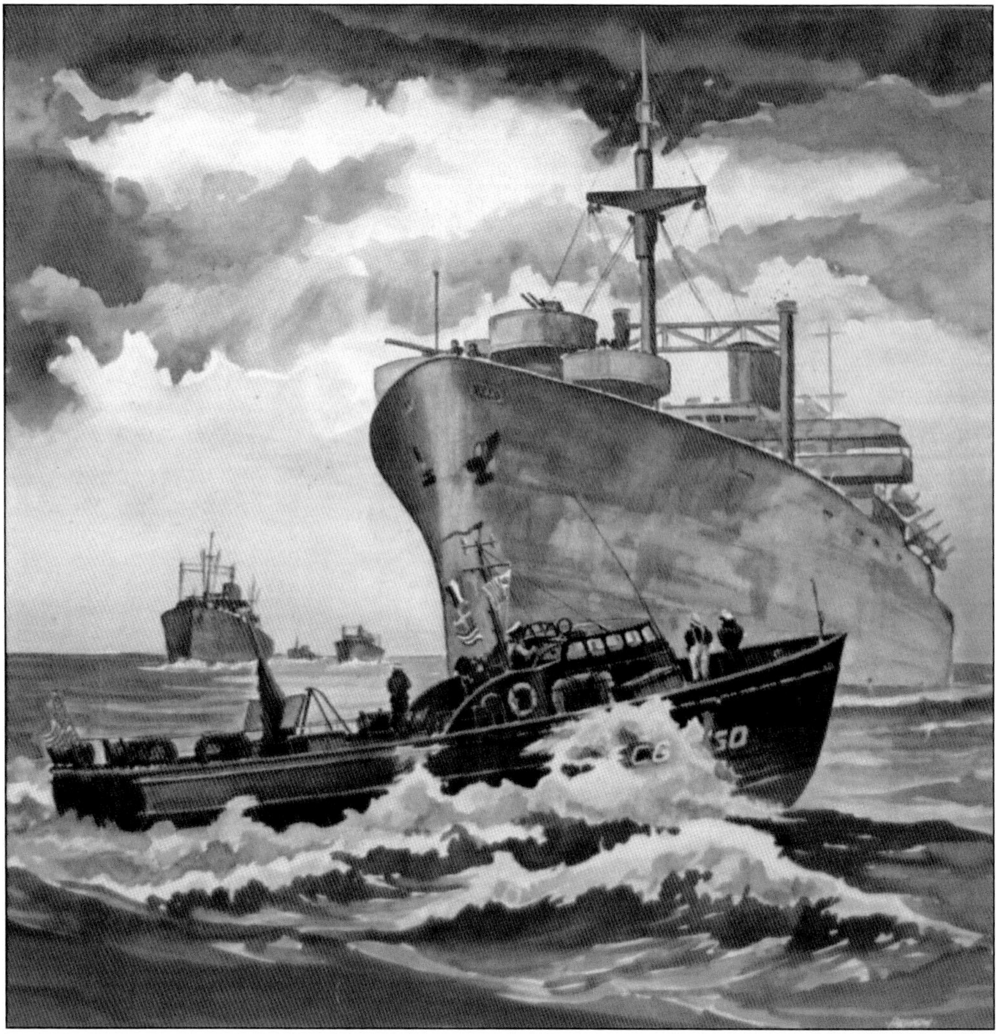

Patrol Boat Painting. World War II Coast Guard veteran Marshall Perrow from Tacoma served on an 83-foot patrol boat during the war while he was stationed at the US Coast Guard Academy in New London, Connecticut. After the war, he recreated this scene of an 83-footer escorting a convoy of Liberty ships returning from Europe. Following his discharge from the Coast Guard, Perrow took his illustrations around to New York magazine publishers, and sold this work to *Motor Boating*, which featured it on its August 1948 cover. Perrow returned to Tacoma and became a well-known and recognized architect as well as artist, and maritime subjects continued to be among of his favorite themes. Recalling his Coast Guard days, he was accepted in the service's public art program, and several of his paintings, one an award-winner, are part of the Coast Guard's permanent art collection and exhibited in traveling shows throughout the nation. (Courtesy Marshall Perrow.)

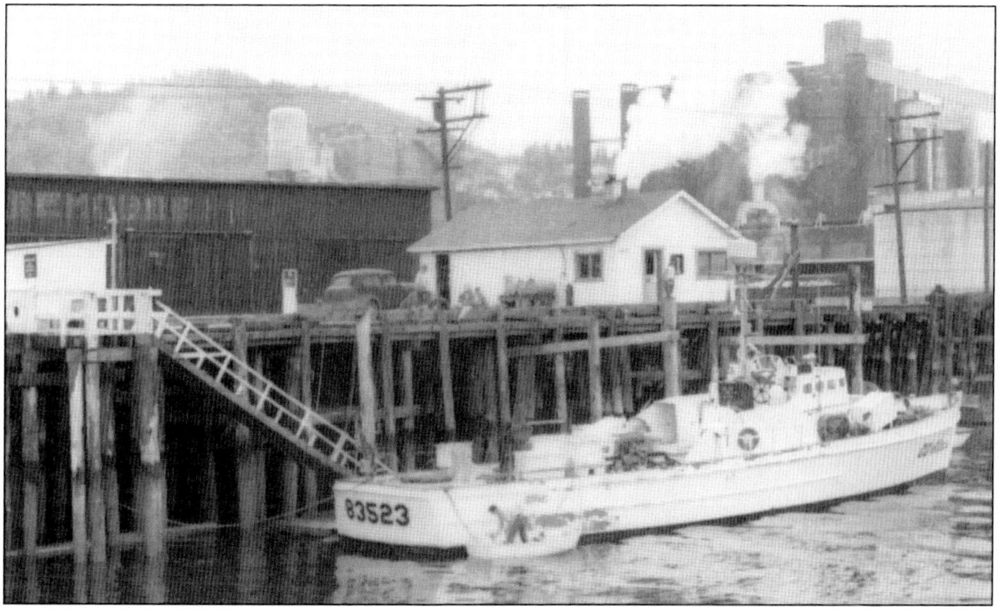

Sound and Strait Scenes. Historically, Coast Guard activities in the northern part of the greater Puget Sound area have been based in Bellingham. The image above, taken in 1954, shows a crew member of the 83-foot CG-83523 involved in a traditional and ongoing maritime maintenance task, painting the hull. Because a key Coast Guard responsibility is preventing the illegal entry of noncitizens into the United States by water, the Bellingham base, near the US-Canada border, is a vital operations location. With three Coast Guard patrol boats in the foreground below, the world's first nuclear submarine, the US Navy's *Nautilus* (SSN-571), is shown dockside at the Port Angeles station in early June 1958 on her way to Seattle. A month later, on a top-secret mission, she became the first submarine in history to transit from the Pacific to the Atlantic under the ice cap at the North Pole. (Above, courtesy Whatcom Museum of History and Art; below, courtesy US Navy.)

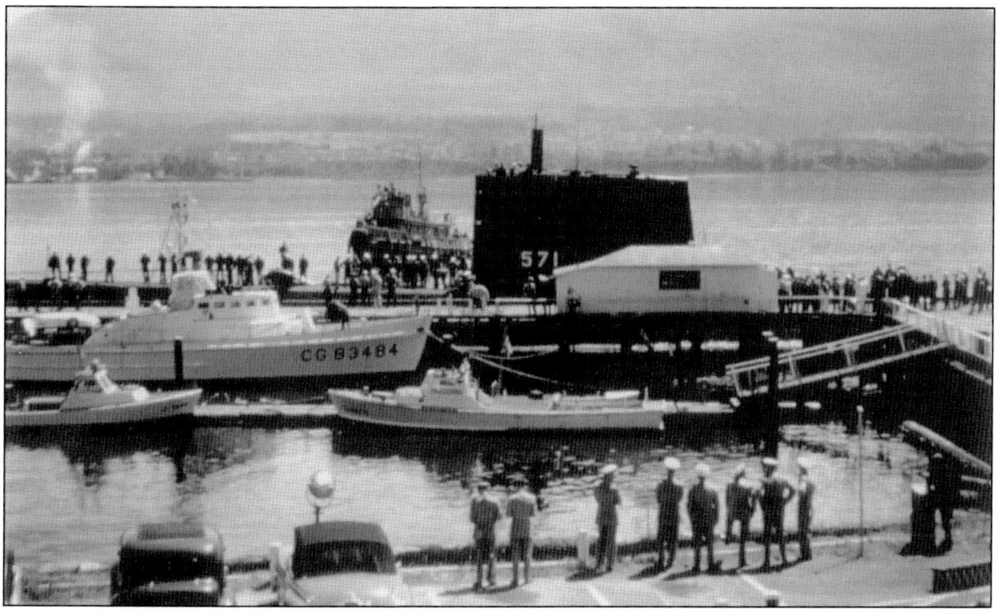

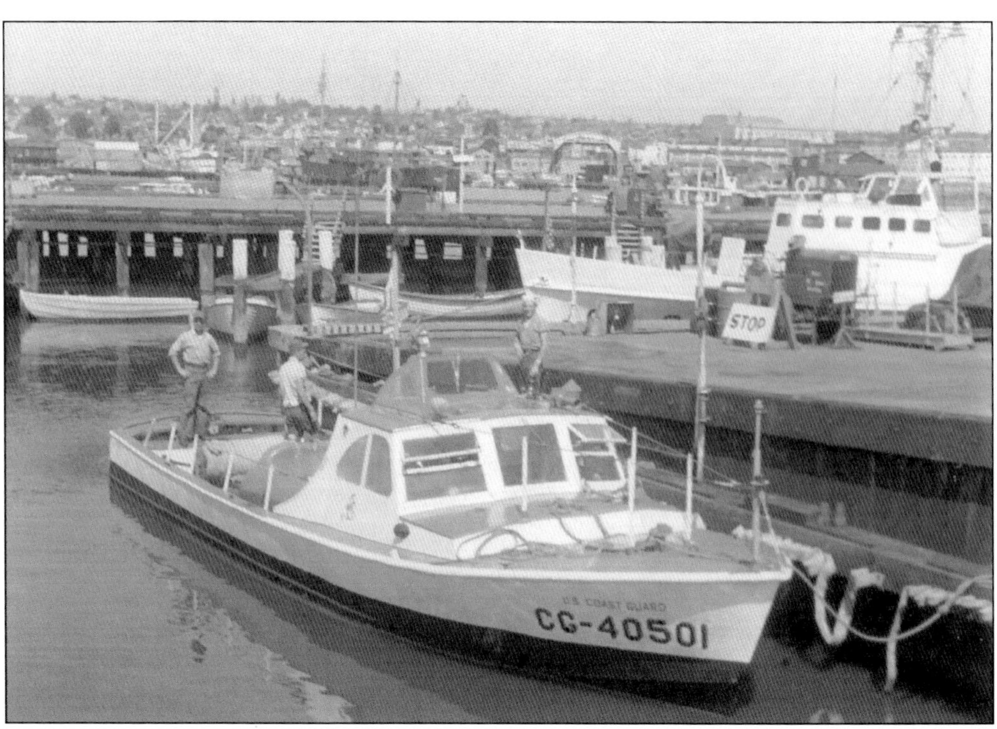

Visible and Versatile. One of the most familiar Coast Guard boats in the Puget Sound region from the 1950s through the late 1970s was the 40-foot utility boat. As depicted above, the 40-footer, together with a larger 83-foot patrol boat, were the primary Coast Guard vessels that handled law enforcement, search and rescue, marine safety, and related duties throughout the sound. CG-40501, commanded by Coast Guardsman Mark Freeman and based at Westport on the Washington coast, was in the sound and Seattle to provide patrol support during the 1958 Gold Cup hydroplane race. Another 40-footer is pictured below in 1953 assisting the famous unlimited hydroplane *Slo-mo-shun IV* prior to a run on Lake Washington. The "Slo-mo," as she was widely known, set the world speed record of 160 miles per hour in 1950 and subsequently won many Gold Cup and other races. (Above, courtesy Mark Freeman Maritime Collection; below, courtesy David Williams, Hydroplane and Raceboat Museum.)

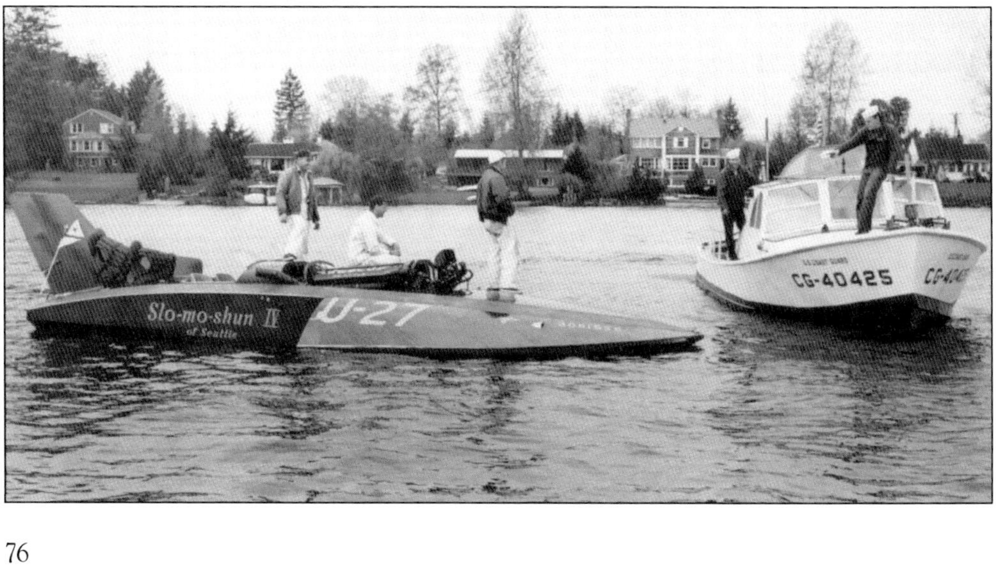

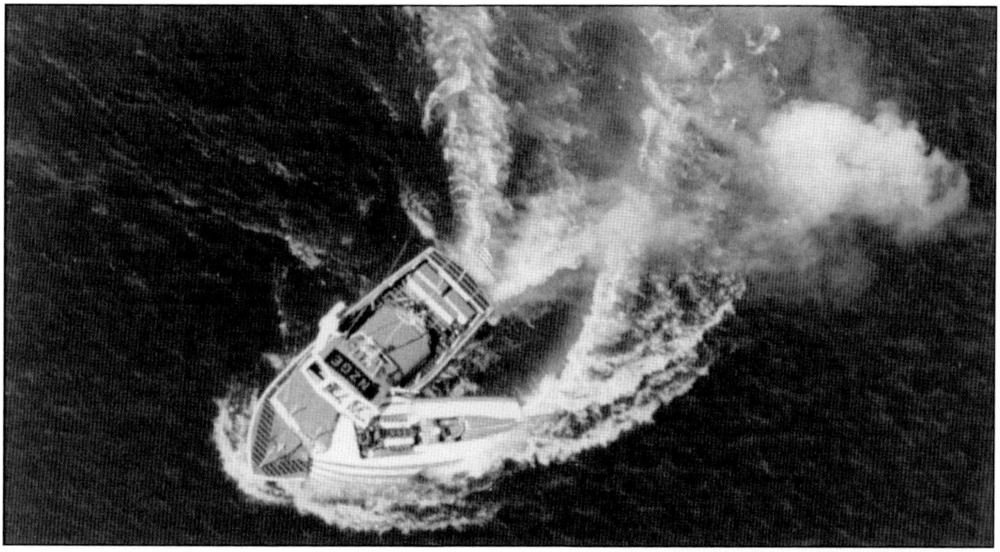

Incredible Incident. Although the Coast Guard in Puget Sound and around the nation often responds to unique emergency incidents, none was more unusual than the collision of the superfast unlimited hydroplane *Miss Thriftway* during the 1958 Gold Cup Race on Lake Washington. As pictured above, just after the start of the race the speeding raceboat lost its rudder, veered off course, and collided with the 40-foot CG-40575. The driver, Bill Muncey, landed safely in the water, and the three Coast Guardsmen aboard the utility patrol boat escaped before she sank. As seen below, the Coast Guard buoy tender *Fir* raised both the 40-footer and the *Miss Thriftway* the day after the race. Shortly after this image was taken, the hydroplane dislodged itself from the patrol boat and again sank, but she was retrieved later. (Above, courtesy Hydroplane and Raceboat Museum, photograph by Howard Vallentyne; below, courtesy Coast Guard Museum Northwest)

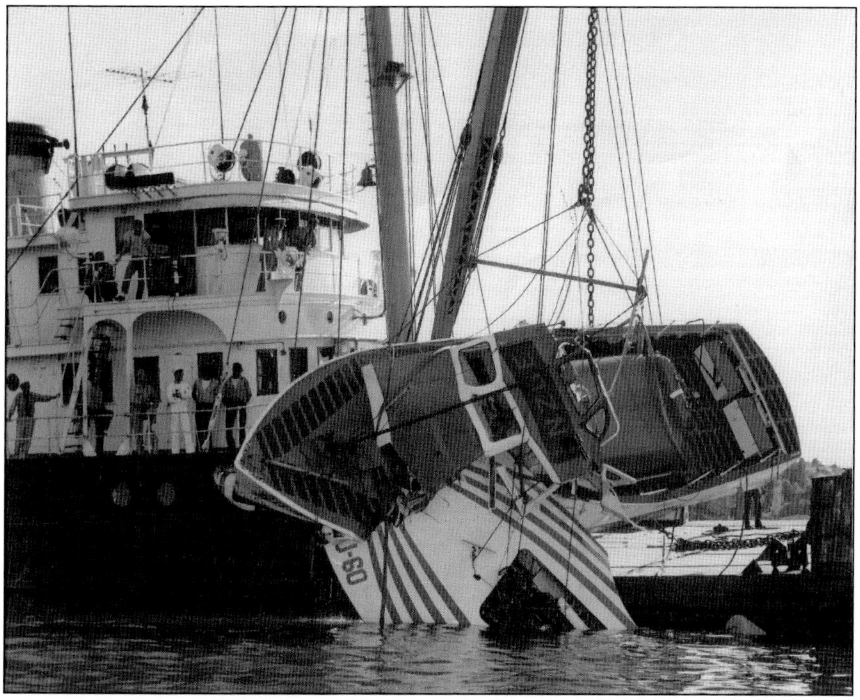

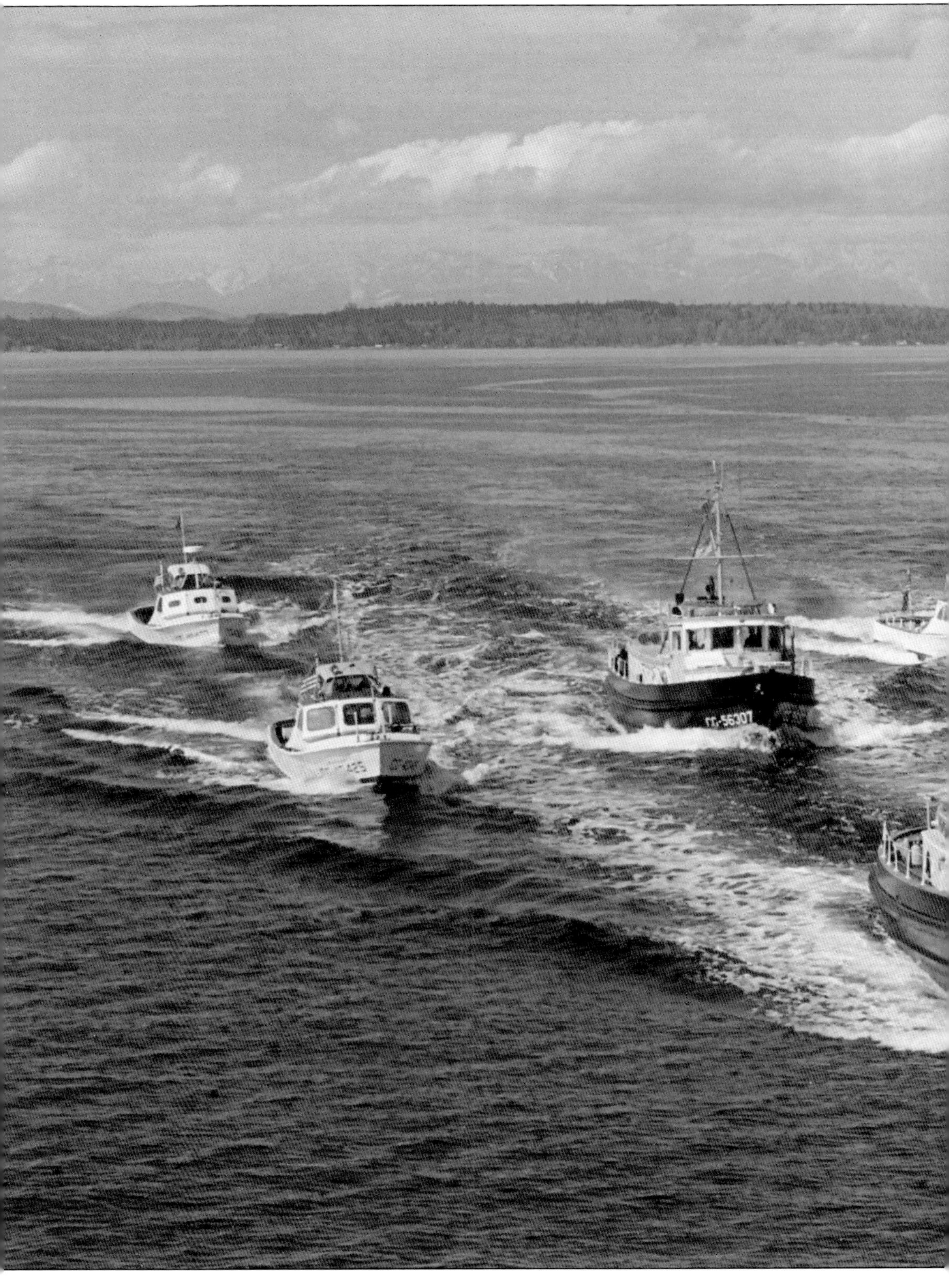

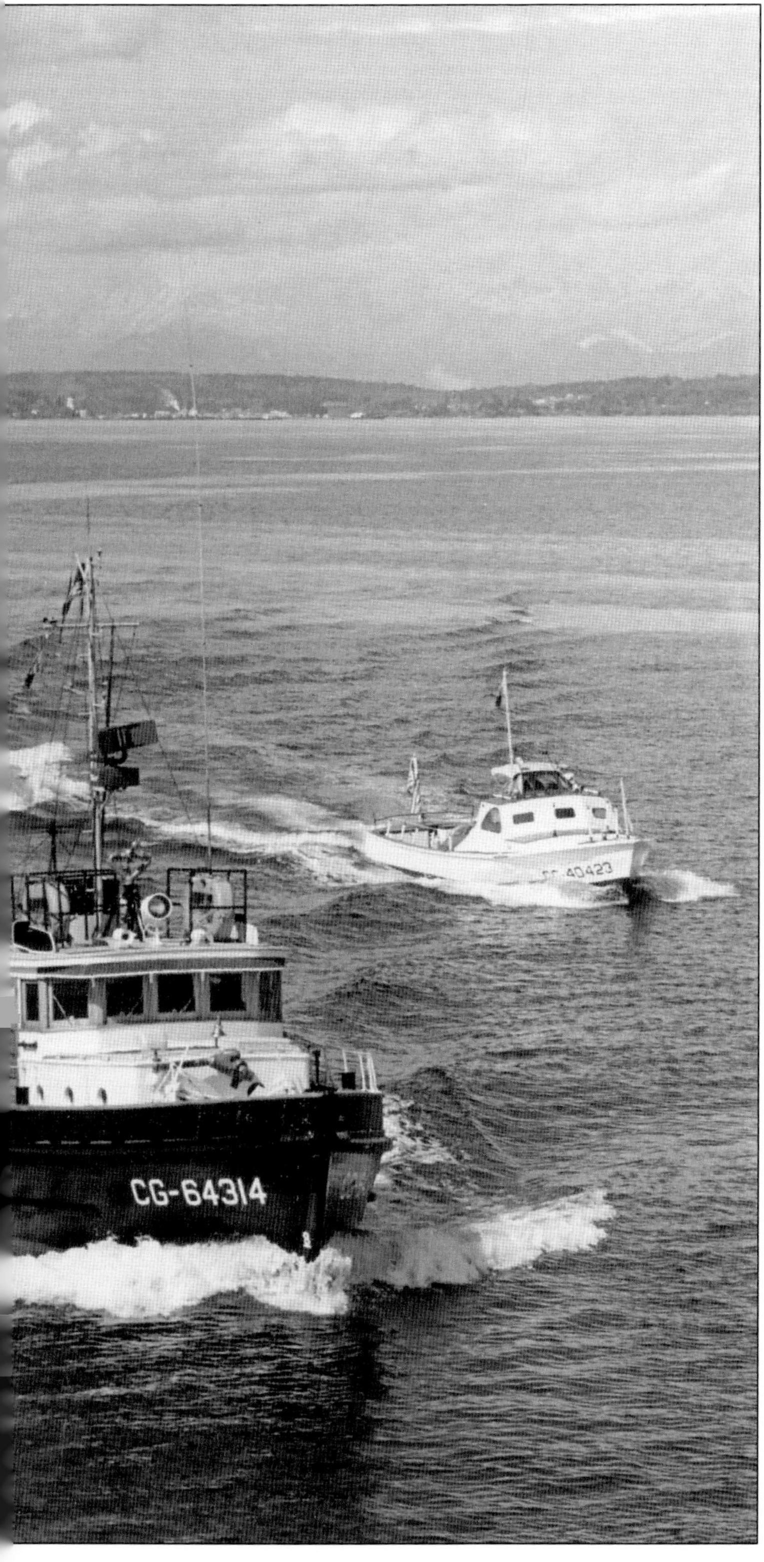

Formidable Formation. A fleet of six Coast Guard boats, including four 40-footers, is seen here in Puget Sound in April 1965. The 40-footers were in active service from the 1950s until the late 1980s. These versatile craft were designed by the Coast Guard and had steel hulls and aluminum superstructures and decks. They were powered by twin diesel engines that produced a total of 380 horsepower and had a top speed of 20 knots (23 miles per hour). The other two vessels shown are a 63-foot harbor tugboat (foreground) used for light towing and patrol duties and a 56-foot support boat. CG-64314 was built in 1944 by Nunes Brothers in Sausalito, California. A stoutly built wooden tug, she was powered by a 160-horsepower diesel engine and had a maximum speed of 11 knots (13 miles per hour). (Courtesy Coast Guard Museum Northwest.)

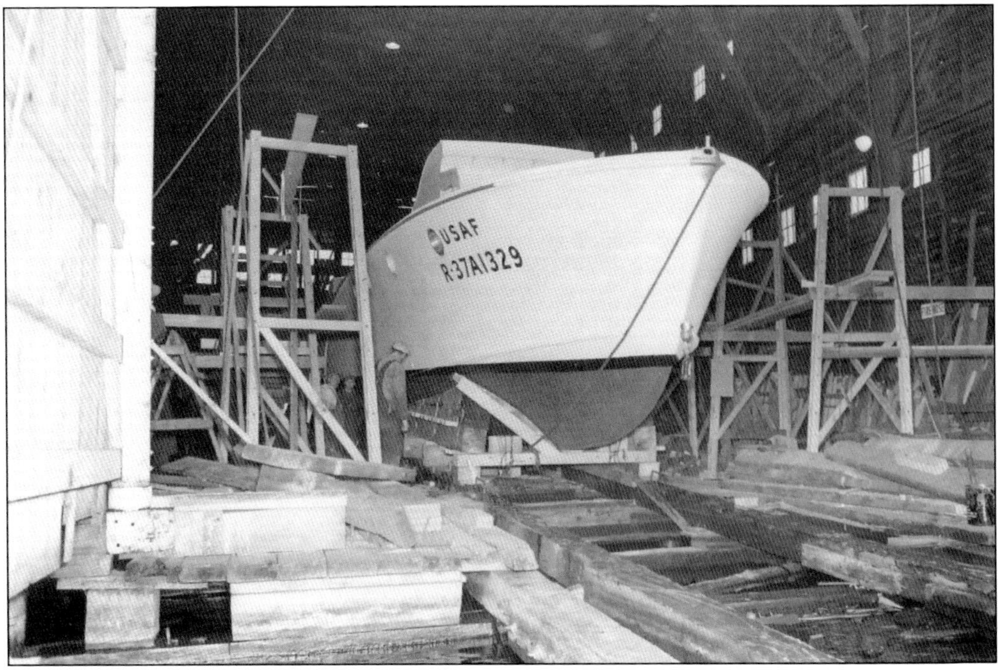

Korean Era Crash Boat. An improved version of the 63-foot US Army Air Force crash rescue boats assigned to Puget Sound during World War II reappeared during the era after the Korean War, when Sagstad Shipyard in Seattle built 20 of the new Mark III craft. The first boat built under contract for the now separate US Air Force was R-37A1329, shown above in the construction shed before launch and below at the outfitting dock. Although featuring a redrawn wheelhouse, the successful Dair Long hull design of the World War II boat was retained. The new 63-footers were again powered by twin Hall-Scott Defender V-12 gasoline engines of 630 horsepower each, giving the boats a top speed of more than 30 knots (35 miles per hour). (Both courtesy Odd Johansen Collection, PSMHS.)

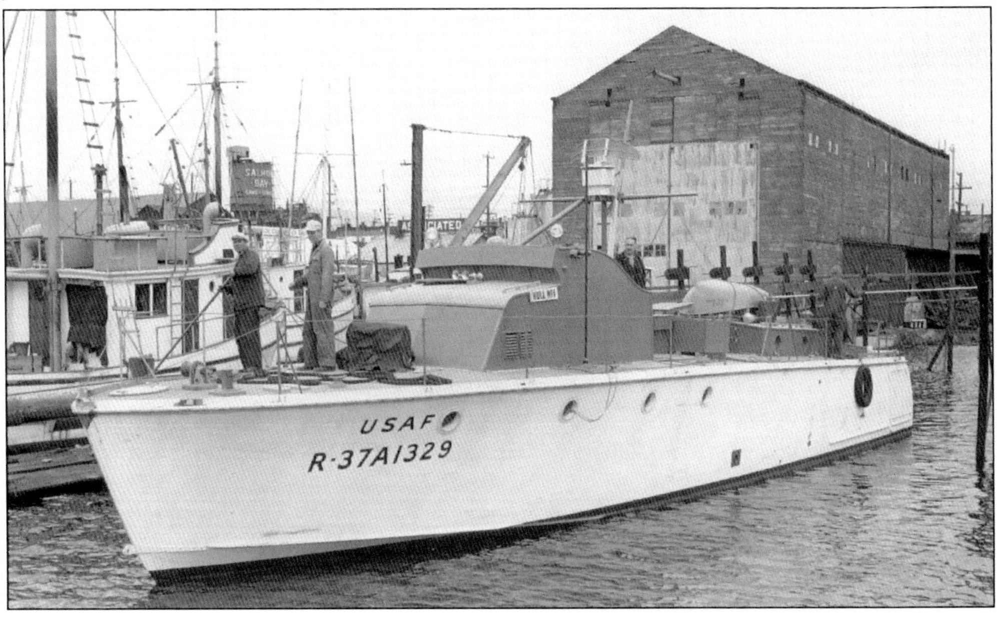

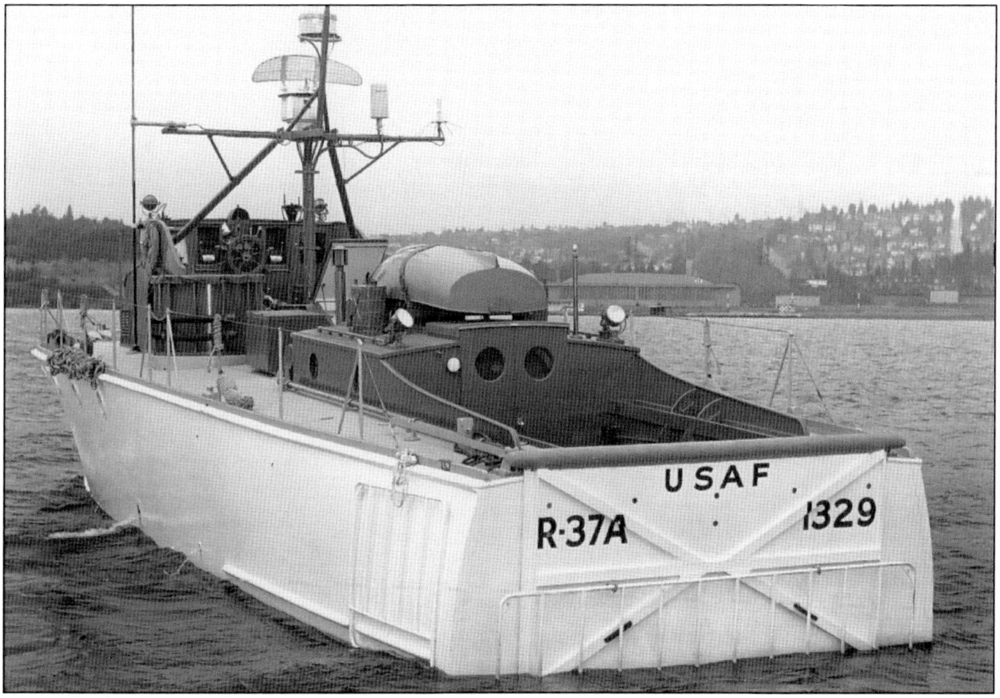

WATERBORNE AND AIRBORNE. A unique aluminum drop-down transom, shown above, was a new innovation on the Mark III 63-foot CRBs. It was designed to make recovery of downed aircrew members easier, bringing them aboard at the stern and near water level instead of over the side aft with the aid of a rope net. The image below shows the eighth boat built by Sagstad being loaded aboard the freighter *Hawaiian Logger* in 1955 at the Seattle Port of Embarkation, located at Pier 36, for transport to Japan. While most of the Sagstad-built 63-footers were sent to Japan and Korea, one was assigned to Mukilteo to support air operations at Paine Air Force Base. (Above, courtesy Odd Johansen Collection, PSMHS; below, US Army, courtesy Chip Marshall.)

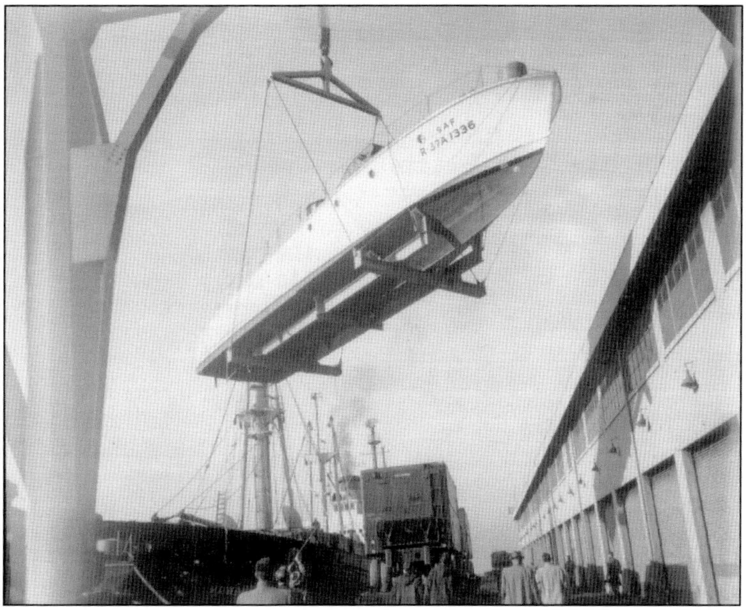

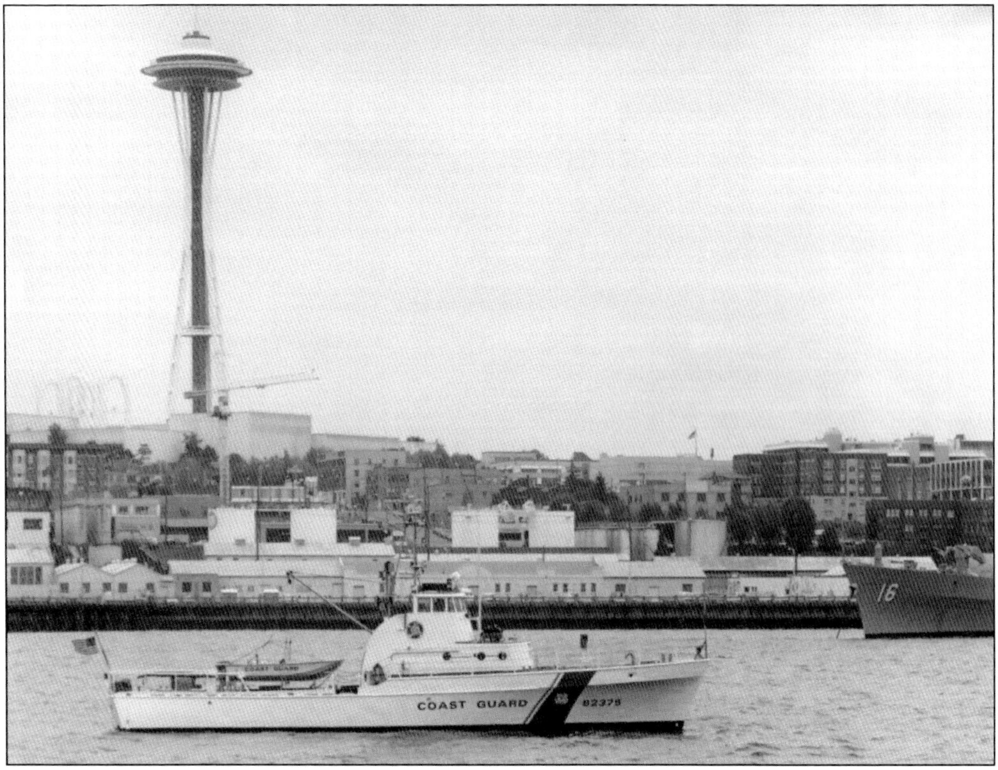

Time of Transition. The early 1960s were a time of transition for Coast Guard patrol boats in Puget Sound, as the wooden 83-footers were decommissioned and the new 82-footers with steel hulls and aluminum superstructures came on line. The 82-foot *Point Doran*, shown above in Seattle's Elliott Bay with the Space Needle in the background, was built at the Coast Guard shipyard in Curtis Bay, Maryland. She was commissioned in January 1970 and began serving in Everett soon after. The *Point Judith* (CG-82345), shown below in Commencement Bay in July 1966, was one of 26 of the 79 produced but not built by the Coast Guard. She was constructed by J.M. Martinac Shipbuilding in Tacoma to replace those 82-footers stationed stateside that were sent to Vietnam for coastal patrol and interdiction duties. (Above, courtesy Coast Guard Museum Northwest; below, courtesy Tacoma Public Library.)

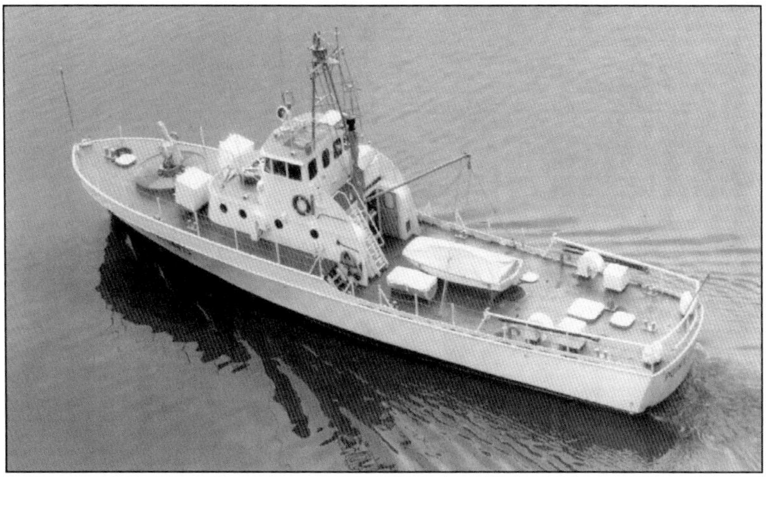

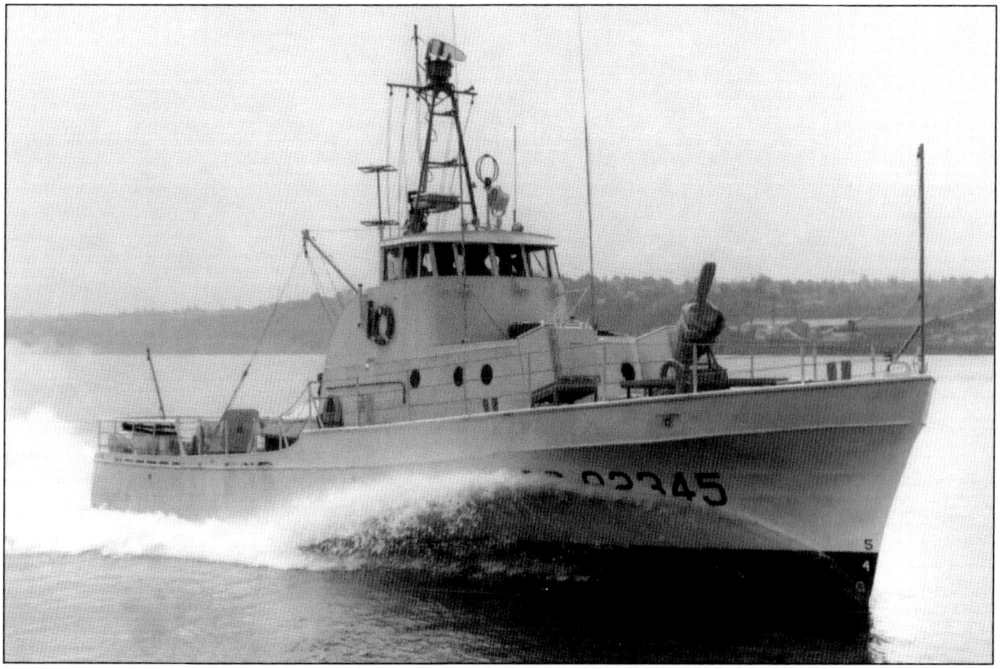

Hauling In, Hauled Out. The first of the Point-class boats built by Martinac, the *Point Judith* is pictured above during sea trials at her full speed of about 22 knots (25 miles per hour). CG-82345 had twin diesel engines that provided a total of 1,600 horsepower. She was armed with a 20-millimeter cannon and four .50-caliber machineguns. The *Point Richmond* (CG-82370), shown below hauled out in Bellingham, was commissioned in August 1967. She was the last 82-footer built by Martinac and among the last 10 of the entire Coast Guard production run. The *Point Richmond* was assigned to Anacortes for law enforcement and search and rescue duties from 1967 to 1990, her entire Coast Guard active duty career. (Above, courtesy Tacoma Public Library; below, courtesy Coast Guard Museum Northwest.)

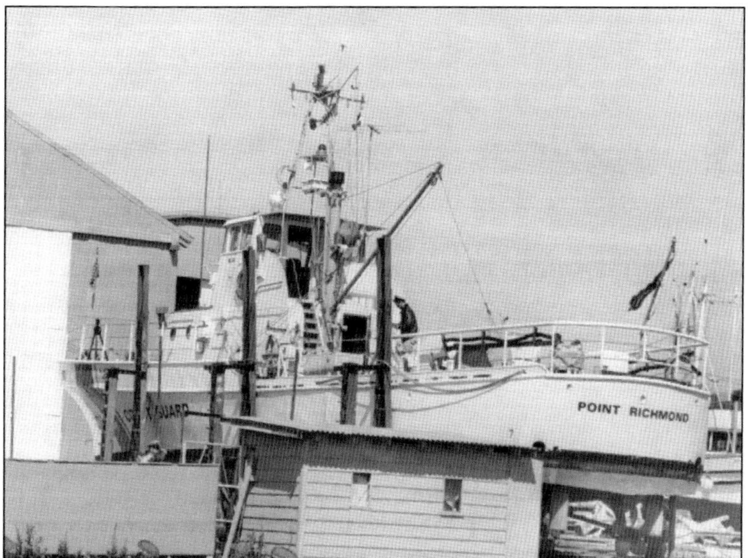

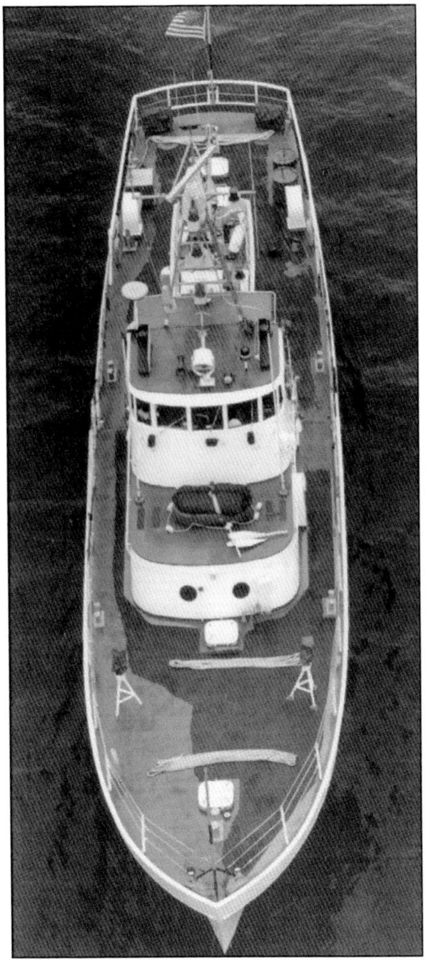

Overhead Observation. The long hull lines of an 82-footer and its spacious 17-foot beam are seen from above in these aerial views of the *Point Doran*. Designed to accommodate two officers and eight crewmen, CG-82375 carried 1,840 gallons of diesel fuel, which provided a 542-mile cruise radius at 14.5 knots (16.5 miles per hour). The engine room of one of the 82-footers, the *Point Thatcher*, allowed the installation of twin 1,000-horsepower gas turbine engines and their equipment to evaluate this type of propulsion system. The test also included the use of variable-pitch propellers to maximize economic operation. But as with other turbine engine tests in smaller vessels, the fuel consumption results did not make the operation of the new power plants feasible. The deck of the 82-footers also allowed a small, offloadable, outboard-equipped fiberglass boat to be stowed aft for rescue and other operations. (Both courtesy Coast Guard Museum Northwest.)

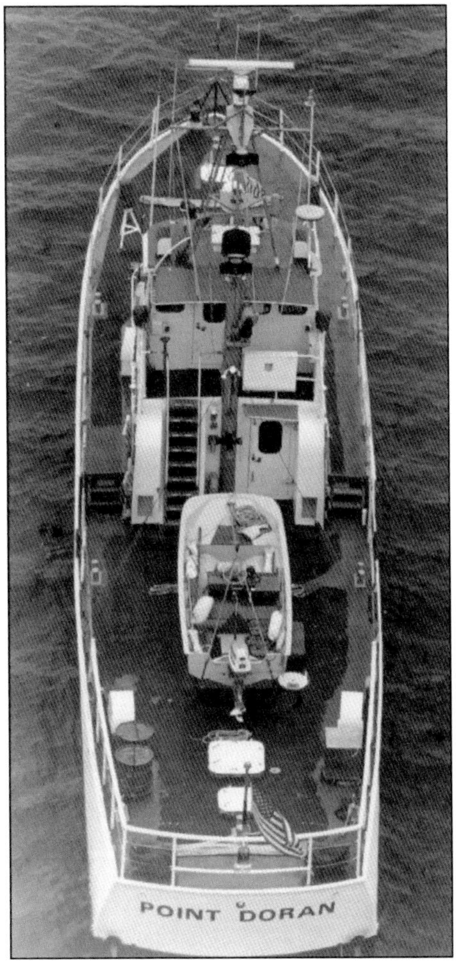

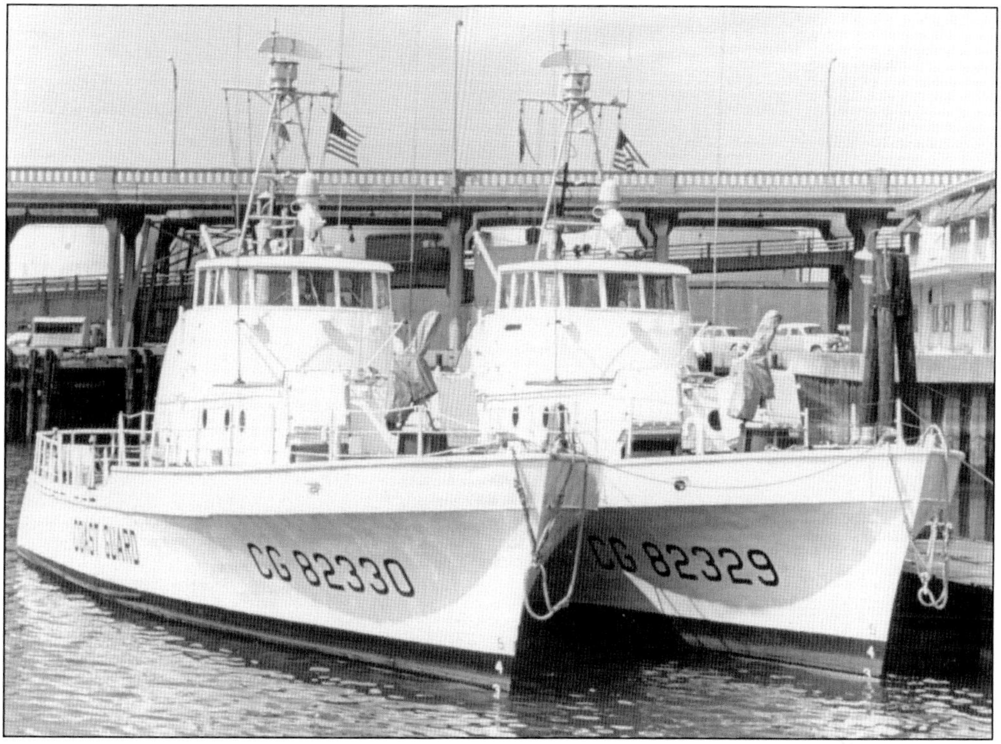

VIETNAM-BOUND DUO. The *Point Ellis*, at left above, was stationed at Port Townsend from 1962 to 1965, and the *Point Welcome* was stationed in Everett during the same period. Both 82-footers were built within the first two years of full production of the Point class patrol boats and were selected for transfer to South Vietnam for coastal patrol and enemy vessel interdiction service. They are shown above on the Seattle waterfront in 1965 waiting to be loaded on a cargo ship. Once in Vietnam, both boats were repainted in combat-zone gray and assigned to Coast Guard Squadron One, Division 12. The image below shows the *Point Welcome* rafted inboard, second from the outside, and the *Point Ellis* fourth from the outside, moored next to a Navy command and barracks barge. (Both courtesy Coast Guard Museum Northwest.)

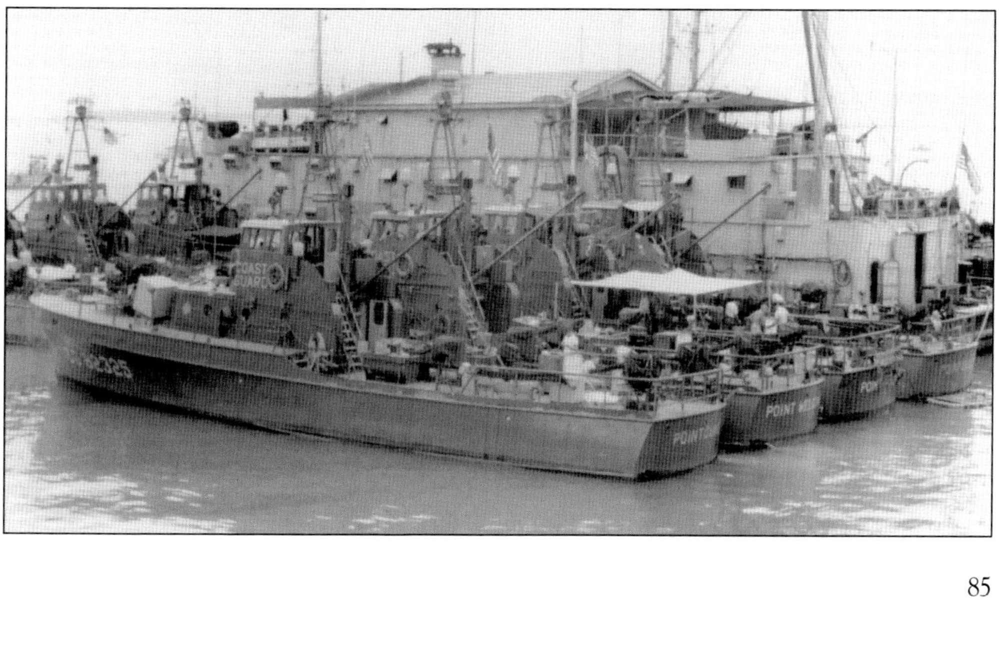

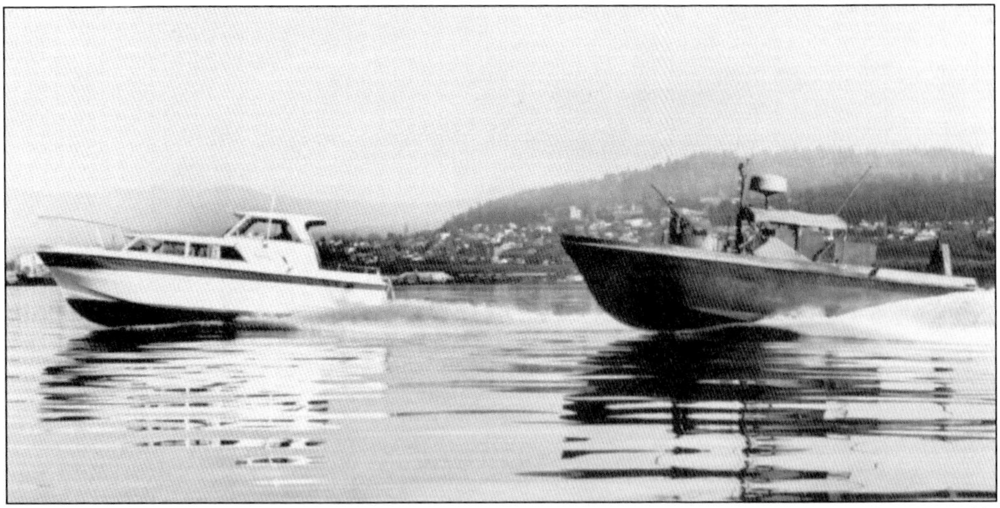

PBR Evolution. The evolution of the Uniflite Patrol Boat River (PBR) is shown dramatically above, as the Bellingham boat builder's 31-foot recreational cruiser leads the company's military PBR across the bay during a demonstration run in 1966. Through careful planning and personal follow-up, Uniflite, also known as United Boat Builders, competed and won several federal government contracts to build an eventual 535 fiberglass river patrol boats for use by the Navy and Army during the Vietnam War. The fast, shallow-draft, highly maneuverable boats were powered by diesel engines driving waterjet pumps and could operate in South Vietnam's shallow river delta environment. Arthur (Art) Nordvedt, Uniflite's president, is seen below with both cruiser and PBR models. He led the company's effort to secure the PBR contracts, which earned the company $11.5 million in 1966. (Above, courtesy Todd Warger; below, photograph by Todd Warger.)

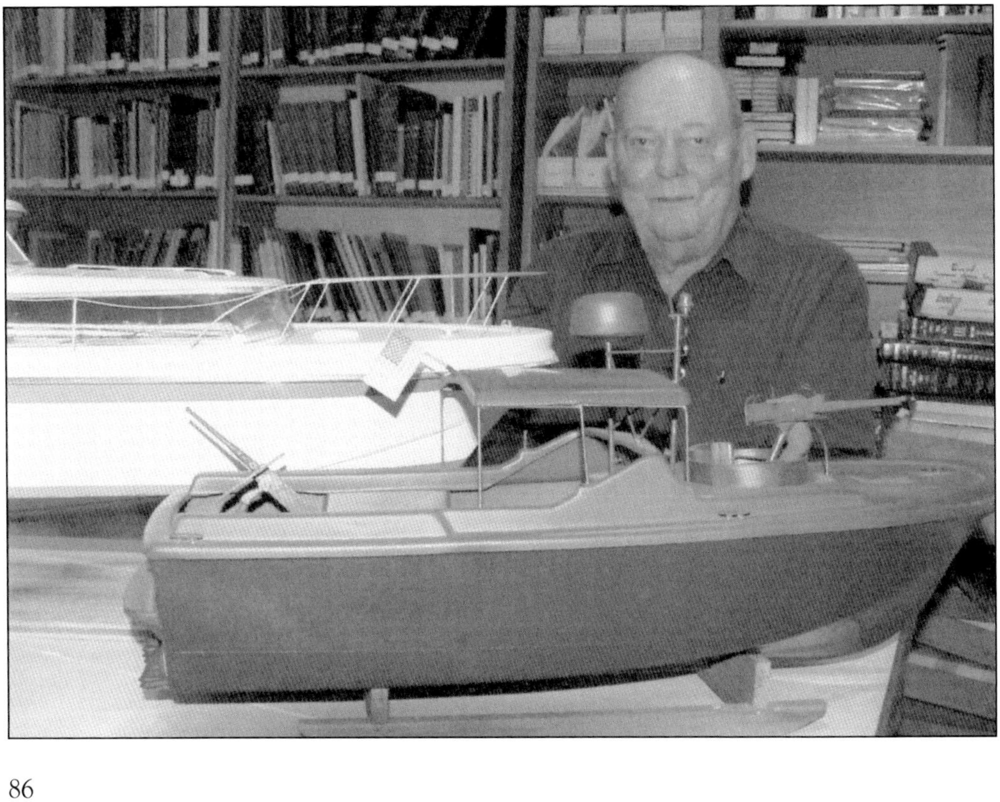

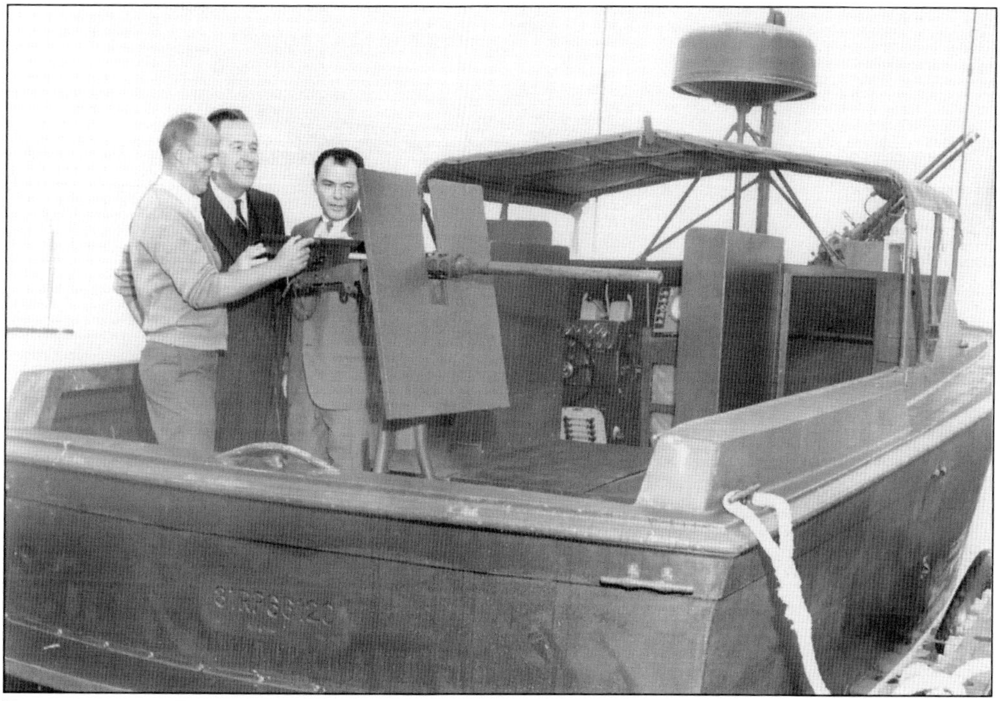

PROMOTION AND PERFORMANCE. The publicity photograph above, taken in 1966, features, from left to right, Art Nordvedt showing Washington senator Henry "Scoop" Jackson and Second District congressman Lloyd Meeds the .50-caliber machinegun mounted on the stern of a newly built PBR on the Bellingham waterfront. The two members of the US Congress supported Uniflite in its successful effort to secure one of the largest boat building contracts in Washington State history. A PBR Mark II is seen below in March 1968 during sea trials to prove its performance for Navy and other government agency officials. Following completion of these tests, Uniflite ramped up its production to 60 boats per month. (Above, courtesy Whatcom Museum of History and Art No. 1995.1.42; below, Tim Southerland, Sea Cure.)

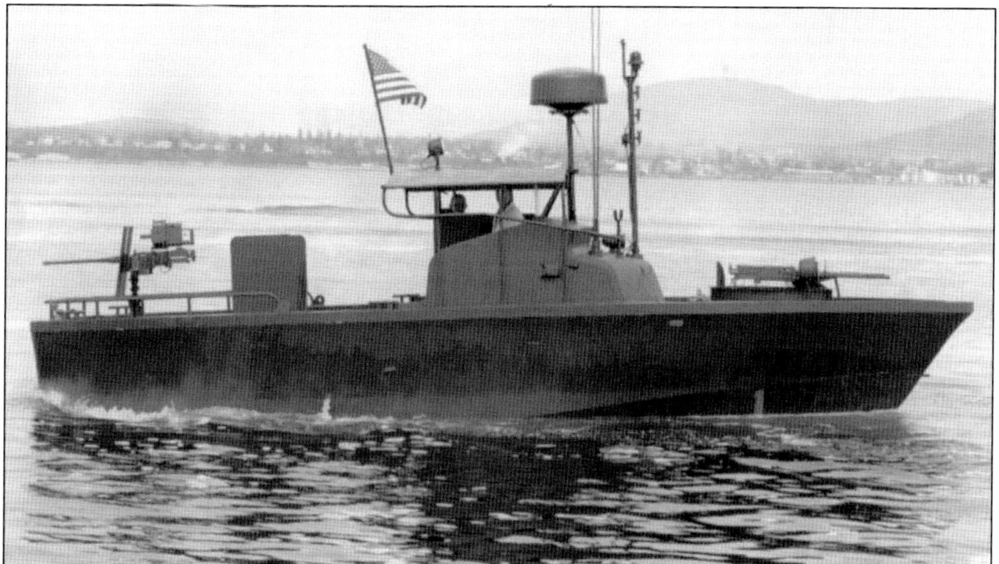

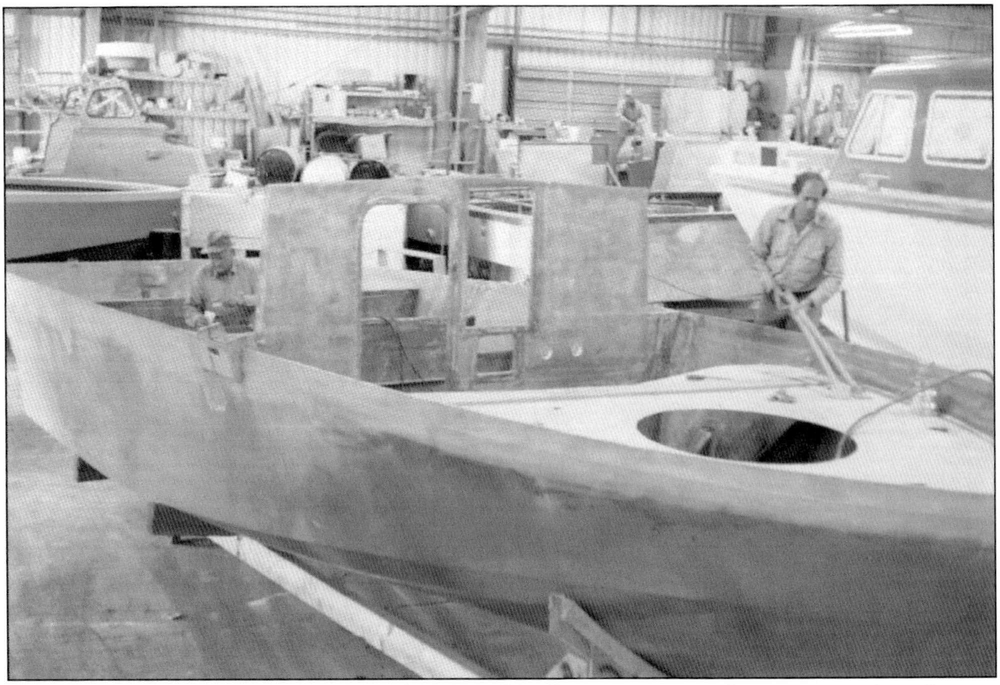

In production, on the Water. With one of Uniflite's recreational cruisers on the adjacent production line, in the image above, two Uniflite boat builders continue assembly of the main bulkhead bow-to-stern stiffening. Efficient construction techniques resulted in the delivery of each PBR, ready for sea trials as shown below, eight days after beginning construction. Following sea trials in Bellingham, boats were loaded on a truck and delivered to Pier 91 in Seattle to be shipped to Vietnam. (Above, courtesy Tim Southerland, Sea Cure; below, Don Rubeneck.)

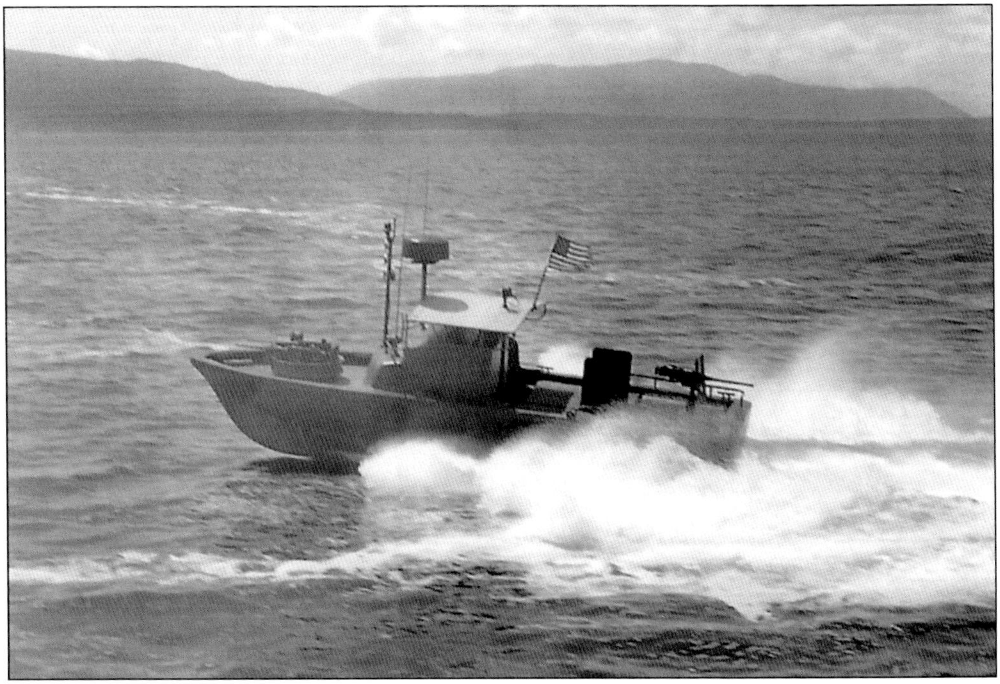

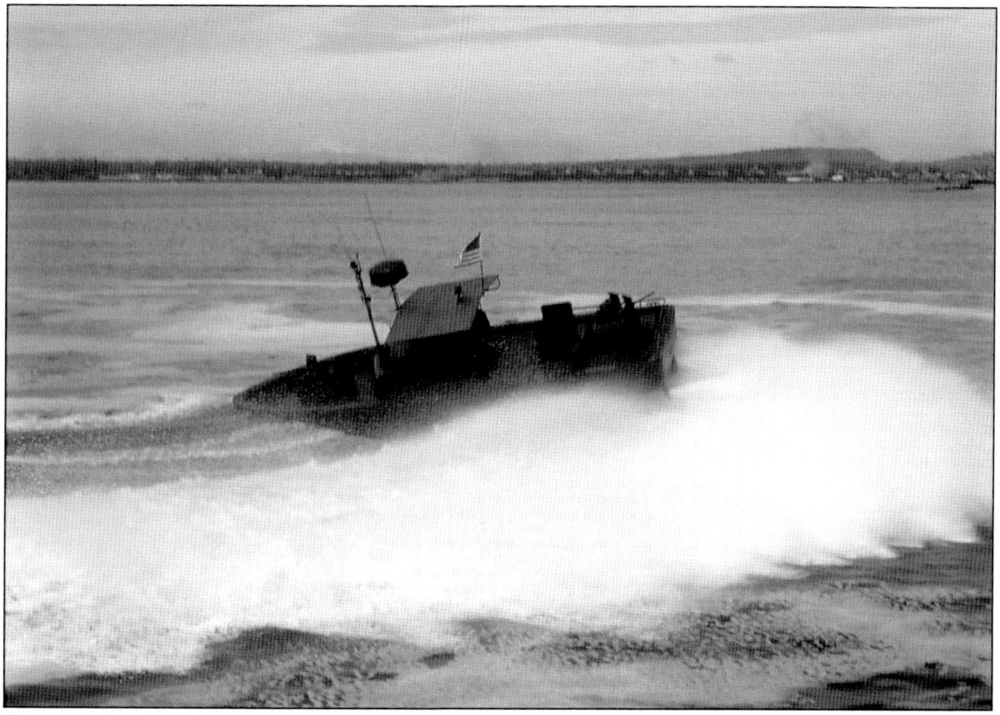

Turning out Boats. A PBR makes a 180-degree turn in its own length, as depicted above, and a crash stop by reversing the jet pump propulsion nozzles while moving forward at full speed. The turn, commonly known as a Hamilton turn or "jet spin," is a high-speed maneuver in which the boat's engine throttle is cut, the steering wheel turned sharply, and the throttle opened again, causing the boat to spin around quickly with a huge water spray. Needing more water-accessible production space, Uniflite moved into a larger building at Padden Creek on the Bellingham waterfront. This facility allowed increased side-by-side production of both military and recreational boats. (Above, courtesy Charles True, project manager, US Navy Shipbuilding; below, Don Rubeneck.)

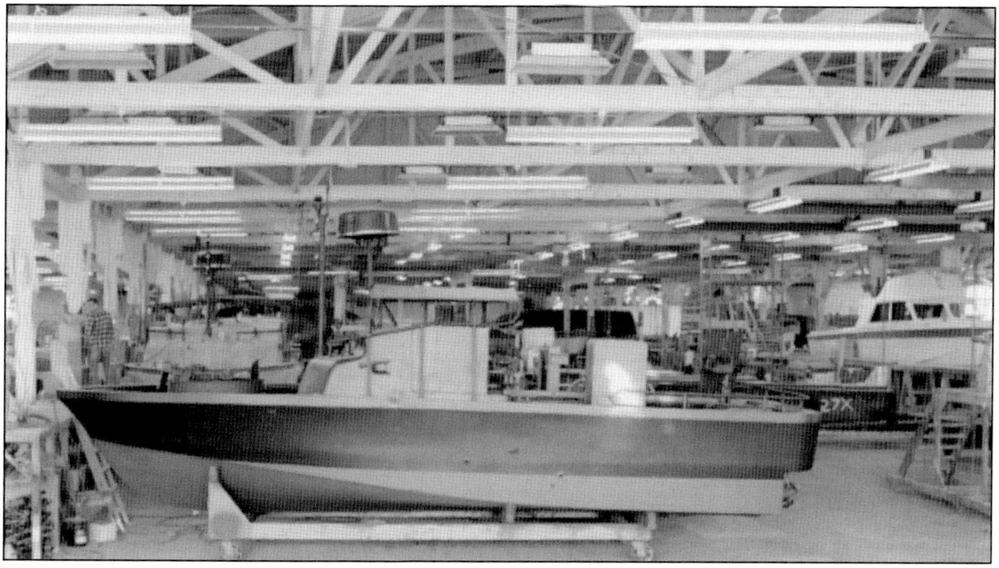

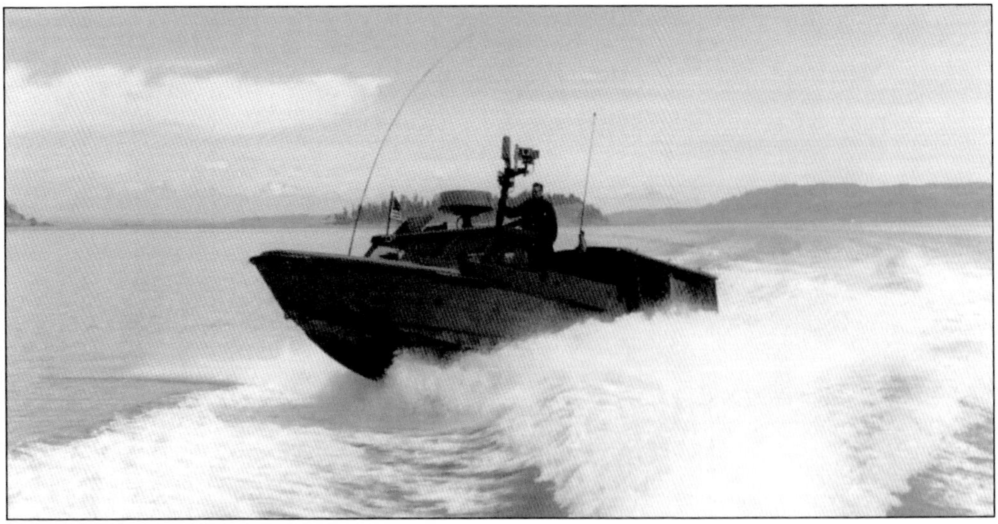

Sea Fox at Sea. Another boat built for the Navy following the Vietnam War period was the Sea Fox or SWCL (Special Warfare Craft Light), shown above crashing through another boat's wake during operational exercises. This special-purpose boat was built by Uniflite beginning in 1981 and used to support Navy SEAL (SEa, Air, and Land) team operations. Sea Foxes were among the Navy boats participating in Exercise Northern Hawk in the mid-1980s, as shown below, along with PBRs, swiftboats, and other combat craft. With Coast Guard coordination, the combat operations games were carried out in the waters and on the shores of Indian and Whidbey Islands. (Above, courtesy of Jeff Hunter, US Navy SBU-13; below, US Navy SBU-11.)

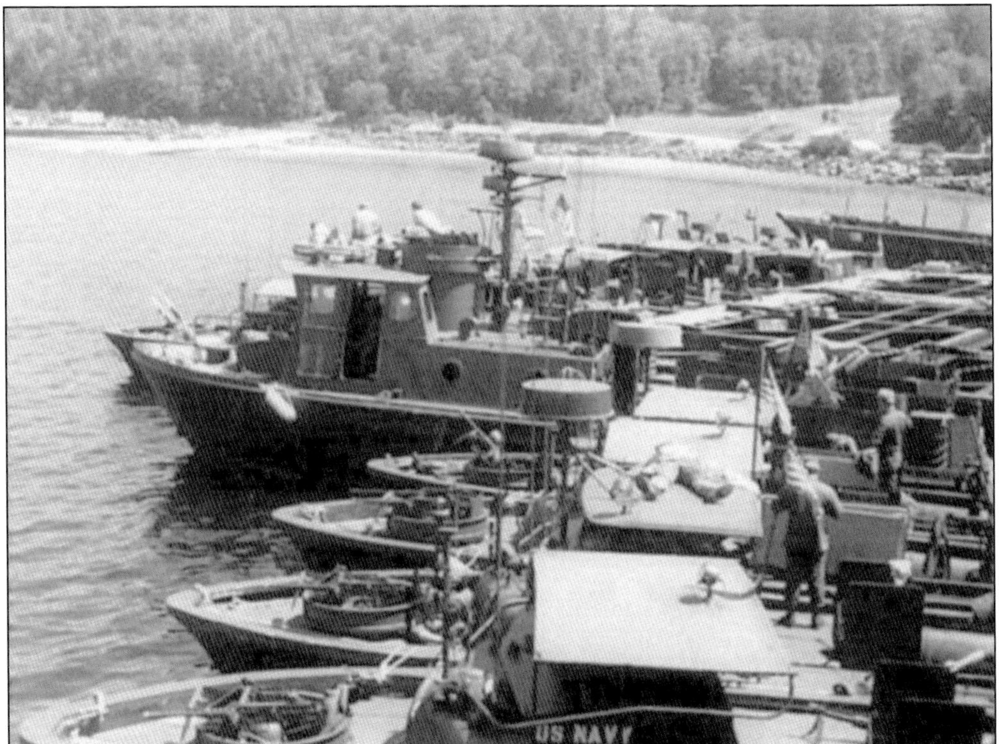

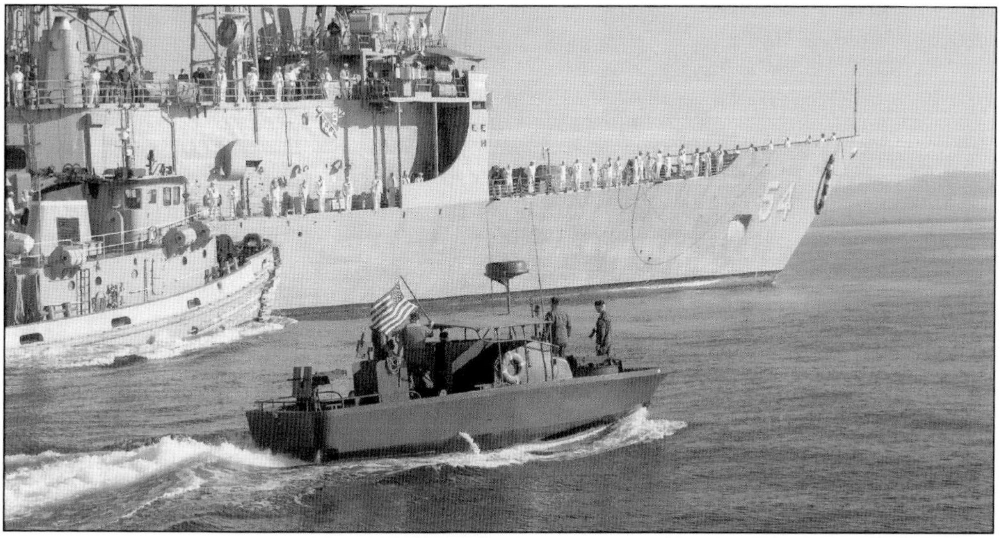

Escort and Exhibit. The fully operational PBR restored by veterans from the Northwest Chapter of Gamewardens, affiliated with the Vietnam Veterans of America, is seen above escorting the Navy frigate USS *Ford* to her moorage at Naval Base Everett in September 2008. The Gamewarden name comes from Operation Gamewarden during the Vietnam War, which used PBRs and other craft to combat Viet Cong enemy activities on inland river and delta waterways. The USS *Ford* was named for a young Navy machinegunner who served on a PBR and was awarded the Navy Cross for bravery after his death in combat. The Gamewardens chapter regularly exhibits its restored PBR during parades, such as the one shown below in Auburn in 2007, and other public events. (Both courtesy Gamewardens of Vietnam, Northwest Chapter.)

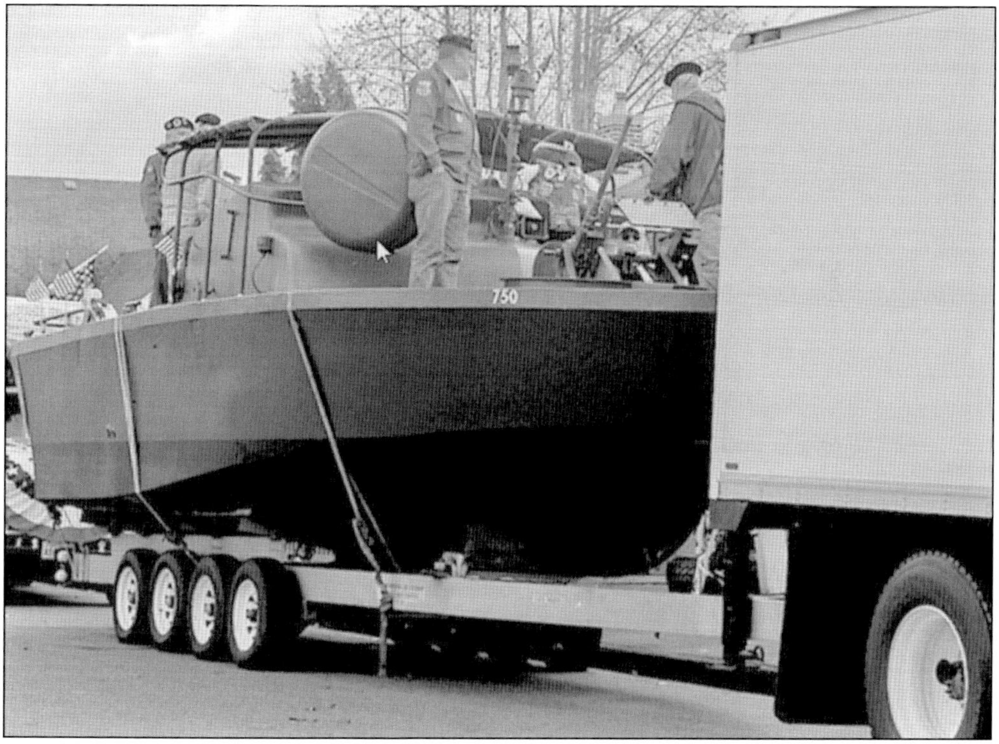

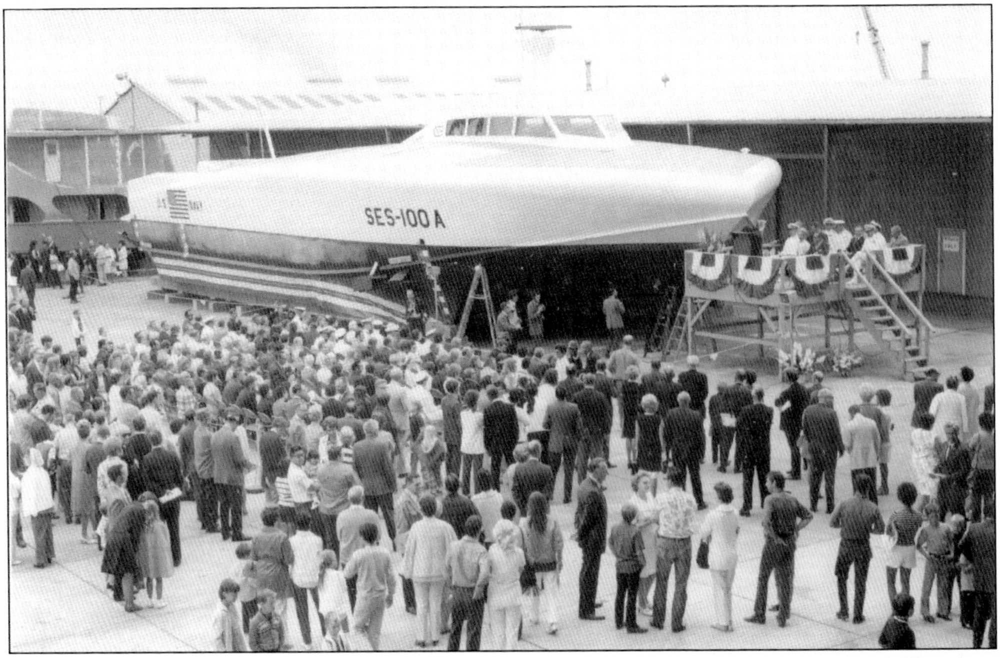

Surface Effect Ship. A radically designed vessel made of welded aluminum alloy and fiberglass, powered by gas turbine engines, and propelled by water-jets was christened in Tacoma in mid-1971 (above). More than 400 people turned out for the event, keynoted by Washington senator Warren G. Magnuson. Named the SES-100A for Surface Effect Ship, the 80-foot, 100-ton, experimental Navy craft was developed by Aerojet General Corporation and built by Tacoma Boatbuilding Company on the Hylebos Waterway. A large hovercraft with rigid sides, the vessel was designed to ride about four feet off the water at speeds faster than 80 knots (92 miles per hour). In the image below, SES-100A sea trials were conducted on Puget Sound in the early 1970s. (Above, courtesy Tacoma Public Library; below, courtesy Navy Photographic Section, Naval History and Heritage Command.)

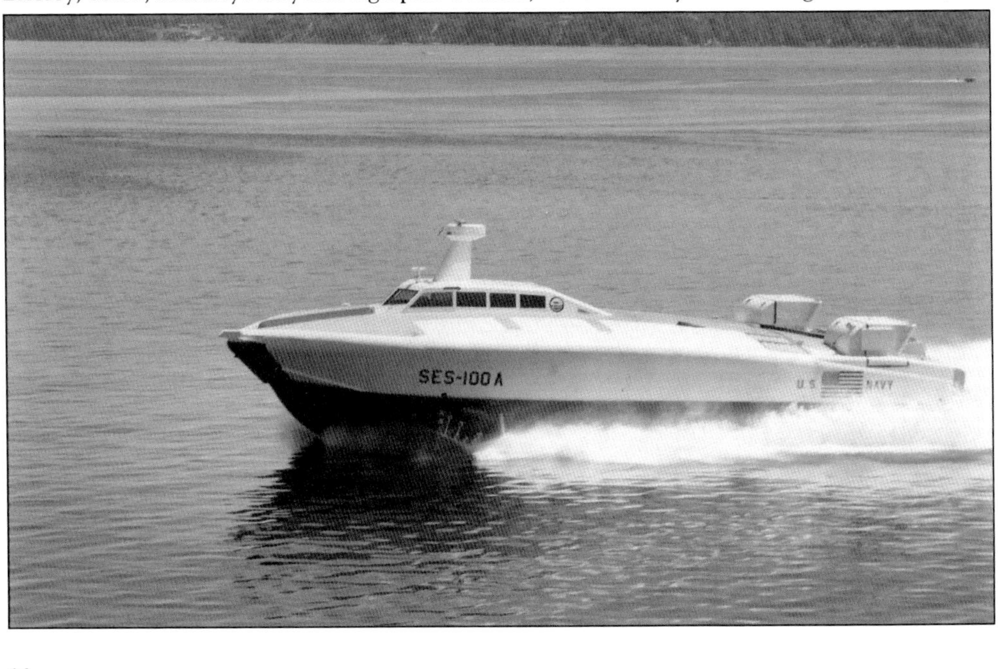

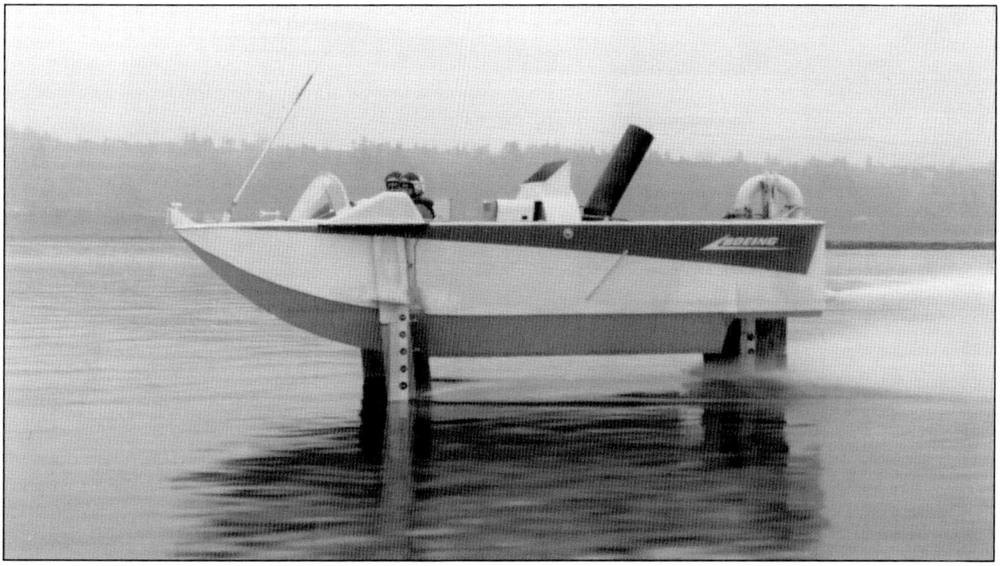

Early Hydrofoils. The *Little Squirt*, pictured above, was built in Seattle in 1962 by the Marine Division of the Boeing Company. Only 20 feet long, it was a company-sponsored research craft designed to test the feasibility of concepts including an automatic control system. The craft was the first to demonstrate the application of waterjet propulsion to hydrofoils. Another Boeing hydrofoil testbed was the FRESH 1 (Foil REsearch Supercavitating Hydrofoil), seen below. A 59-foot craft of high-deadrise catamaran design powered by a conventional turbofan jet engine, it was the first hydrofoil to achieve a foilborne speed of 84 knots (97 miles per hour). The FRESH I was damaged in July 1963 in a rollover crash during testing on Puget Sound but was reconstructed and passed its Navy acceptance trials. (Both courtesy of Hal Turner.)

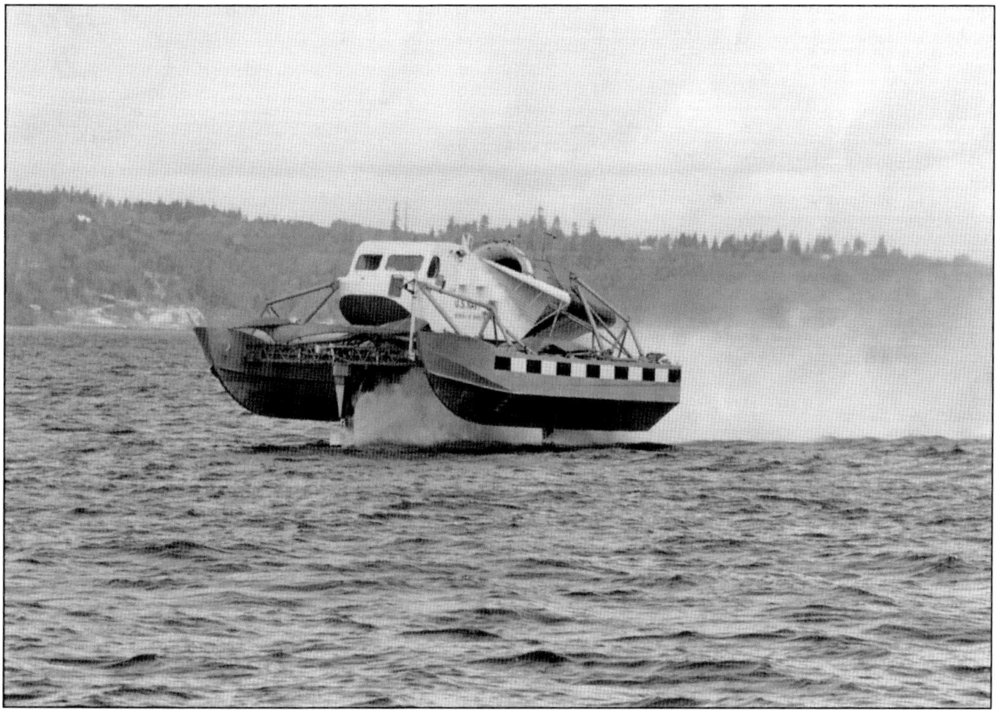

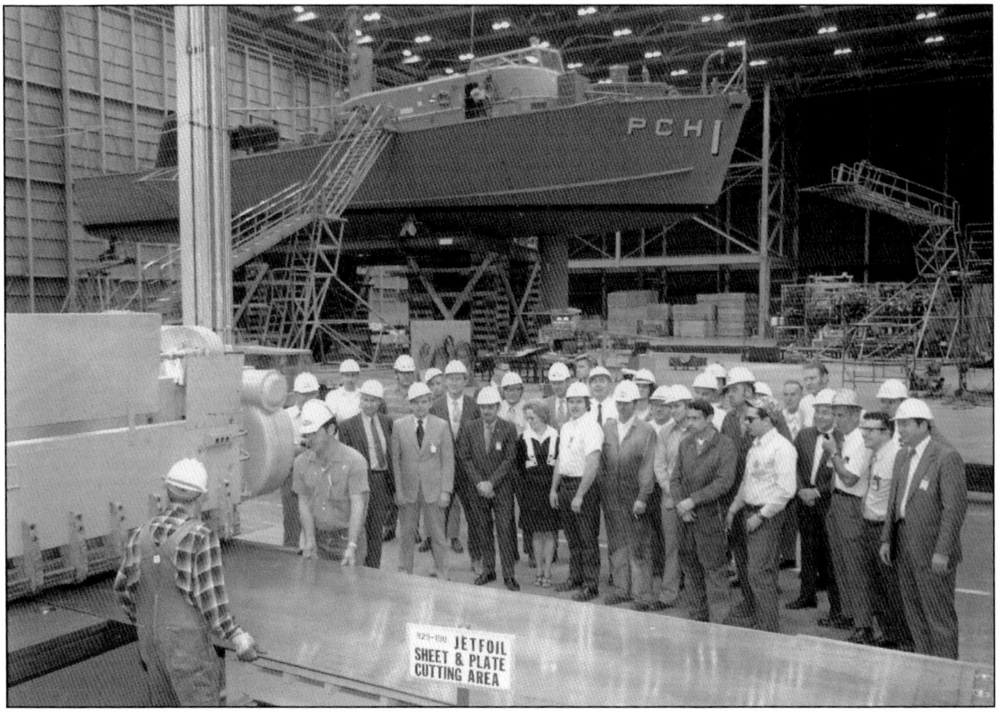

HIGH POINT HIGHLIGHTS. Another Boeing product, the 116-foot PCH-1 patrol craft, was the first military hydrofoil developed for the US Navy. It is shown above behind a group of visitors touring the production plant in the early 1960s. After a competitive process, Boeing won the construction contract for the craft in 1960 and subcontracted the hull and superstructure work to Martinac Shipbuilding Company of Tacoma. The completed hydrofoil was placed into service by the Navy in 1963. It was powered by twin Rolls-Royce marine gas turbines that drove counter-rotating propellers in pods on the foils, and reached a speed of 50 knots (58 miles per hour) during sea trials on Puget Sound, pictured below. (Both courtesy Hal Turner.)

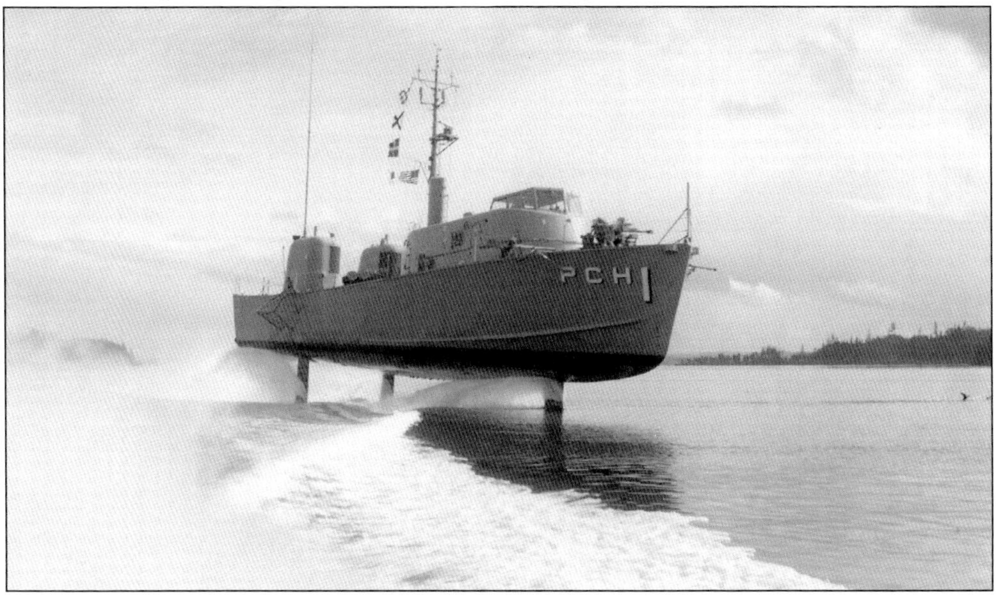

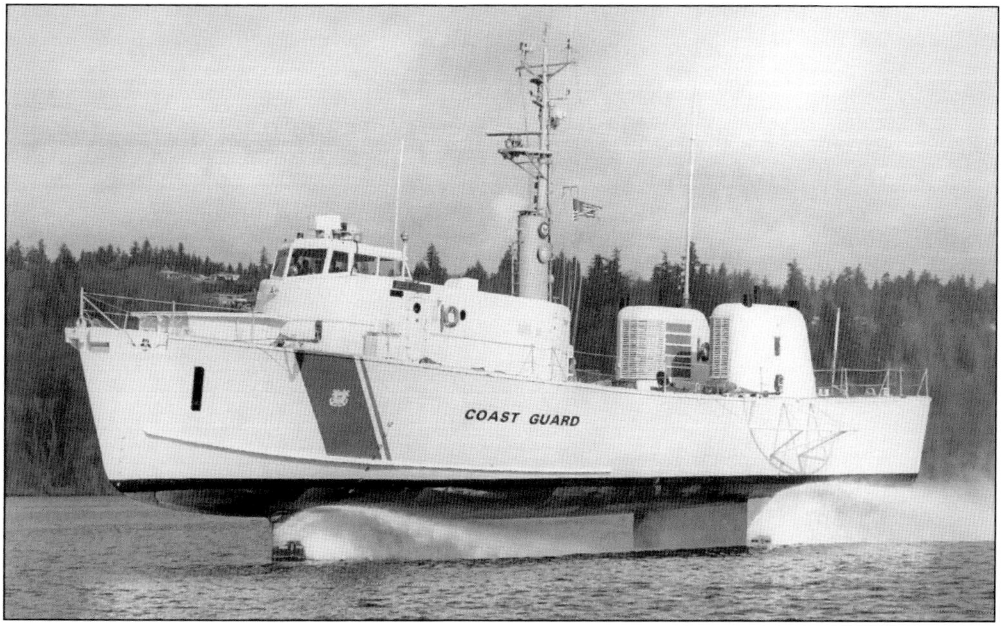

High and Dry. In addition to testing by the Navy, the *High Point* (PCH-1), above, was loaned to and evaluated by the Coast Guard on Puget Sound in the spring of 1975. After a series of trials, the hydrofoil was sent to San Francisco for additional open-ocean testing, and she was ultimately returned to the Navy. The *High Point* returned to Puget Sound and is seen below in July 1978 running together with the largest Navy hydrofoil, the *Plainview* (AGEH-1). The 220-foot hydrofoil was built by Lockheed Shipbuilding and Construction Company in Seattle and commissioned by the Navy in March 1969. After nine years of testing various hydrofoil systems, operations, and tactics, the vessel was decommissioned in September 1978. (Above, courtesy Coast Guard Museum Northwest; below, courtesy Navy Photographic Section, History and Heritage Command.)

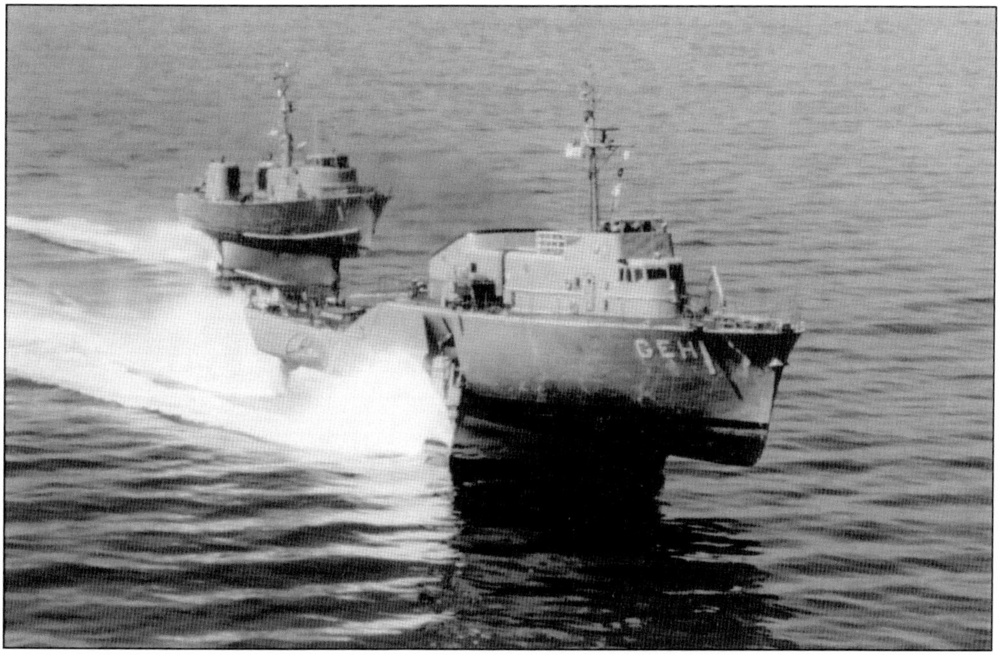

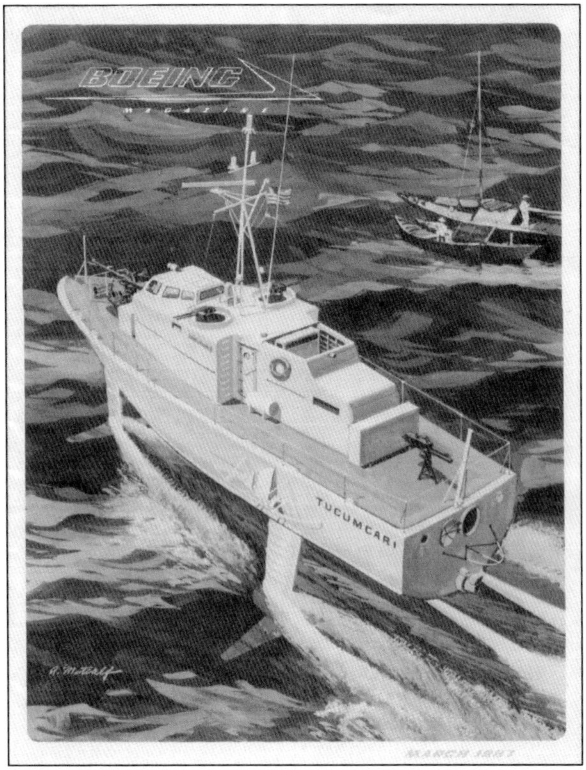

TUCUMCARI TRIALS. Shown on the cover of the March 1967 issue of *Boeing Magazine*, the 70-foot *Tucumcari* was the company's second military hydrofoil. When foilborne, the 74-foot craft was powered by a Rolls-Royce Proteus gas turbine engine that drove waterjet pods at the ends of its main foils. As seen below, the *Tucumcari* (PGH-2) reached 50 knots (58 miles per hour) during sea trials, and together with another hydrofoil, the *Flagstaff* (PGH-1), was sent to Vietnam for combat-zone evaluation. The *Tucumcari's* features were also chosen as requirements for North American Treaty Organization (NATO) military hydrofoils. Armament for the hydrofoil consisted of one 40-millimeter cannon on the bow, two twin .50-calibre machineguns in side turrets, and one 81-millimeter mortar on the stern. (Both courtesy Hal Turner.)

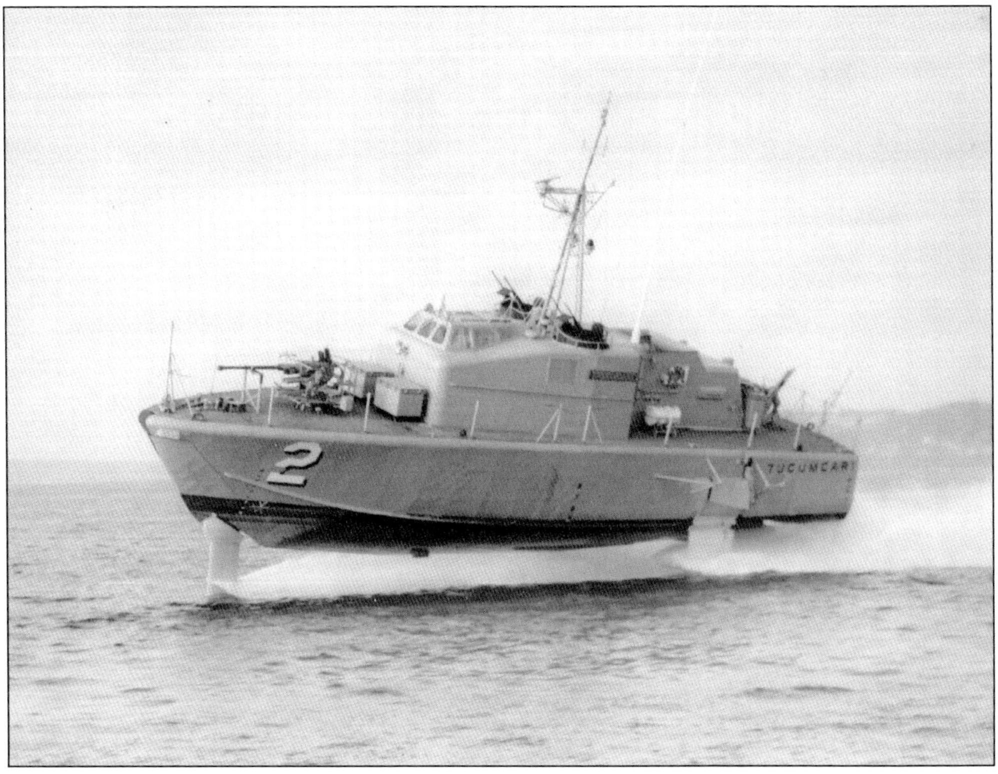

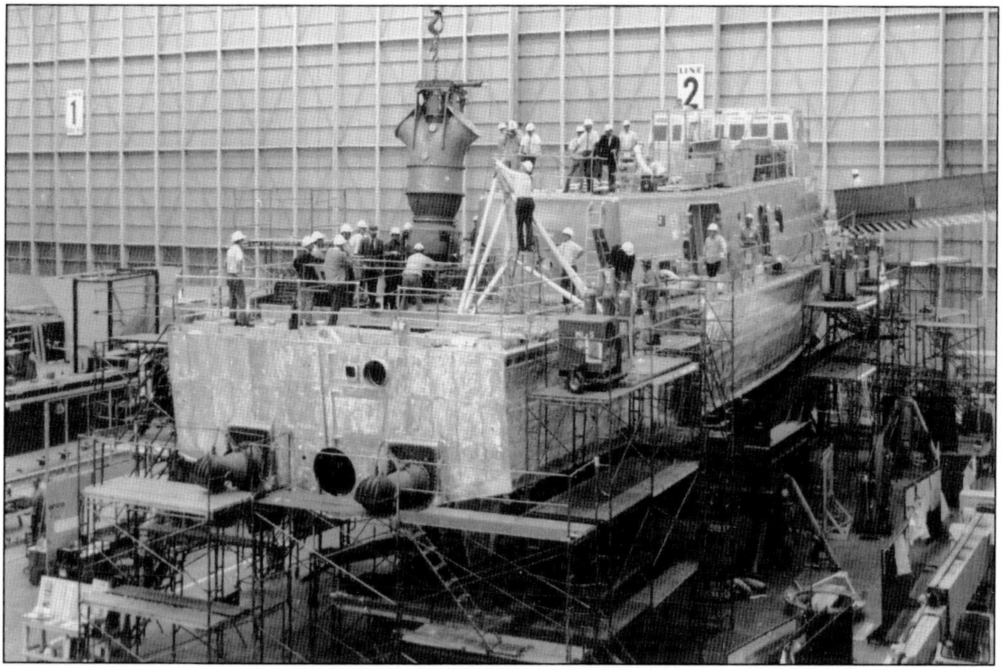

Pegasus Prototype. The USS *Pegasus* (PHM-1), shown above under construction in Seattle, was the first of six missile-armed patrol hydrofoils built by Boeing for NATO nations. The United States, Germany, and Italy all received and evaluated the 131-foot craft under military operating conditions. All were powered by a single 18,000-horsepower General Electric gas turbine engine driving a main waterjet pump built by Aerojet General (pictured being installed). This propulsion system gave the Pegasus a speed of more than 45 knots (51 miles per hour) while on her foils. In the photograph below, taken outside the Boeing Renton plant, the hydrofoil is seen on the ramp leading to Lake Washington on a cradle dolly. (Both courtesy Hal Turner.)

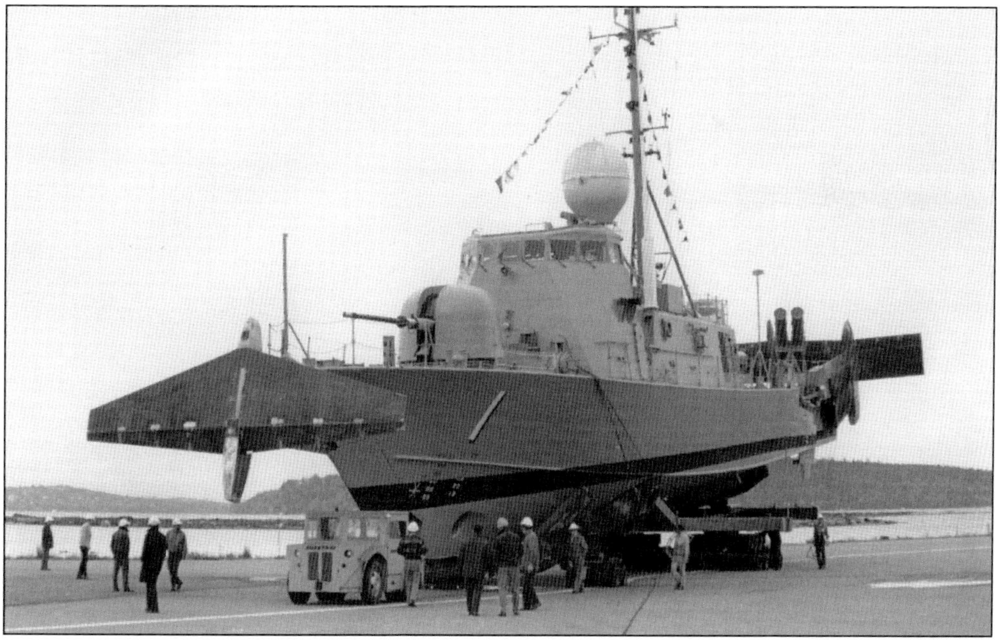

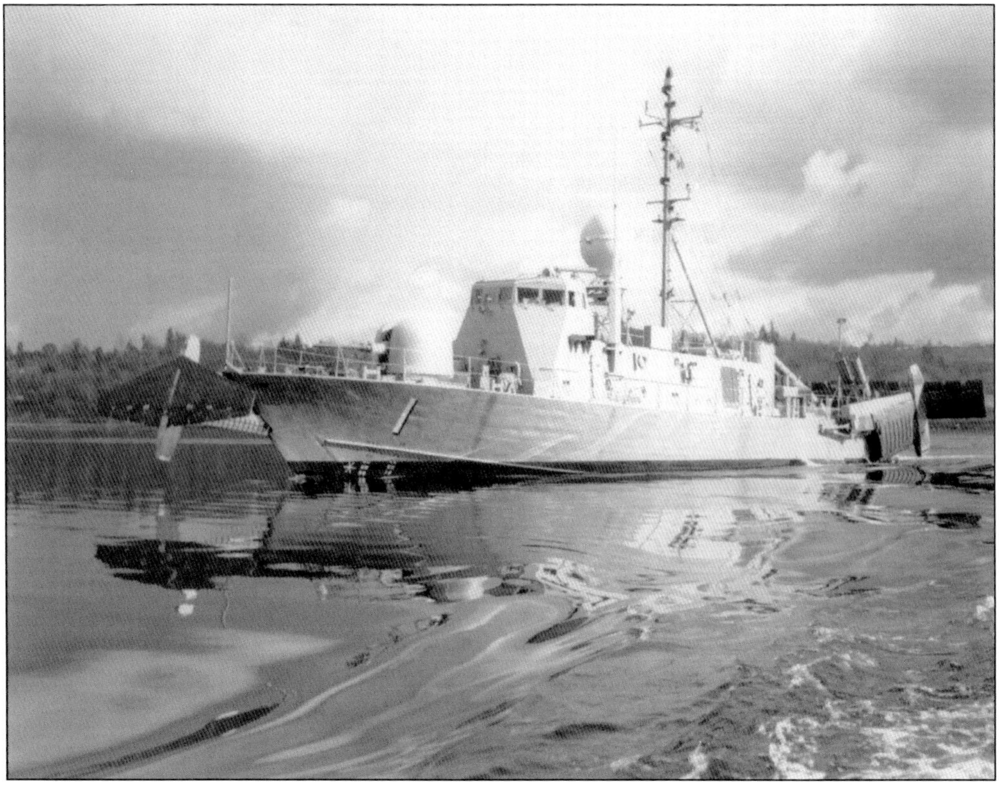

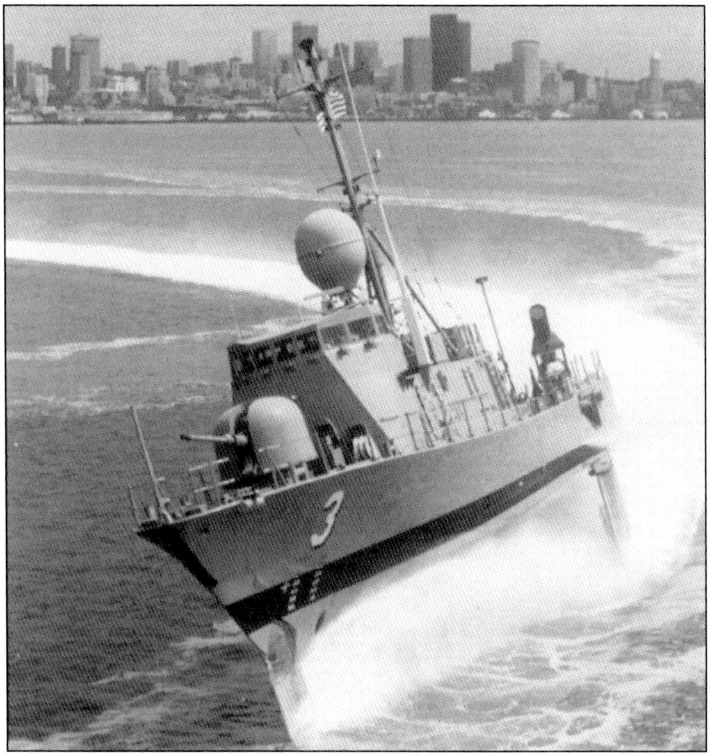

AFLOAT AND FLYING. Shown hullborne after launch at the south end of Lake Washington in 1974, the USS *Pegasus* (PGH-1) was commissioned at the Puget Sound Naval Shipyard in July 1977. The craft's twin foils, one at the bow and the other at the stern, are seen retracted for slow-speed hull operation. While "flying" above the water on their foils, the Pegasus-class hydrofoils, like the USS *Taurus*, shown at left during sea trials on Seattle's Elliott Bay, could fire eight missiles carried on their aft decks. (Above, courtesy Hal Turner; left, US Navy.)

Four

A Patrol Boat Rescued
The CG-83527 Story

Among the six 83-foot Coast Guard patrol boats that served in the greater Puget Sound area for more than 15 years beginning in 1945 is one particular cutter in near-original military condition that still graces its waters, CG-83527. The third from the last of 230 similar boats built in 1944 during World War II by Wheeler Shipyards in Brooklyn, New York, this important part of living Coast Guard history was stationed in Tacoma from 1945 until 1962.

Following her sale in a federal government surplus auction in 1962, CG-83527 was taken down the Pacific coast to Alameda, California, where her new owner used her as a live-aboard summer home for four decades. Upon his death, the patrol boat was donated to the nonprofit American Patrol Boats Museum in Rio Vista on the Sacramento River. In 2003, the boat was discovered by Dan Withers, a Navy destroyer veteran of the Vietnam War, and his wife, Roxane, residents of Port Ludlow, Washington.

Following initial restoration in the San Francisco Bay area, CG-83527 began a 1,000-mile return voyage up the west coast. She arrived back in Puget Sound and paid a homecoming visit to Tacoma 41 years after she had completed her Coast Guard active duty in Washington State.

But the discovery in Seattle's Lake Union of another former Coast Guard 83-foot patrol boat with an even more illustrious background, *Tiburon*, former CG-83366, enhanced the importance of the CG-83527. *Tiburon* was purchased as surplus in California, brought up the coast to Seattle, and converted to a recreational yacht for cruising Puget Sound. Historically, the boat was part of Coast Guard Rescue Flotilla No. 1 during the fabled World War II invasion at Normandy, France, in June 1944. With the discovery of the last two surviving crewmembers of the boat from D-Day, emotion-filled onboard reunions were arranged by the nonprofit Combatant Craft of America organization in 2006 and 2007. CG-83366 and CG-83527 provided an authentic historical context during these memorable occasions.

The story of Puget Sound's CG-83527 is an ongoing one, with her continued restoration and participation in maritime heritage and other events. The historic patrol boat and her legacy deserve to be honored and preserved for future generations.

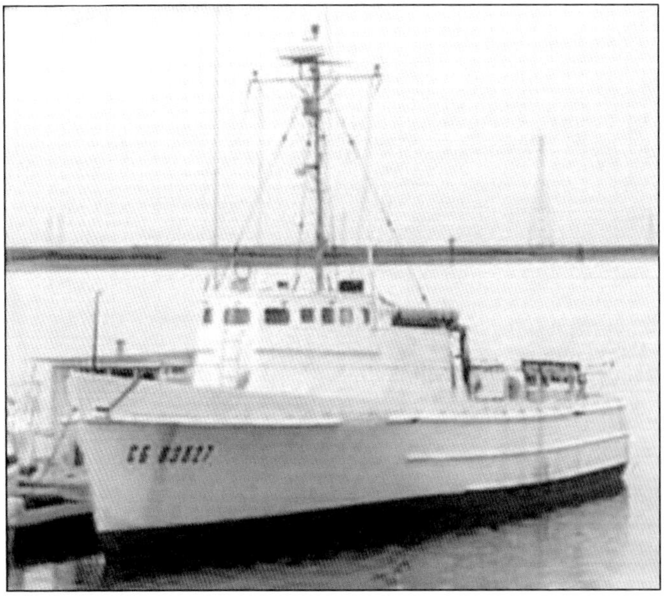

RESCUE BOAT REDISCOVERED. Dan and Roxane Withers discovered the Coast Guard CG-83527 sitting at the dock at the American Patrol Boat Museum (APBM) in Rio Vista in 2003. The 83-foot wooden boat was based in Tacoma and served south Puget Sound during her 18-year military career. She was built in 1944, among the last three of 230 such wooden patrol and rescue boats constructed by Wheeler Shipyards, Inc., in Brooklyn, New York, during World War II. (Courtesy APBM.)

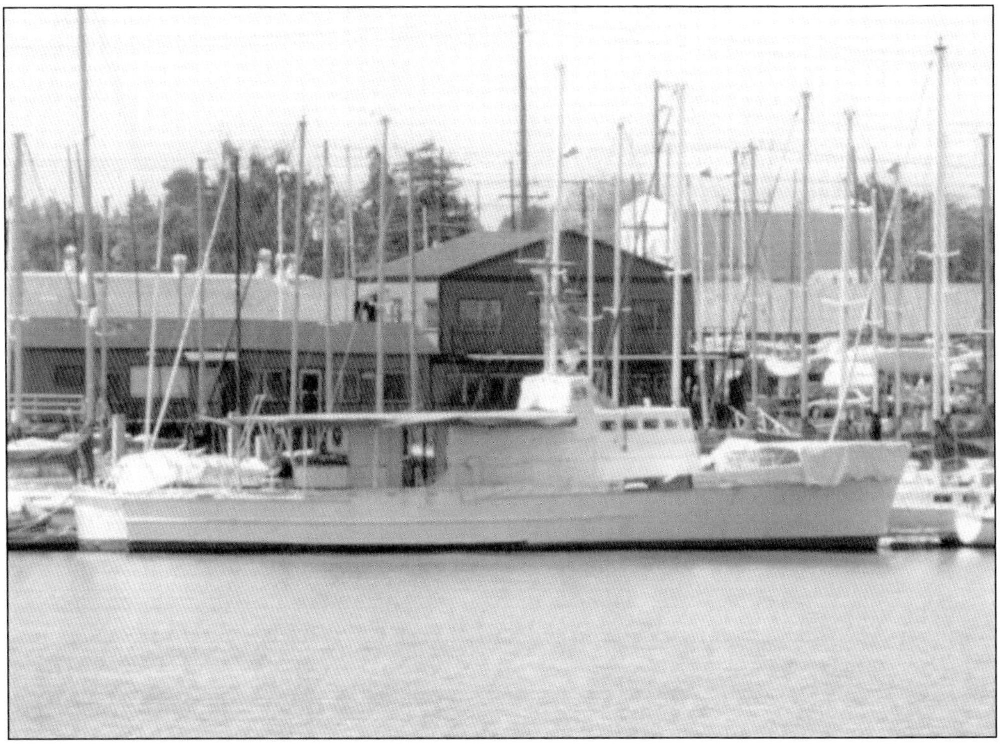

LIVE-ABOARD LIFE. Following her 1962 decommissioning and subsequent sale at a federal government surplus auction, the former CG-83527 became a live-aboard summer home at Alameda in the east San Francisco Bay area. The boat's new private owner did some limited renovation of the interior spaces and used them for storage but left the wheelhouse and other on-deck features in basic military configuration. (Courtesy APBM.)

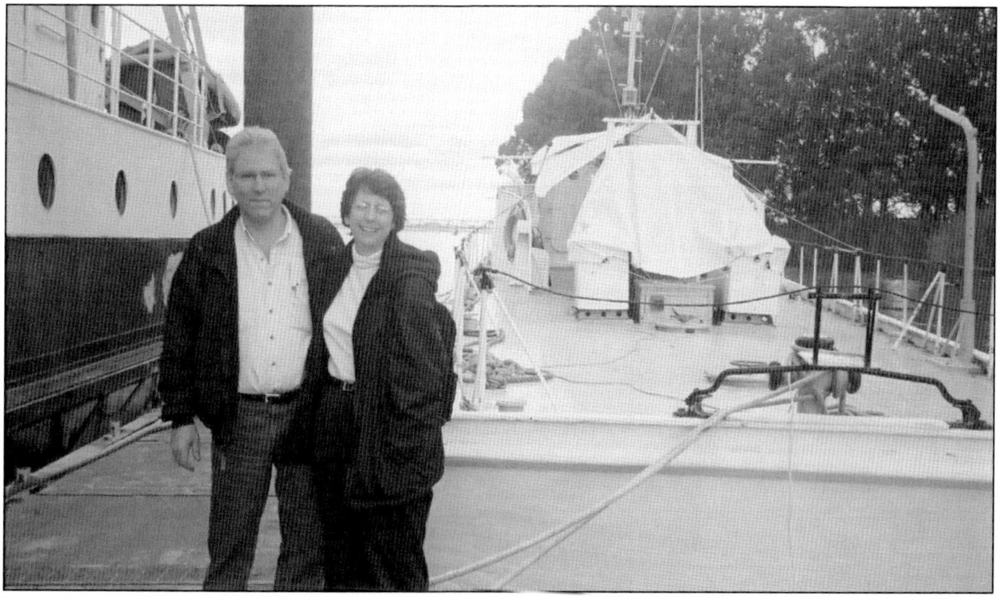

Resourceful Renovators. The Withers are shown with the historic patrol boat after the nonprofit Combatant Craft of America (CCA) purchased the former CG-83527. As a Navy Vietnam War destroyer veteran and president of the CCA, Dan wanted to find and restore a relatively small historic military sea service boat. With support from Roxane, the couple and their friends began the initial on-site restoration process of the interior and engine room, which took nine months of part-time but difficult and hard work. (Photograph by Chuck Fowler.)

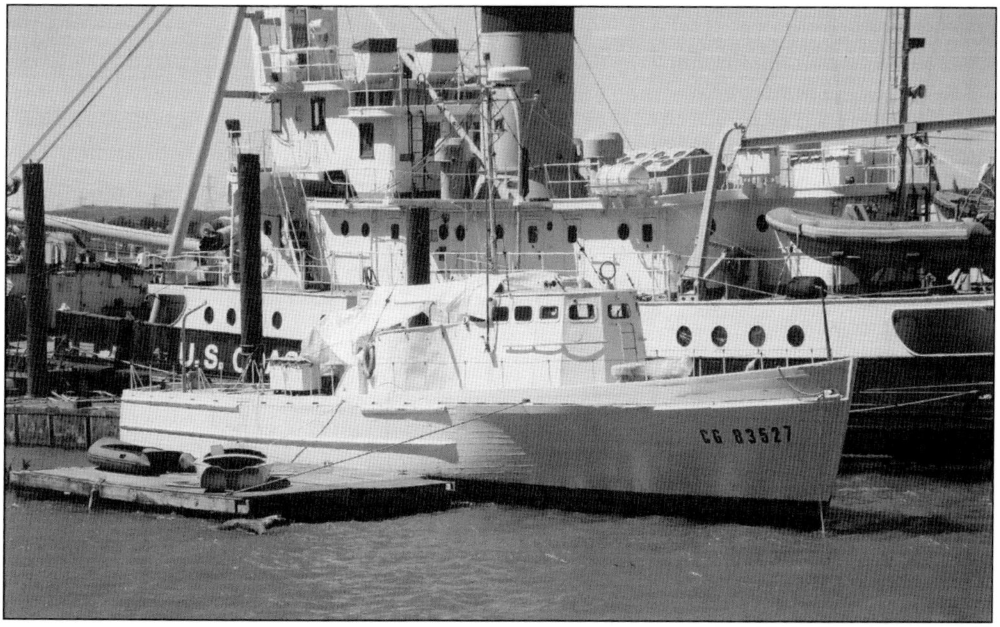

Coast Guard Companions. In 2004, CG-83527 and the retired 174-foot Coast Guard buoy tender *Fir* (WLM-212) were photographed moored together as part of the nonprofit American Patrol Boats Museum fleet. The museum fleet of historic military vessels was located on the eastern shore of the Sacramento River across from Rio Vista. White tarpaulins aft of the wheelhouse cover early restoration efforts. (Photograph by Chuck Fowler.)

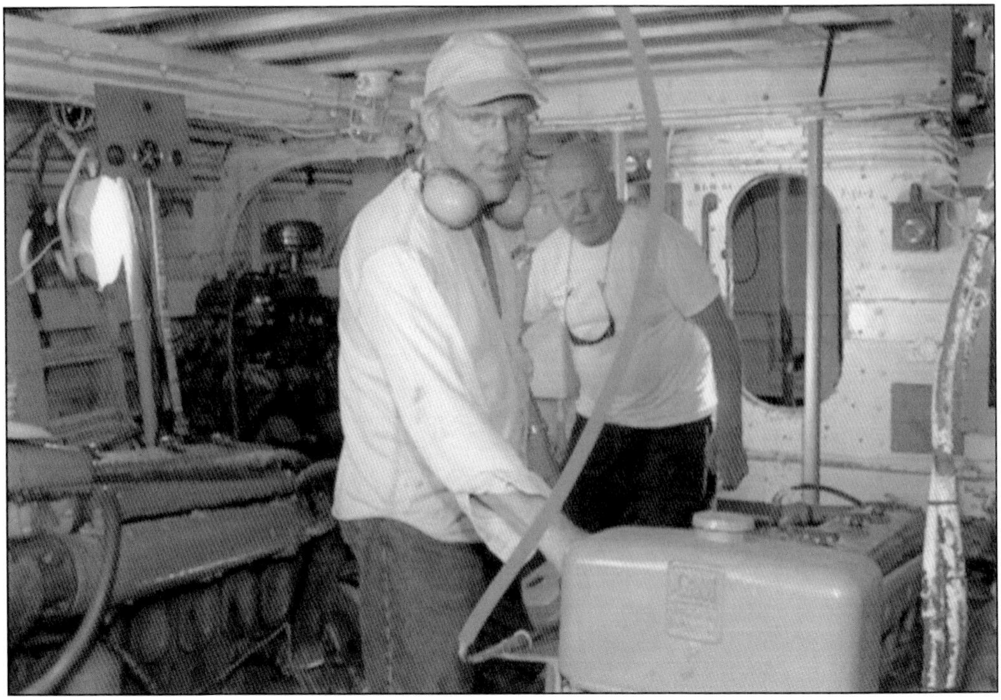

Engine Readied for Return. Dan (left) and Air Force veteran friend Royal Journey are shown working on one of CG-83527's twin General Motors 671 diesel engines, readying them for the patrol boat's long return voyage up the Pacific coast to Puget Sound. The 83-foot vessel was originally powered by two 600-horsepower Sterling Viking gasoline engines. These fuel-thirsty wartime-era power plants were removed in the late 1980s after her sale by the government. (Photograph by Marc Bracken.)

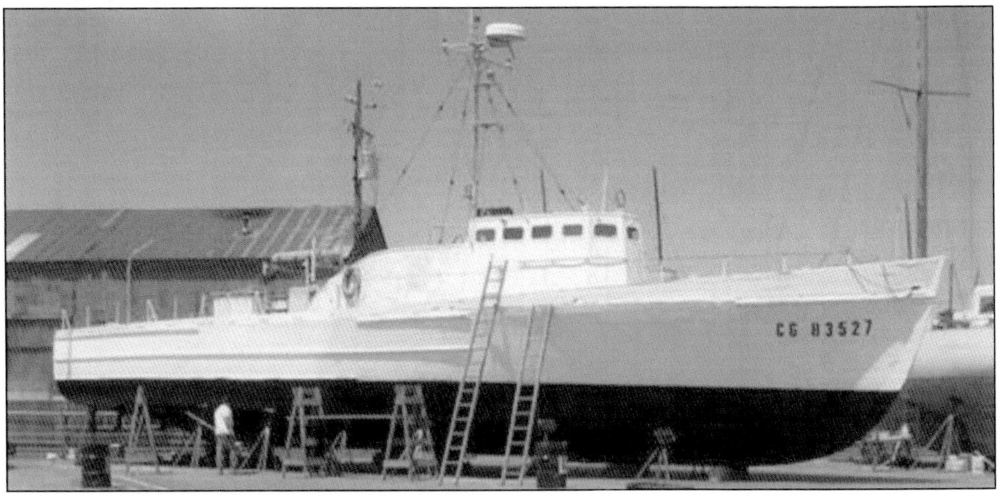

High-Standing Haulout. With towing assistance from Rio Vista by the Liberty Maritime Sea Scout unit's Vietnam-era patrol boat, CG-83527 was taken downriver to Richmond, California, in the north San Francisco Bay area for haulout, hull inspection, and pre-voyage maintenance. One of the last of more than 200 similar boats produced during World War II, the craft's wooden planked hull and overall structural integrity were found to be in remarkably good condition six decades after she was built. (Photograph by Dan Withers.)

Long Seaway Home. This chart, or map in non-nautical terminology, shows the route of CG-83527 in 2004 as she returned to her home waters in Puget Sound, more than 1,000 miles north. The passage included nine port calls before entering the Strait of Juan de Fuca in Washington State and arrival at Port Townsend on Puget Sound. (Courtesy CCA.)

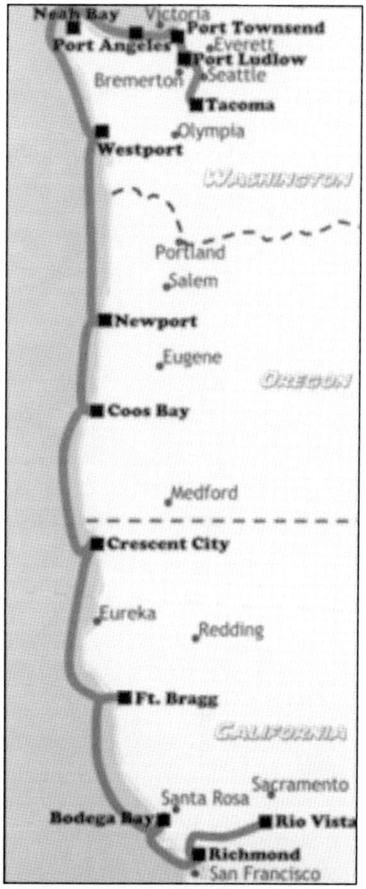

Coast Guard Station Stopover. The Coast Guard station at Fort Bragg, California, was one of several CG-83527 stopovers made en route up the Pacific coast. The "Coasties" welcomed the 60-year-old patrol boat and the chance to see and tour part of their own service history. More than two dozen similar 83-foot patrol and rescue craft served on the coast after World War II until the early 1960s, when all were decommissioned and replaced by newer vessels. (Photograph by Selby Drew, former Coast Guard 83-foot patrol boat skipper.)

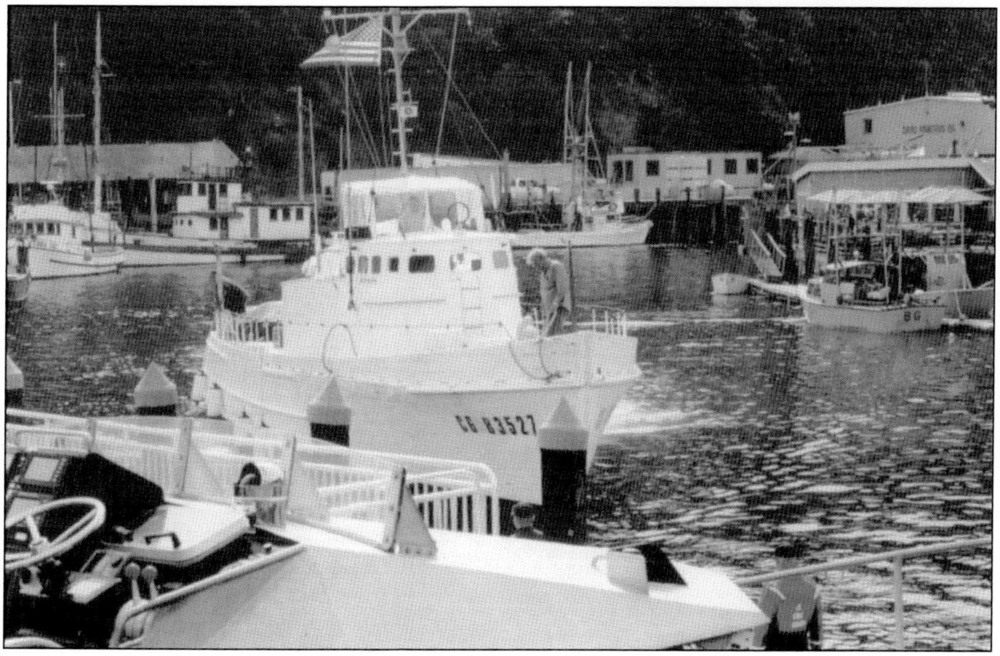

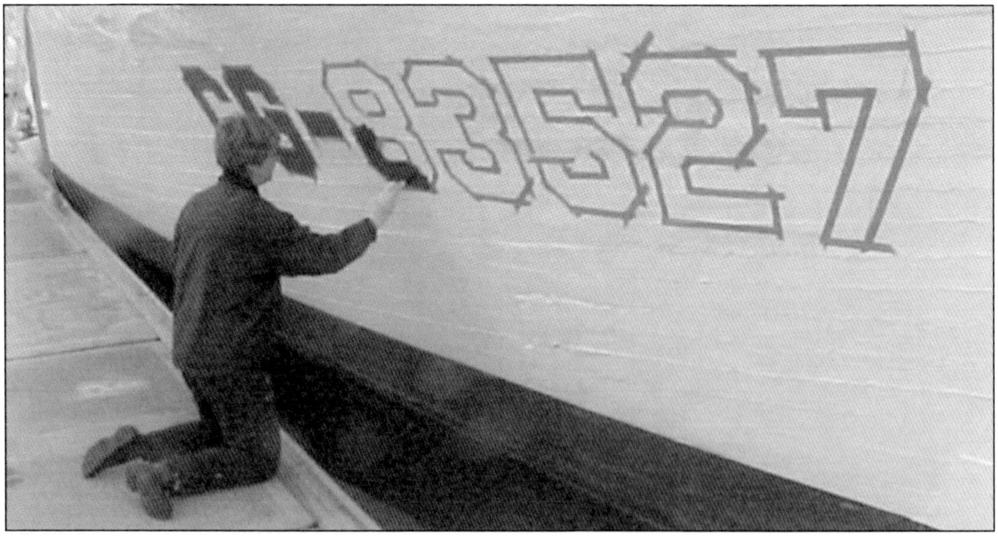

PAINTING WITH PRIDE. After CG-83527 arrived at Port Ludlow, Washington, Roxane Withers is shown repainting the regulation large-size Coast Guard identification numbers on the boat. The stopover in Port Ludlow, the Witherses' home community, allowed for crew rest and final cleanup before the historic vessel returned to her original homeport station in Tacoma. (Photograph by Dan Withers.)

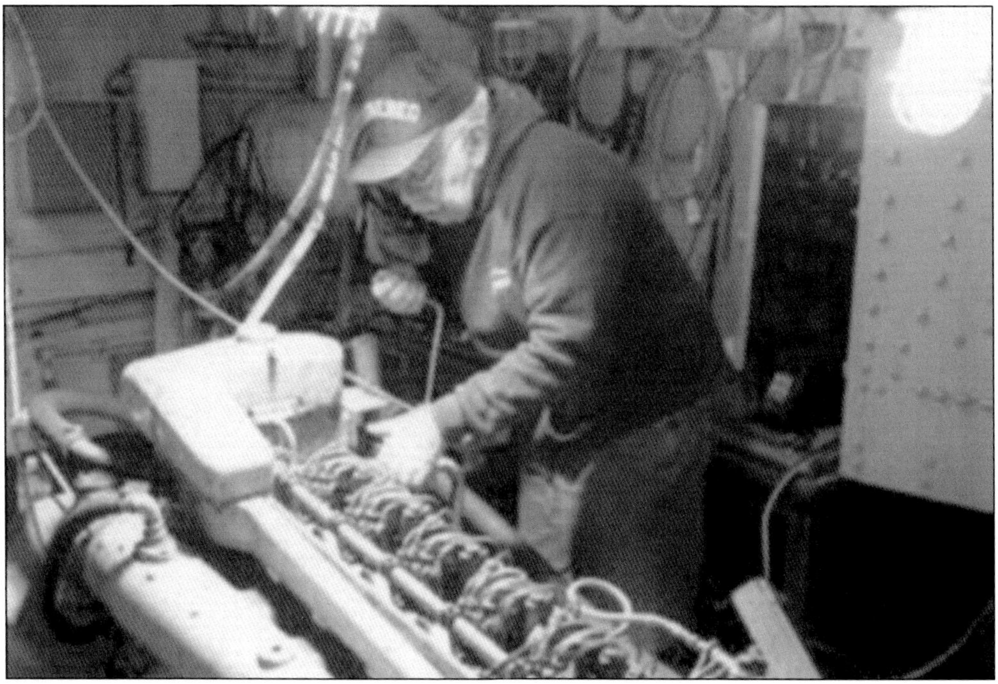

ENGINEERING THE ENGINES. Keeping the CCA's patrol boat's engines operating requires ongoing periodic maintenance. Here, CG-83527 veteran and volunteer Len Brue, from Virginia Beach, Virginia, checks over one of CG-83527's twin 165-horsepower General Motors diesel power plants in April 2005. The craft's original gasoline engines developed 600 horsepower each, driving the 76-ton boat at a top speed of more than 18 knots (21 miles per hour) and burning 120 gallons per hour. (Courtesy CCA.)

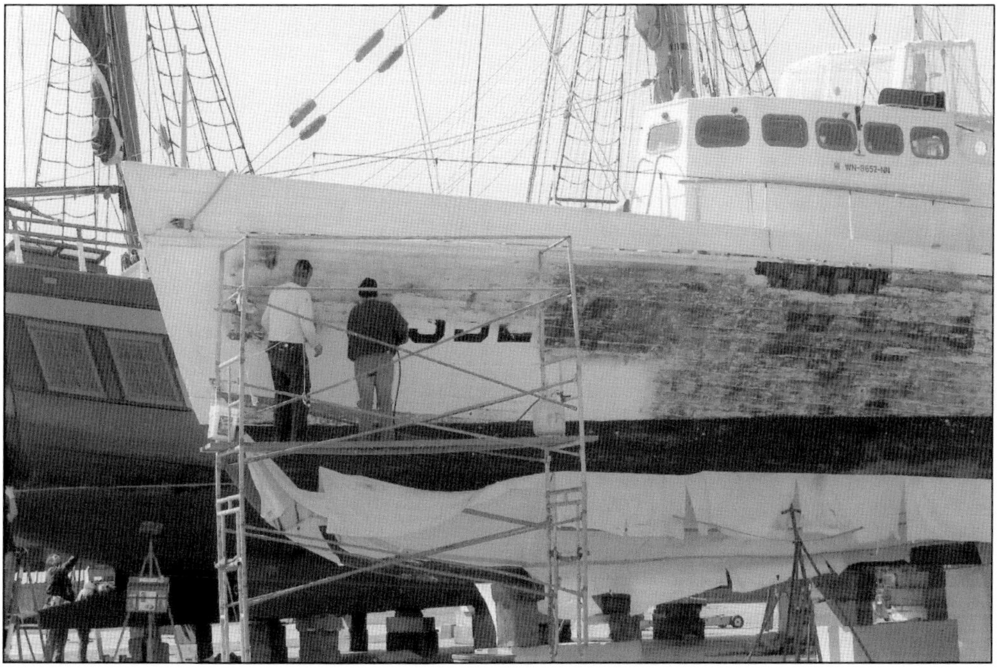

Bow Paint Burnoff. Two shipwrights are pictured on scaffolding at the Port Townsend Boat Yard burning old paint off the bow of CG-83527 during a 2007 haulout. The boat's hull was being repaired after a collision with an unidentified underwater object caused propeller and shaft strut damage. While out of the water, it was decided to strip and repaint the historic boat's hull in preparation for her participation in the Tacoma Tall Ships 2008 event. (Photograph by Dan Withers.)

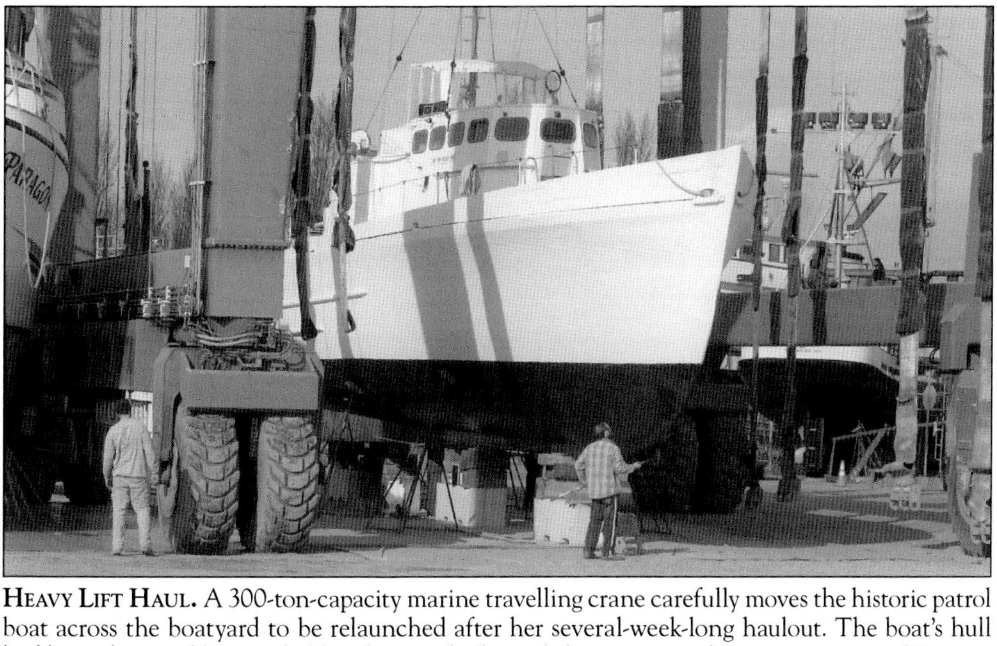

Heavy Lift Haul. A 300-ton-capacity marine travelling crane carefully moves the historic patrol boat across the boatyard to be relaunched after her several-week-long haulout. The boat's hull had been damaged by a probable submerged piling while en route to her moorage east of Everett, and she was sent to Port Townsend for repair. (Courtesy CCA.)

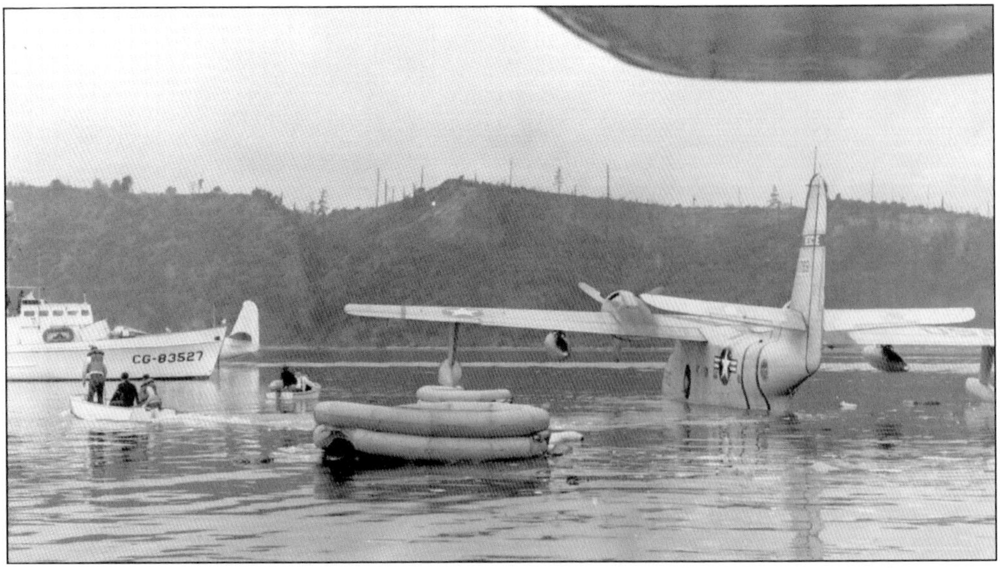

Ditching Rescue Drama. CG-83527 is shown on the scene during the dramatic rescue of passengers aboard a Northwest Airlines airliner following its ditching in Puget Sound on April 2, 1956. Following engine failure shortly after takeoff from Seattle-Tacoma International Airport, the disabled airliner made a water landing off Point Robinson on Maury Island. Also pictured is one of two US Air Force amphibian rescue aircraft that happened to be on a training mission in the area at the time and responded to the accident. (Photograph by Howard Vallentyne, courtesy of the *Seattle Times.*)

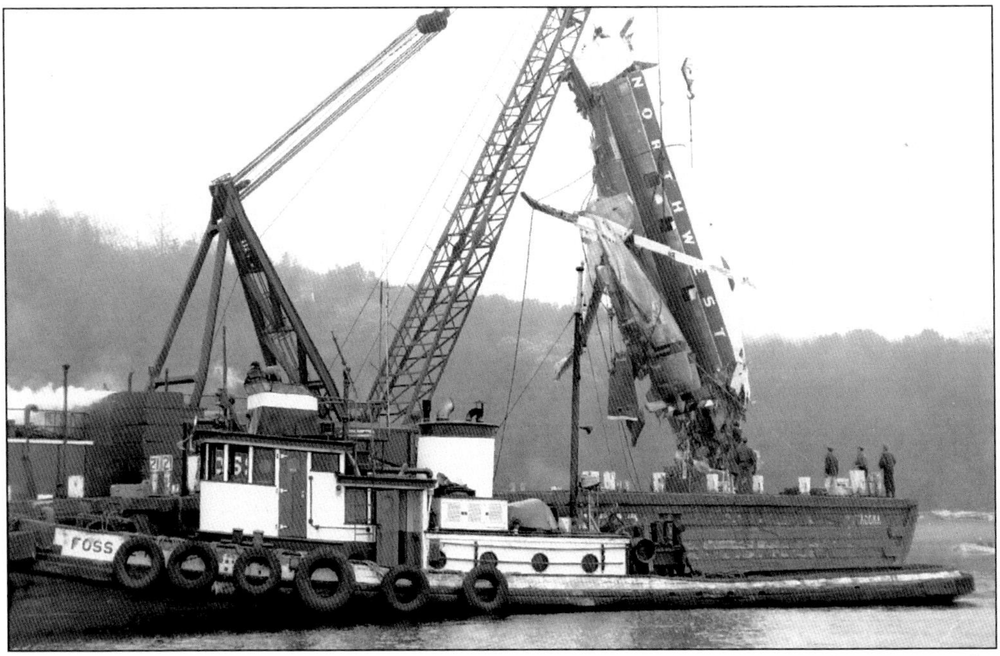

Raised and Recovered. The Foss 300 steam crane aboard a barge is shown here raising the Northwest Airlines airliner that ditched in Puget Sound after takeoff from Seattle-Tacoma International Airport. Thirty-three passengers were rescued and assisted by the crews of CG-83527, two Air Force amphibious seaplanes, tugboats, and also nearby island residents in rowboats, but five passengers perished. (Courtesy Foss Maritime.)

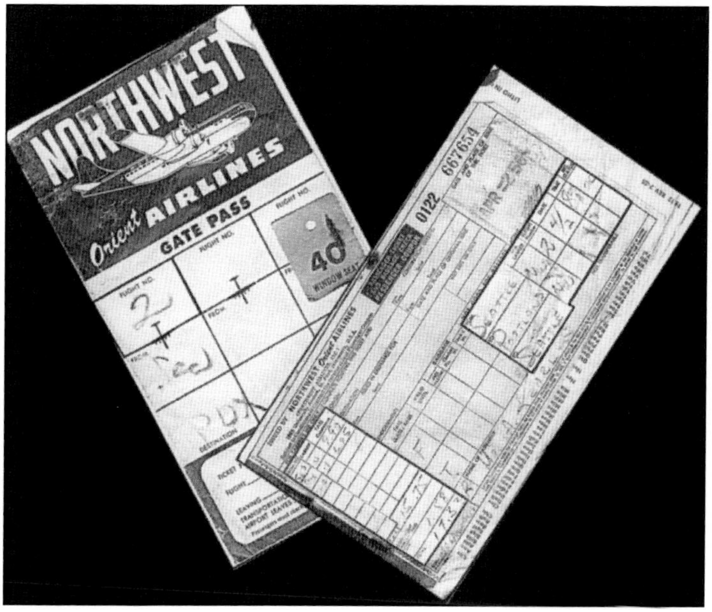

Tattered Ticket. The tattered, water-soaked airline ticket of survivor J. Alten (Al) Kerl is pictured at right. He was a window-seat passenger on a short flight from Seattle to Portland when the aircraft plunged into the sound shortly after takeoff. Kerl's only request for compensation for his own watery dunking was return of his $17.33 airfare, which he received several weeks after the crash together with the airline's apologetic letter. (Courtesy Al Kerl.)

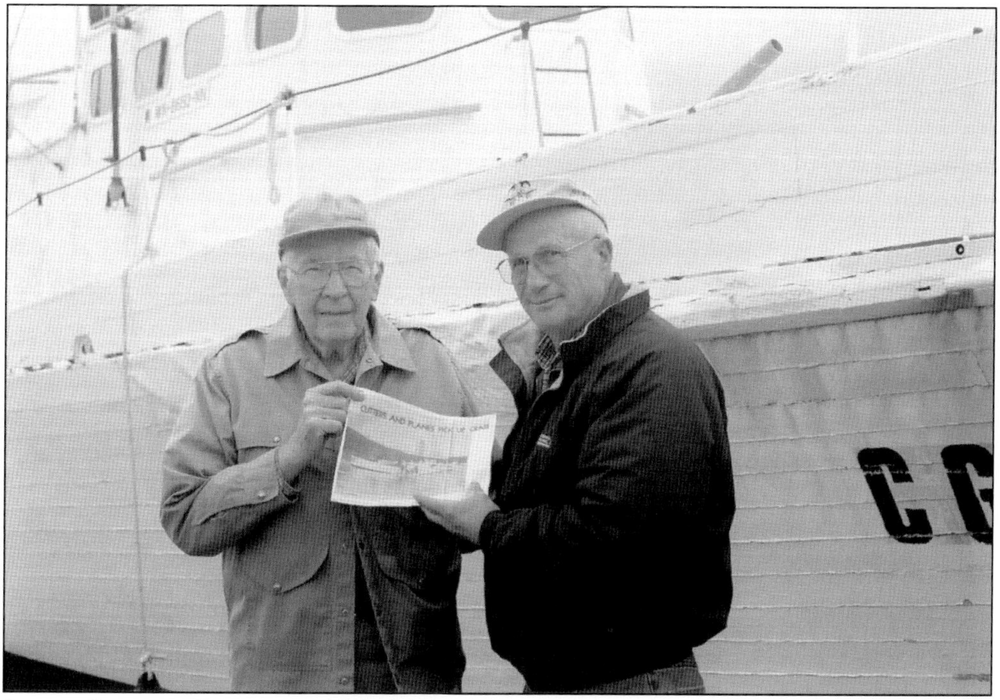

Sailor, Survivor Reunited. Al Kerl, left, was a passenger on Northwest Airlines Flight 2 from Seattle to Portland, Oregon, when the airliner ditched in the sound on April 2, 1956. Here he is shown in 2004, almost 50 years later, with Myron "Tike" Hillman, the CG-83527 crewman who helped save him after the accident. They are holding a copy of the front-page story about the crash in the *Seattle Times*. Kerl was en route to a business meeting when the ditching occurred four minutes after takeoff. (Photograph by Chuck Fowler.)

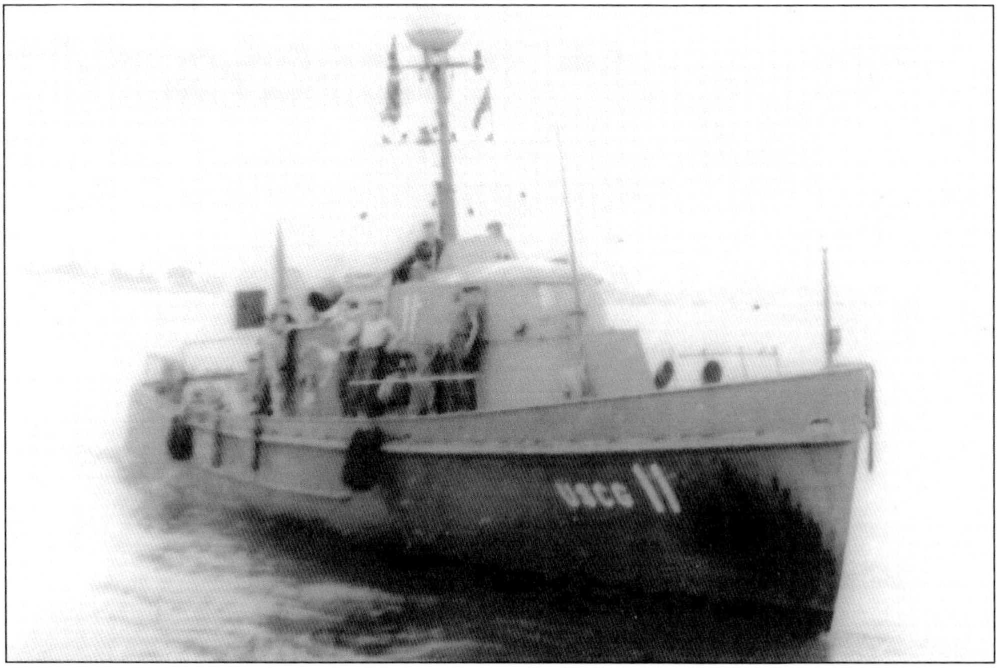

D-Day Rescue Boat. USCG-11 was one of sixty 83-foot patrol boats that formed Coast Guard Rescue Flotilla No. 1, which participated in the D-Day invasion at Normandy, France, on June 6, 1944. Following her wartime and subsequent peacetime service as CG-83366 in Santa Barbara, California, she was decommissioned in 1962, sold to a private owner, brought to Seattle, converted to a recreational yacht, and named *Tiburon*. As pictured below, World War II Coast Guard veteran Wilfred "Bud" Eberhardt, a signalman third-class aboard the USCG-11 on D-Day, was reunited with his wartime patrol boat in 2006 during ceremonies at Seattle's Lake Union Park Historic Ships Wharf. Accompanied by family members, he was recognized for his combat service at Normandy. (Above, courtesy of Wilfred "Bud" Eberhardt; below, photograph by Chuck Fowler.)

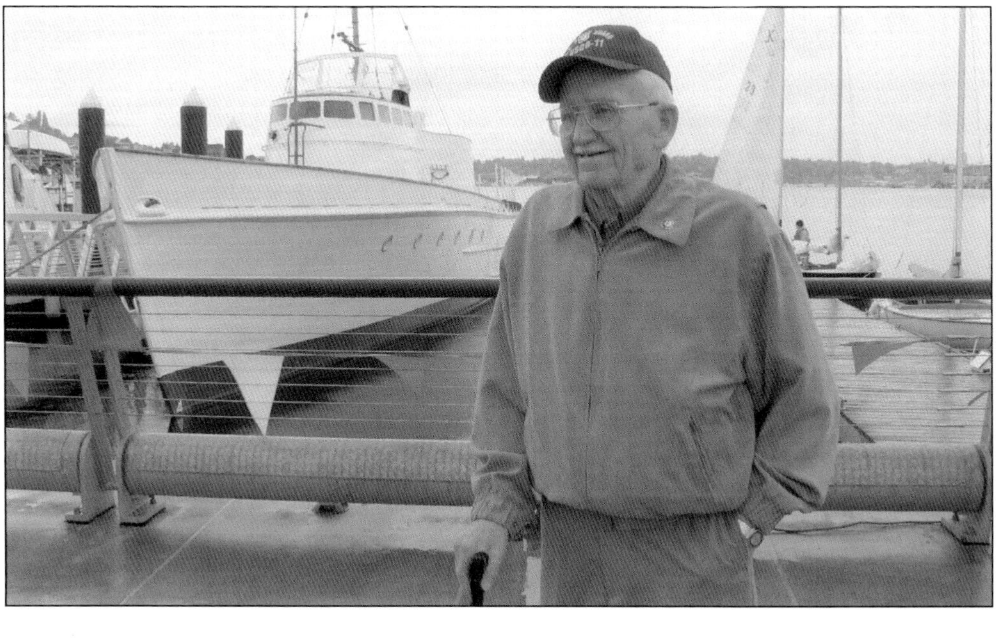

SKIPPER, SAILOR MEET AGAIN. Following Bud Eberhardt's 2006 reunion with the ex-USCG-11, additional research located her only other known living crewmember, former Coast Guard lieutenant (junior grade) Arthur (Art) Lehne (at right), who was the patrol and rescue boat's skipper on D-Day. Again with the help of family members, in 2007, Lehne and Eberhardt met aboard their historic boat, more than 60 years after their service together at Normandy. Eberhardt passed away at 85 a year later. (Photograph by Chuck Fowler.)

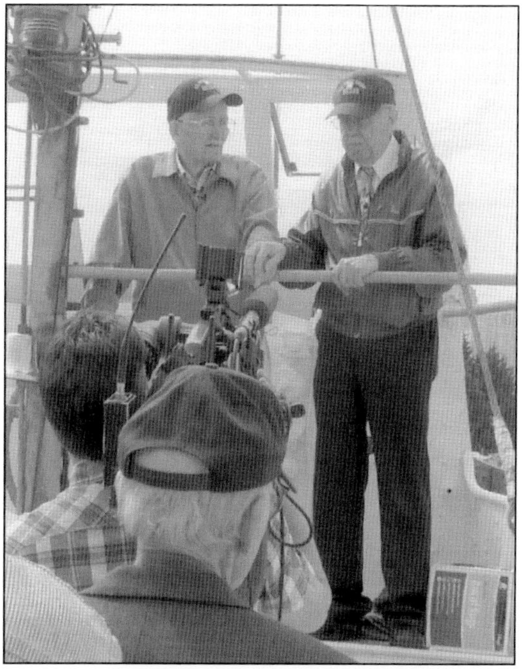

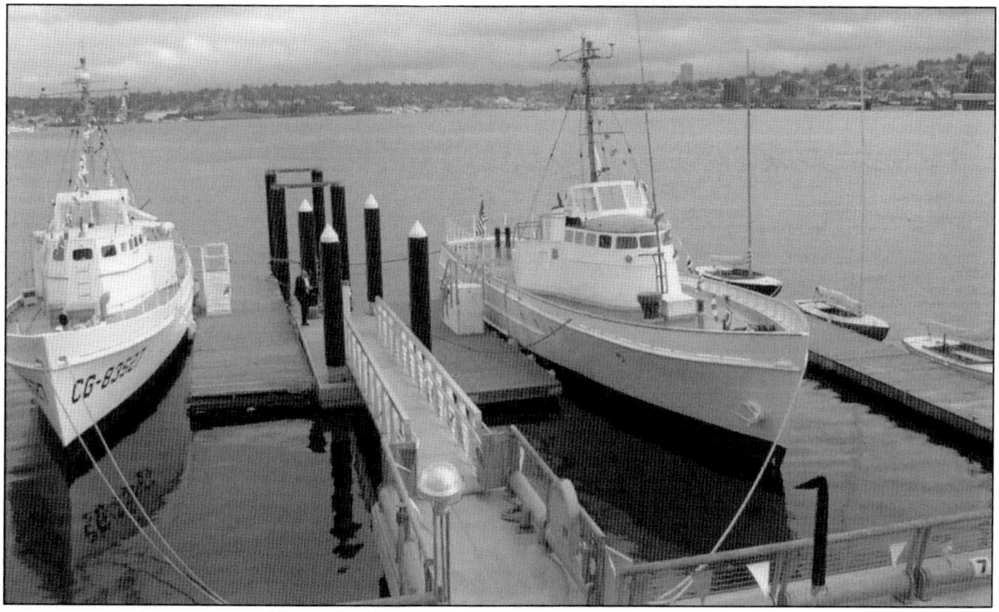

COMPANION CUTTERS. Although they never served together during their active duty days, the CCA's CG-83527 (left) and USCG-11, later CG-83366 and finally *Tiburon*, were exhibited side-by-side at the Historic Ships Wharf at Lake Union Park during ceremonies in 2006 and 2007. During the 2007 Armed Forces Day event, retired Coast Guard rear admiral and former District 13 commander John Lockwood presented D-Day veterans Eberhardt, Lehne, and retired captain Earl McAuliffe commemorative medals. The photograph above was taken from the second floor of the Naval Reserve Armory building, which served as a Navy, Marine, and Coast Guard training facility from 1941 to the late 1990s and was scheduled to become Seattle's new Museum of History and Industry (MOHAI) in 2012. (Photograph by Dan Withers.)

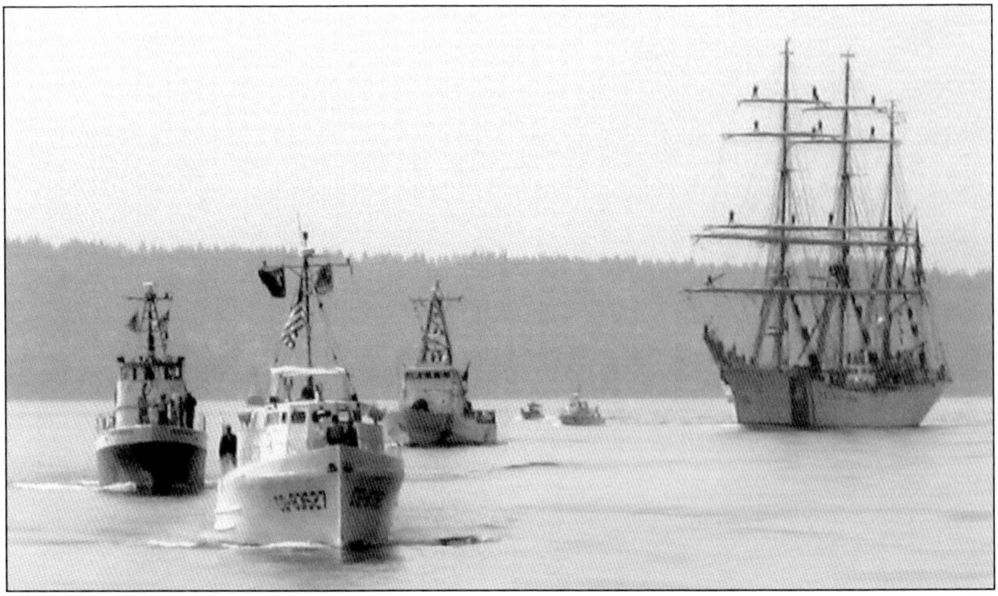

Eagle Escort. When the widely known USCGC *Eagle*, the square-rigged training ship based at the Coast Guard Academy, visited Puget Sound in 2008, a fleet of heritage patrol boats escorted her into Seattle's Elliott Bay, as pictured above. The vessels in the escort fleet were Mark Freeman's 1941 buoy tender *Blueberry* (WLI-65302), not shown, and the 1944 CG-83527 (foreground) and at left, the 1961 former *Point Divide* (CG-82337), owned and operated by the Seattle Maritime Academy as the *Maritime Instructor*. (Photograph by Mark Freeman.)

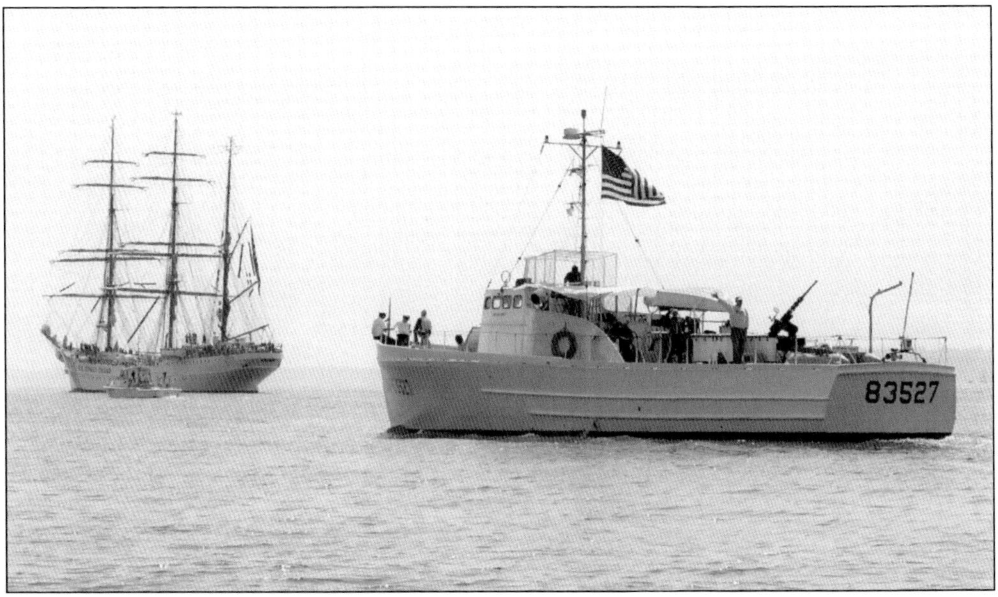

Historic Sister Ships. CG-83527 is shown astern of the USCGC *Eagle* during her 2008 Puget Sound visit. Built in 1936 as the *Horst Wessel* for the German Navy, the three-masted barque was a World War II war reparation prize to the United States, assigned to the Coast Guard in 1946 and renamed the *Eagle*. Known as "America's Tall Ship," the *Eagle* visited Puget Sound twice, in 1965 and 1978, before her 2008 appearance in Seattle and at the Tacoma Tall Ships event. (Photograph by Chuck Fowler.)

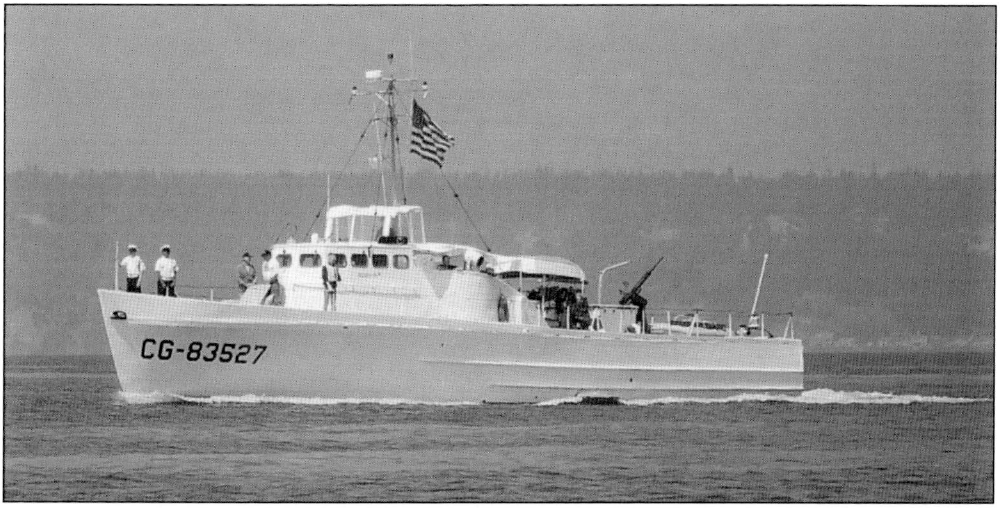

Participating Patrol Boat. In addition to participating in the Coast Guard Heritage Fleet escort for the USCG tall ship *Eagle* in 2008, CG-83527 was involved in many public events following her return to Puget Sound in 2004. She has visited many port communities through the years, from Port Townsend to Olympia, during maritime festivals, veterans' reunions, military memorials, and historical commemorations. (Photograph by Chuck Fowler.)

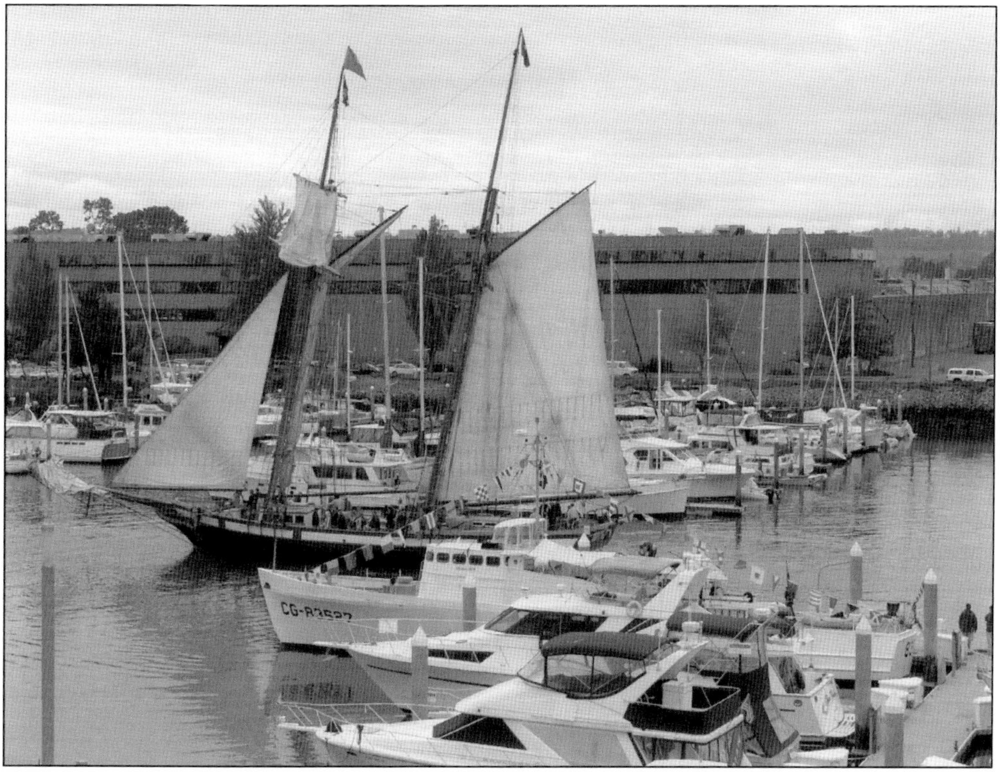

Tall Ship Setting. With the topsail schooner *Lynx* from Newport Beach, California, sailing by behind, CG-83527 is shown on public exhibit on the Foss Waterway during the Tacoma Tall Ships event in 2008. She was moored less than a half-mile away from her active duty station moorage at the former Tacoma Municipal Dock building from 1945 to 1962. (Courtesy CCA.)

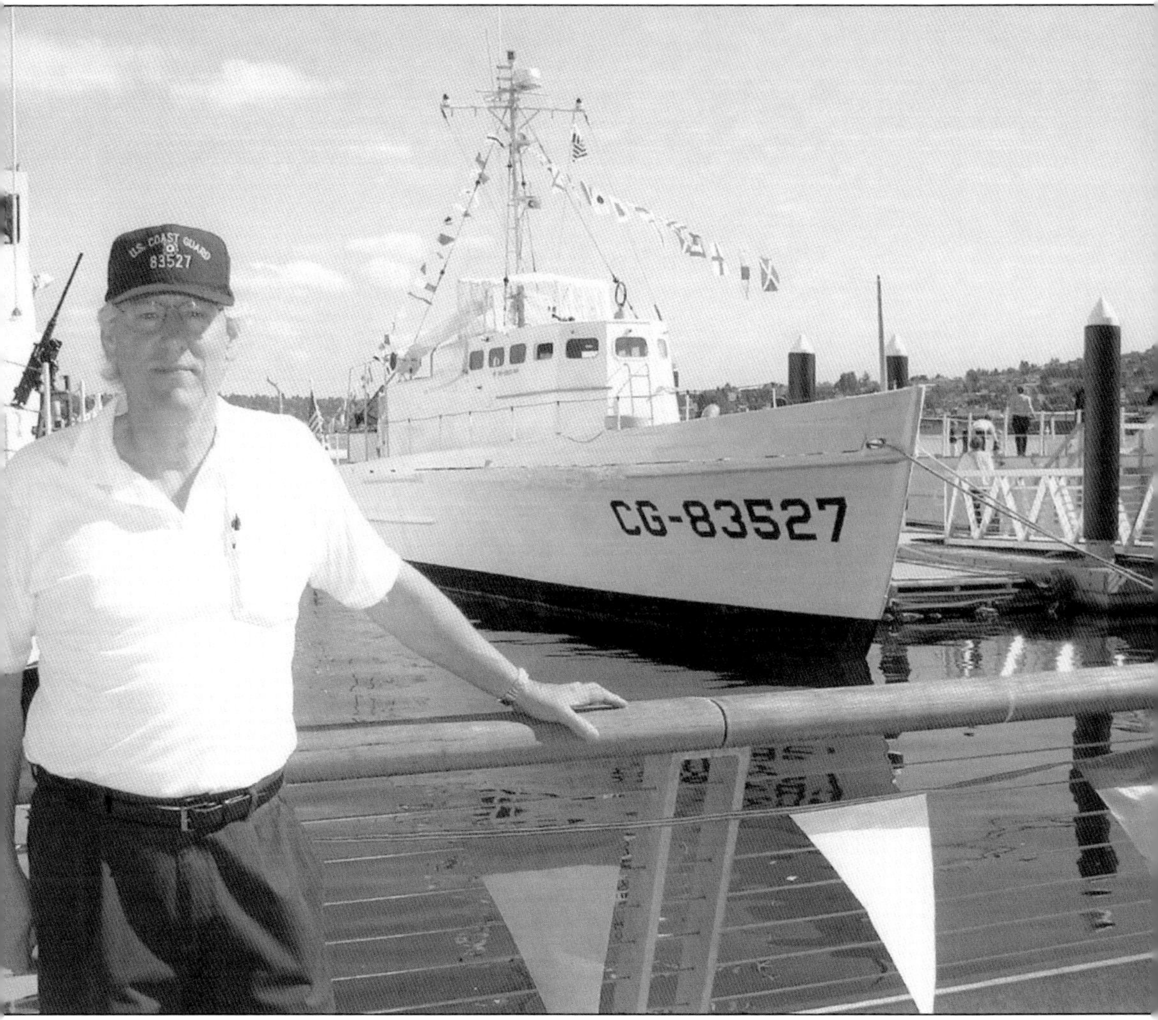

Rescue Boat Rescuer. Combatant Craft of America president Dan Withers stands in front of the World War II–era patrol boat that he and his wife discovered and rescued with the help of many Coast Guard and other dedicated volunteers. Since her return to Puget Sound and ongoing restoration, CG-83527 has revisited many of the south sound cities she once served while on active duty beginning more than six decades earlier. The restored heritage vessel symbolizes the Coast Guard's proud Pacific Northwest and national history and continuing legacy. (Photograph by Chuck Fowler.)

Five

Terrorism and Sound Security 1992–2010

In 1991 the Cold War threat of a nuclear exchange between the United States and the Soviet Union ended, and the next two decades saw the rise of international terrorism in local and regional areas. Insurgent warfare and suicide bombings of civilian targets in the Middle East, Africa, Southeast Asia, and even Europe were carried out to achieve political purposes. This new strategic reality came to the United States with the surprising, dramatic civilian airliner suicide attacks of September 11, 2001, in New York City and Washington, DC.

The patrol boat response to these new threats to national security abroad and later on the home front had begun in the 1990s with more emphasis on armed, maneuverable Vietnam War–style inland and coastal small craft. At first, off-the-shelf, relatively high-speed civilian workboats were adapted for military use. But following the 9/11 attacks, the Coast Guard began seeking purpose-built boats for homeland security duties.

Subsequently, following a competition and extensive sea trials, a contract was awarded to SAFE Boats International of Port Orchard, Washington, for up to 700 of its 25-foot Response Boat–Small (RB-S) boats, at the time one of the largest boat purchases in the world. The Coast Guard had decided to standardize its small patrol craft fleet, and the SAFE boat Defender-class design was its choice.

Another major achievement in Puget Sound patrol boat design and construction came in June 2006, when Marinette Marine Corporation of Wisconsin and subcontractor Kvichak Marine Industries of Seattle were awarded a contract for 180 new Response Boat–Medium (RB-M) patrol boats.

Again, as they had during World War II and the Korean and Vietnam Wars, Puget Sound boat builders produced superior solutions to meet changing military needs for fast, multi-mission patrol and rescue craft.

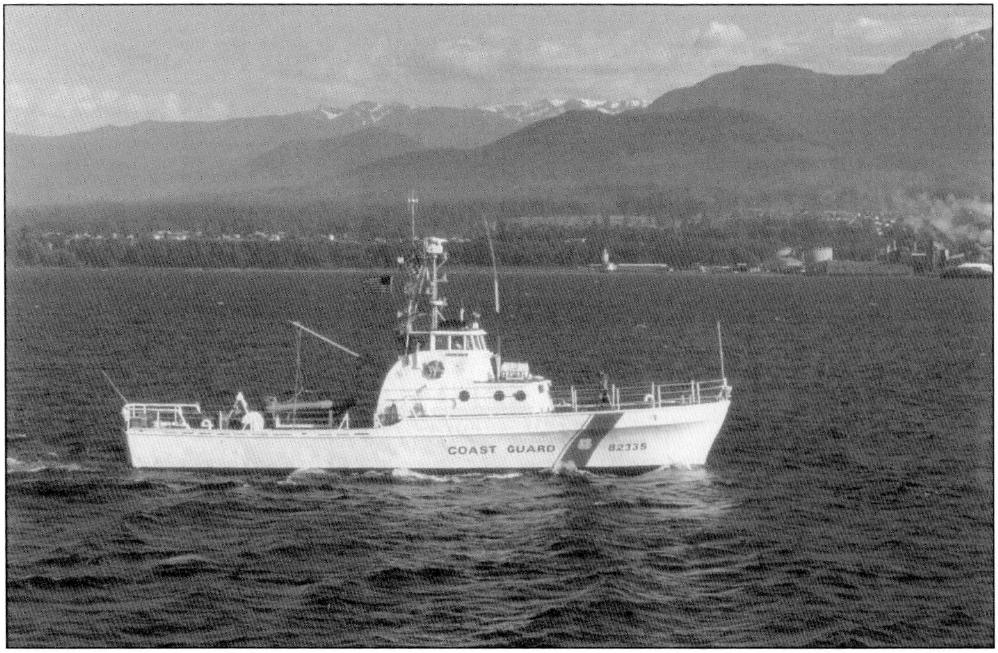

Senior Guardians. The 82-foot Coast Guard patrol boats, first commissioned in 1960, continued to be the service's major law enforcement and search and rescue force in Puget Sound into the 1990s. Pictured above with the Olympic Mountains in the background is the *Point Countess* (CG-82335), which entered active service in 1962 and is shown here while stationed at Port Angeles for 20 years between 1968 and 1988. While she was built at the Coast Guard shipyard at Curtis Bay, Maryland, the *Point Bennett* (CG-82351), shown below, was constructed by J.M. Martinac Shipbuilding in Tacoma and commissioned in 1966. Both patrol boats served more than 25 years in the sound before being replaced by the 87-foot Marine Protector–class craft beginning in the mid-1990s. (Both courtesy Coast Guard Museum Northwest.)

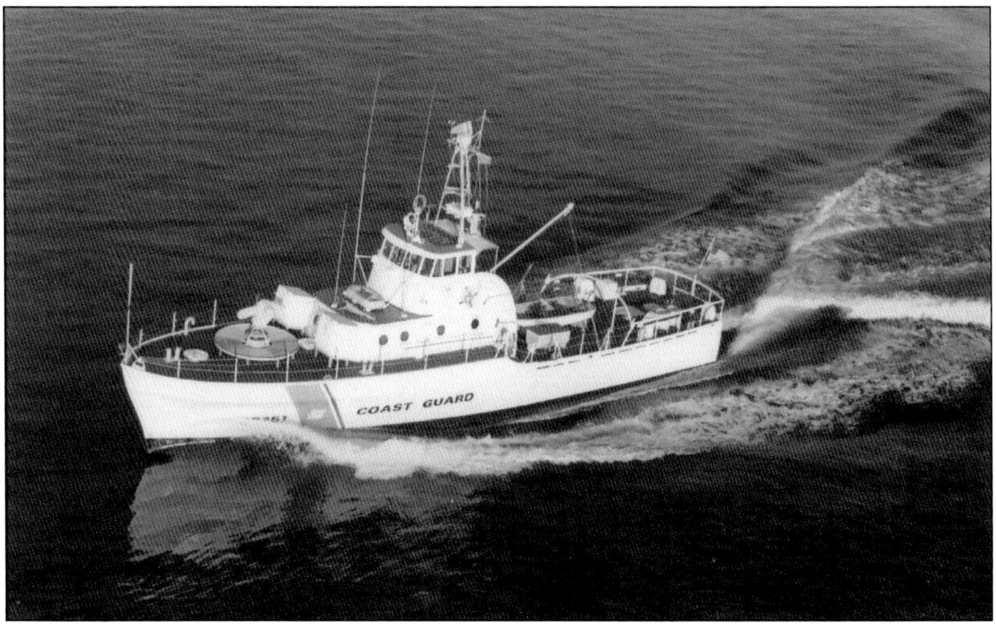

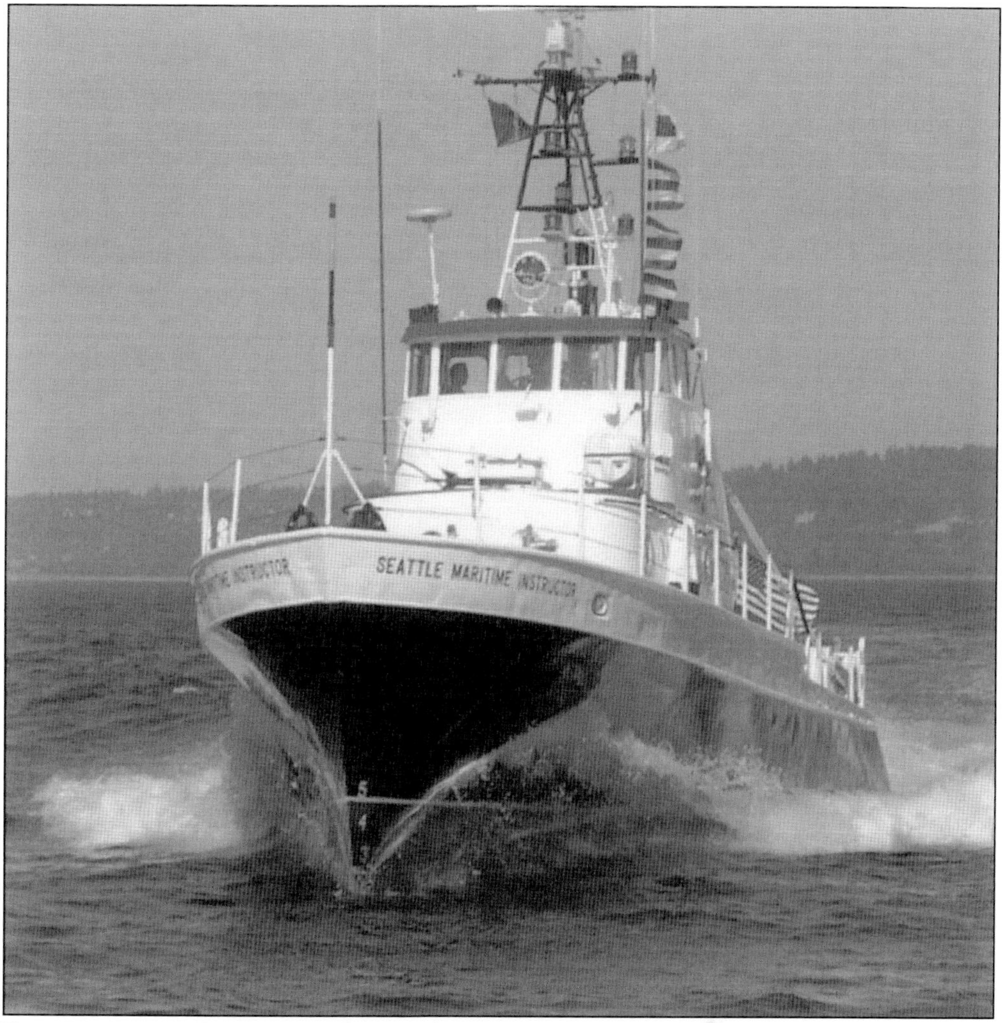

ENFORCEMENT TO EDUCATION. The Seattle Maritime Academy's 82-foot floating classroom, the *Marine Instructor*, was formerly the Coast Guard's *Point Divide* (CG-82337), commissioned in 1962. Built by the Coast Guard, the ex–patrol boat was stationed at Newport Beach and then Corona del Mar, California, from 1962 until she was decommissioned in 1995. One of the cutter's most notable law enforcement actions was the 1985 seizure of the fishing vessel *Ocean Joy* of San Clemente with 10 tons of marijuana onboard, preventing the crew from scuttling her. The 82-footer also had a small- and large-screen career, appearing in the *Baywatch* series and a documentary about the drug war on television as well as in cameo roles in several films. Acquired from the federal government in 1995, the *Maritime Instructor* is used for marine technical and vocational training at the academy. (Courtesy Seattle Maritime Academy, Seattle Central Community College.)

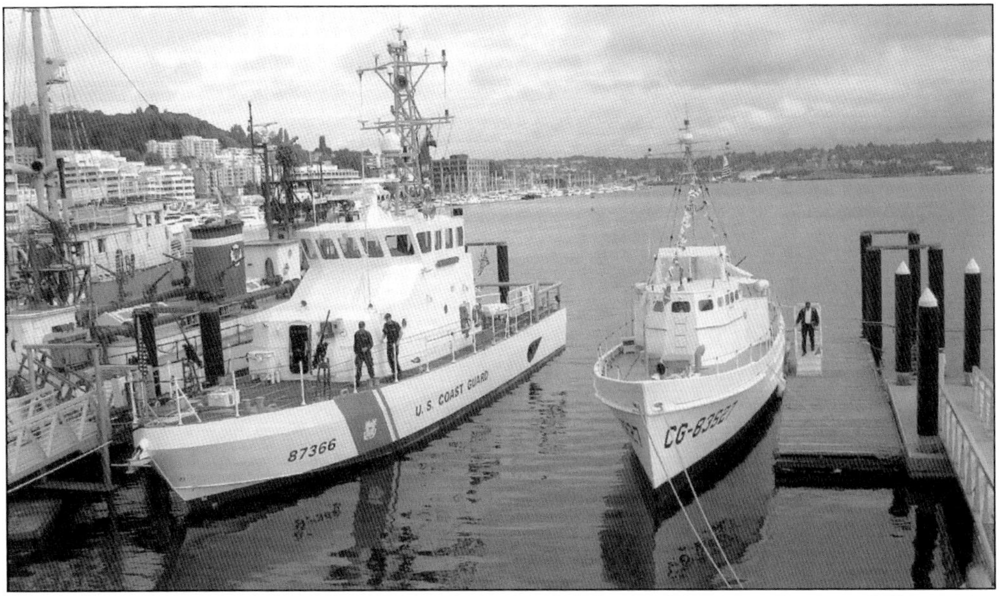

Generational Shift. Two generations of Coast Guard patrol boats are pictured above, the CG-83527 at right and the *Terrapin* (CG-87366) at left, at South Lake Union Park in 2006, spanning the 65-year period from World War II to 2010. The 83-foot CG-83527, stationed in Tacoma, was constructed of wood. Originally powered by twin gasoline engines totaling 1,200 horsepower, she could reach speeds of more than 20 knots (23 miles per hour). By contrast, the *Terrapin* and *Blue Shark* (below), assigned to Everett, are built of steel and aluminum and powered by twin turbo-diesel engines with a total output of 1,650 horsepower, and have a top speed of 26 knots (30 miles per hour). The *Blue Shark* was the 60th of 65 of the 87-foot Marine Protector–class patrol boats built for the Coast Guard. (Above, photograph by Dan Withers; below, US Navy.)

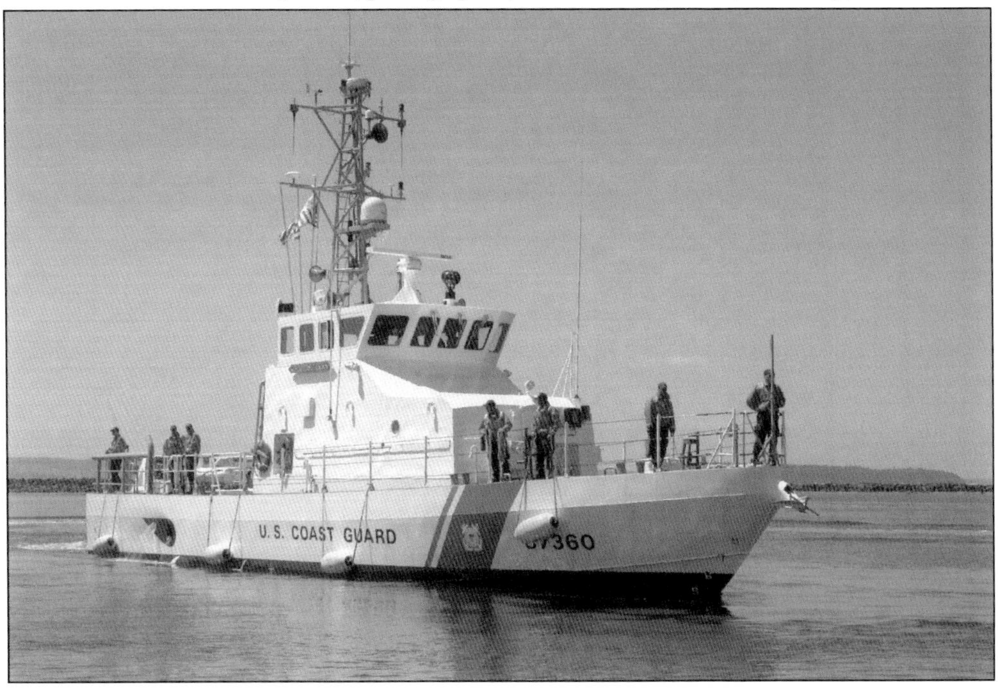

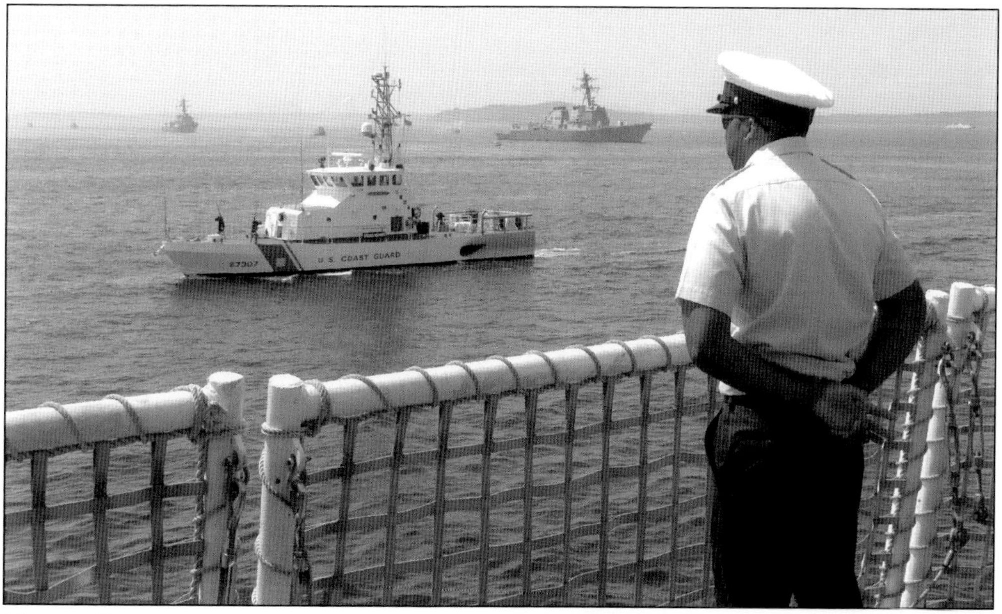

MARINE PROTECTOR PROFILE. In addition to carrying out search and rescue, law enforcement, marine environmental protection, and port security responsibilities, Coast Guard 87-foot patrol boats also provide marine safety support at community events such as the 2009 Seattle Seafair Fleet Week parade on Elliott Bay. The *Osprey*, stationed at Port Townsend and the first of the Marine Protector–class craft to be assigned to Puget Sound in 1999, is shown above with two Navy guided missle destroyers in the background. The image at right shows the unique stern launch and recovery ramp of the *Osprey* and other 87-footers, which allows the boat to be launched while the craft is underway. (Both photographs by Chuck Fowler.)

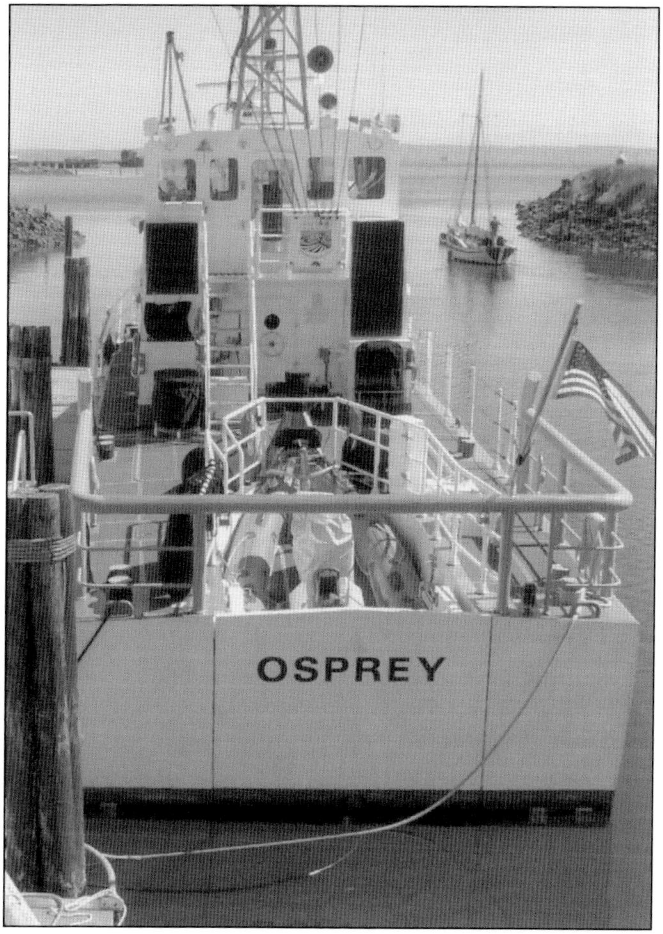

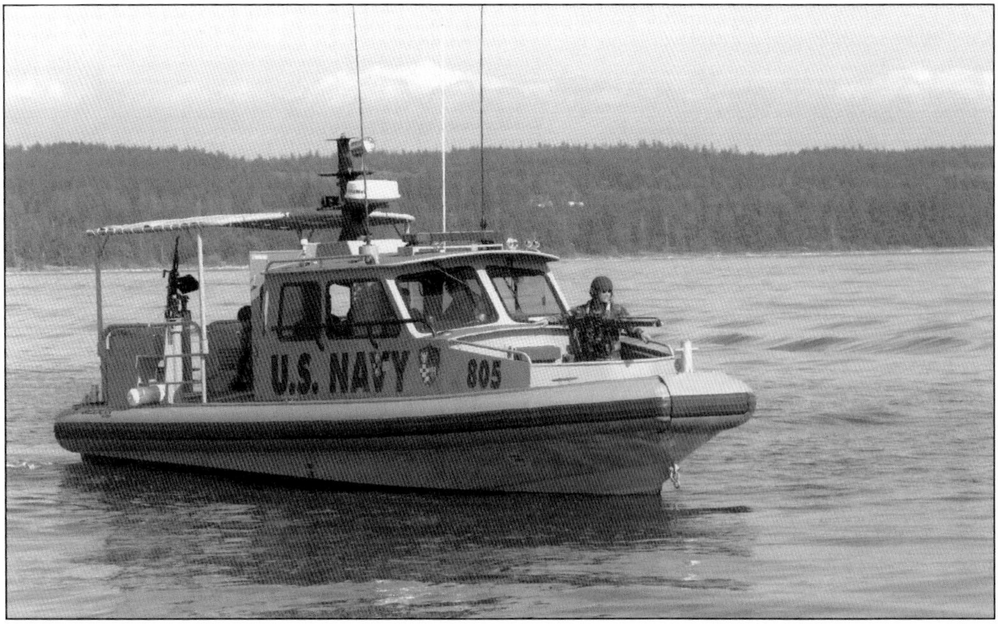

Navy Maritime Security. The US Navy also has security responsibilities in Puget Sound. Operating the 34-foot Sea Ark Dauntless patrol boats seen above, Navy Maritime Expeditionary Security Squadron 9 (MSRON9) crews are assigned to protect high-value assets such as the major Navy ships that are based in the sound at Everett and Bremerton, arrive for repairs and maintenance, and visit during special events like Fleet Week in Seattle. Part of the Navy Expeditionary Combat Command and staffed by Navy Reserve forces, as shown below, MSRON9 plays an essential role in maintaining military maritime security on Puget Sound and in the Pacific Northwest. (Both courtesy US Navy, Lt. Robert Harris.)

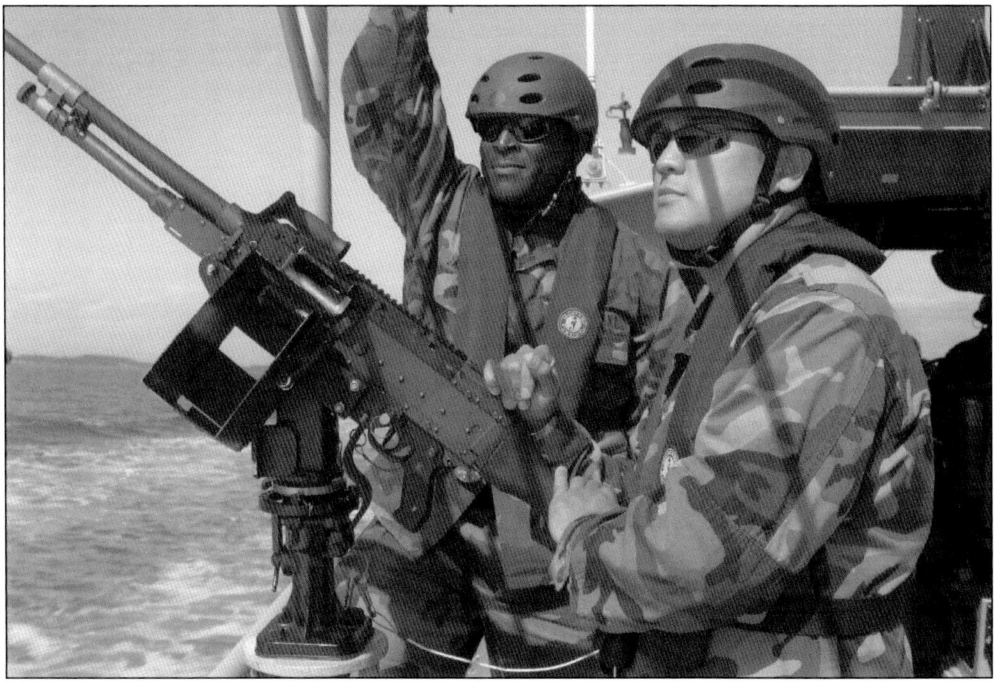

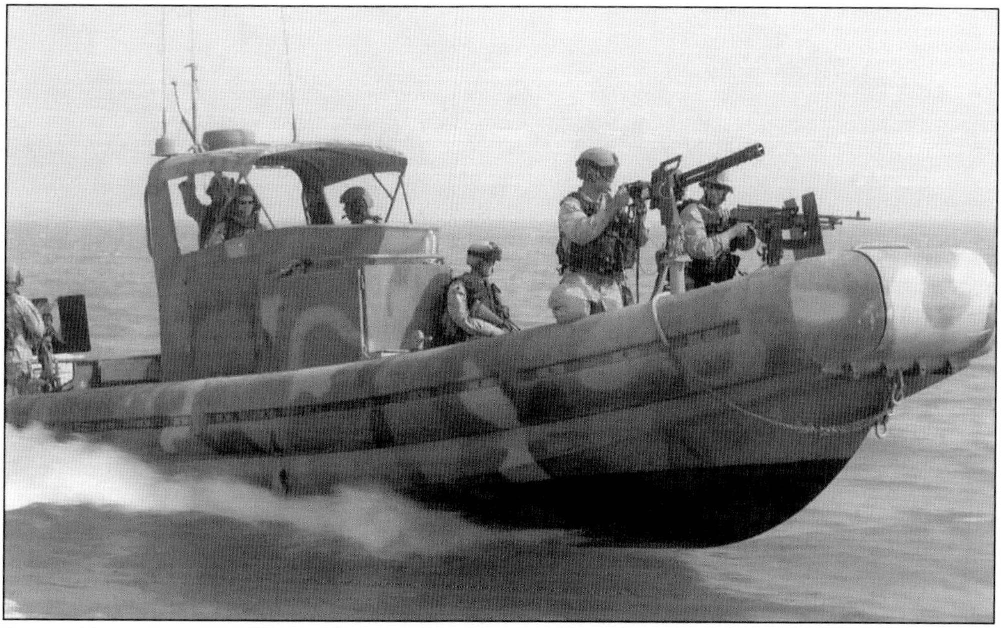

Sound-Built Riverine Boats. Among the newest and least known of the military boats produced in Puget Sound are the riverine combat craft built by SAFE Boats International, Inc., located in Port Orchard. More widely recognized for their successful RB-S (Response Boat–Small) for the Coast Guard, the company has manufactured a fast, maneuverable craft designed to operate in river and delta areas at more than 35 knots (40 miles per hour). Developed for the US Marine Corps, the riverine patrol boat shown above can carry and unload 16 armed troops into inshore combat zones. A larger craft built for the Navy under license from a Swedish boatbuilding company, the riverine command boat below uses diesel and water jet propulsion, carries modern electronics and communication equipment, and has a speed of more than 40 knots (46 miles per hour). (Both courtesy SAFE Boats International.)

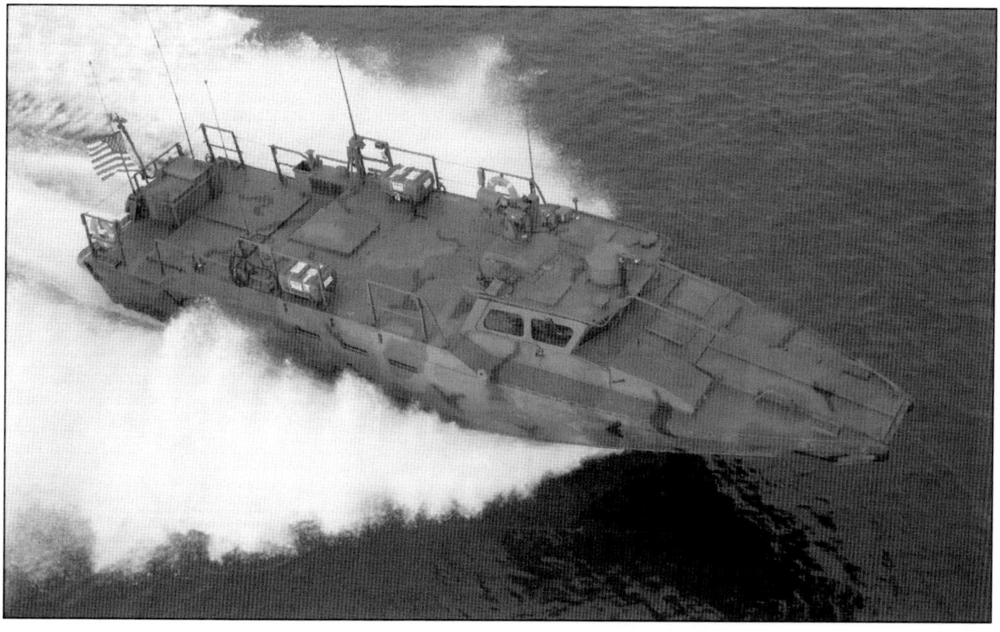

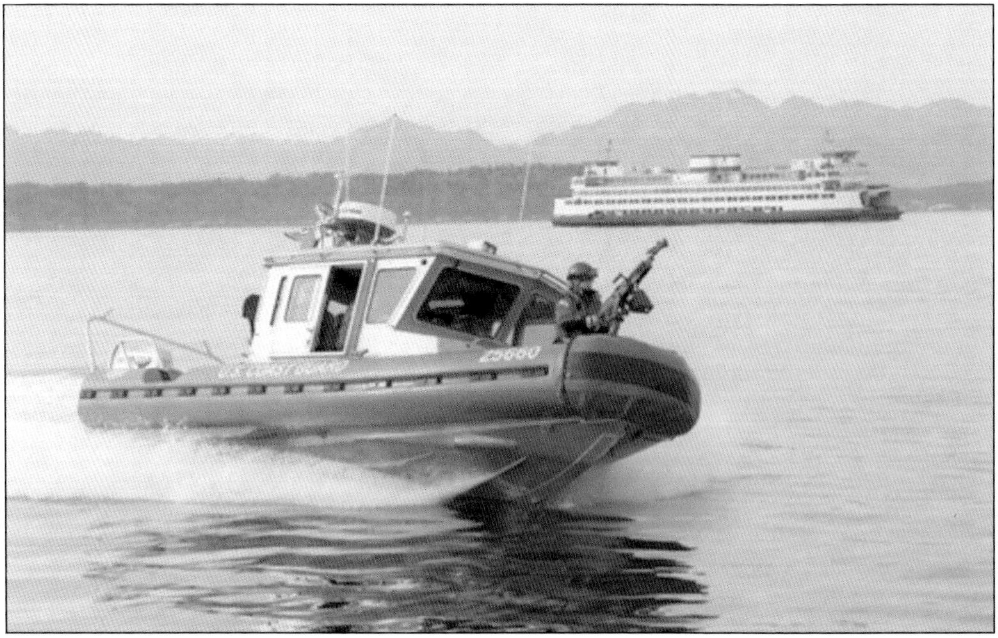

ARMED AND ACTIVE. The Coast Guard's 25-foot RB-S class craft based in Puget Sound exemplify the service's motto, *Semper Paratus*, "always ready." After the September 11, 2001 terrorist attacks, a key mission of the maneuverable, well-armed patrol boats in the Pacific Northwest became the protection of Washington State ferryboats and their passengers on cross-sound routes, as pictured above. Training in the use of the .30-caliber machinegun carried on all the boats is an ongoing activity. In the photograph below, a senior petty officer instructs a young RB-S crewmember in the operation of the weapon at the Coast Guard Sector Puget Sound base on the Seattle waterfront. (Both courtesy US Coast Guard.)

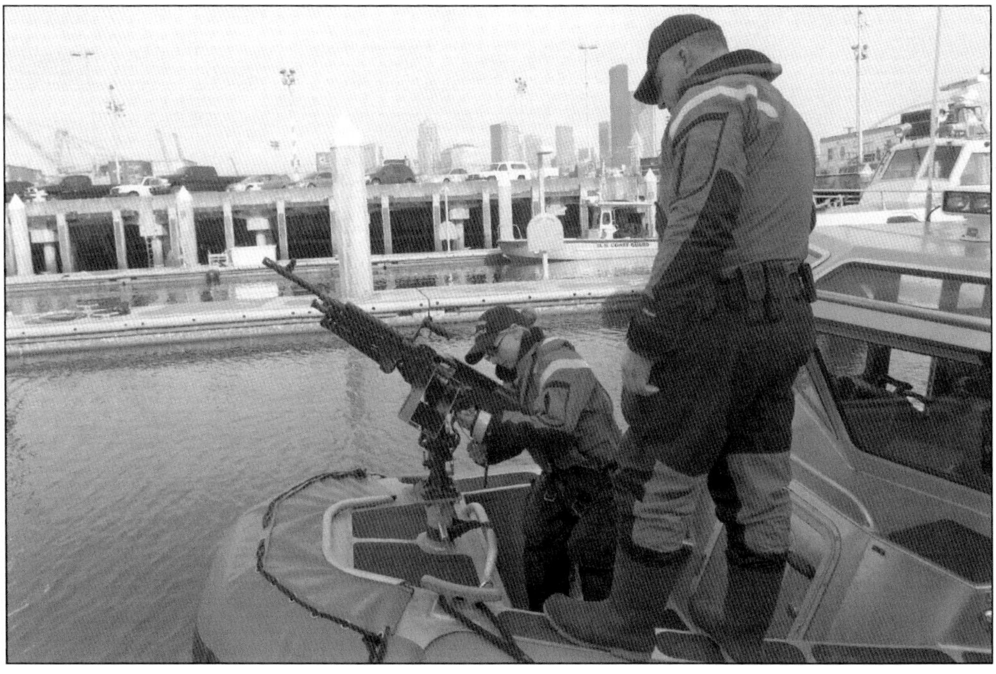

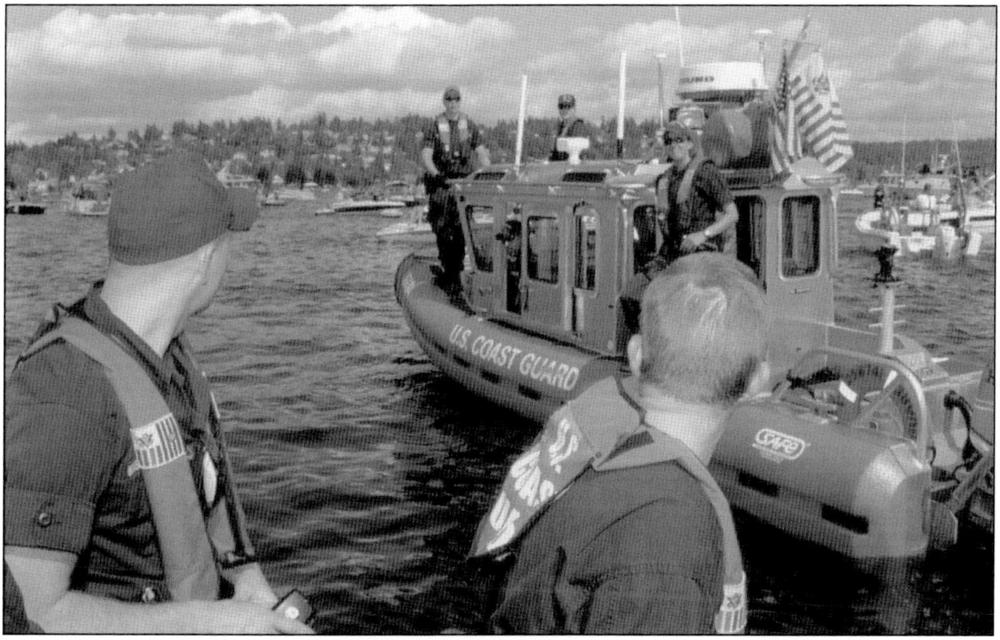

Ready to Respond. Whether providing law enforcement and safety patrol services at a large public event or responding to an emergency incident, Coast Guard RB-S crews are ready to respond professionally and quickly. A significant presence at events that attract large numbers of private vessels, such as Seattle Seafair (shown above) or the Opening Day of yachting season, Coast Guard crews stress the need for good boating safety practices. However, if an emergency arises anywhere in Puget Sound, a balanced force of Coast Guard vessels and trained crews are prepared to take immediate action. The RB-S craft, with their reliable twin high-performance outboard motors totaling 450 horsepower and capable of more than 45 knots (52 miles per hour), are an essential part of this force. (Above, courtesy US Coast Guard; below, courtesy SAFE Boats International.)

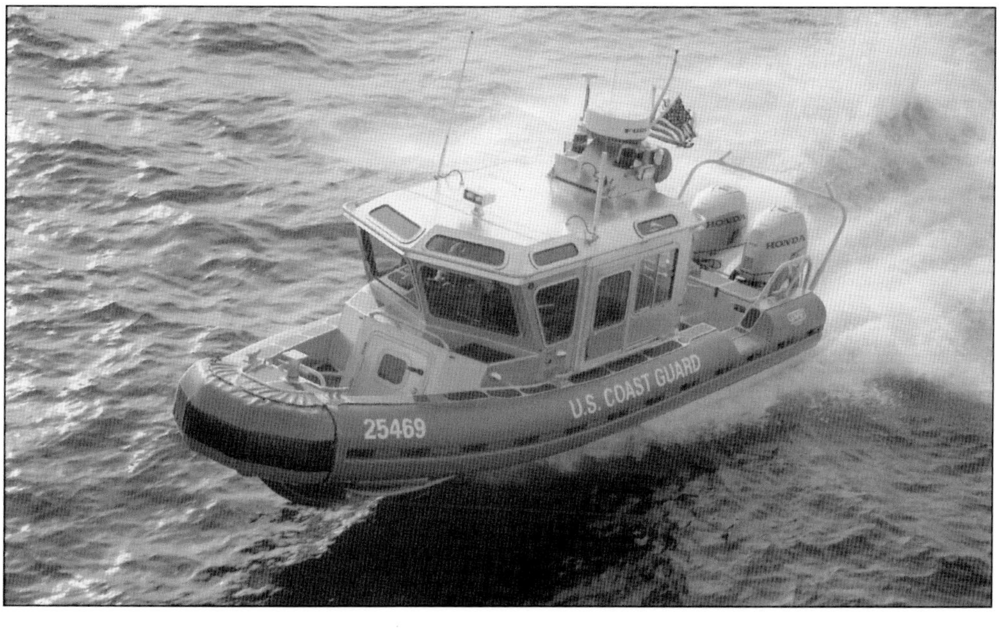

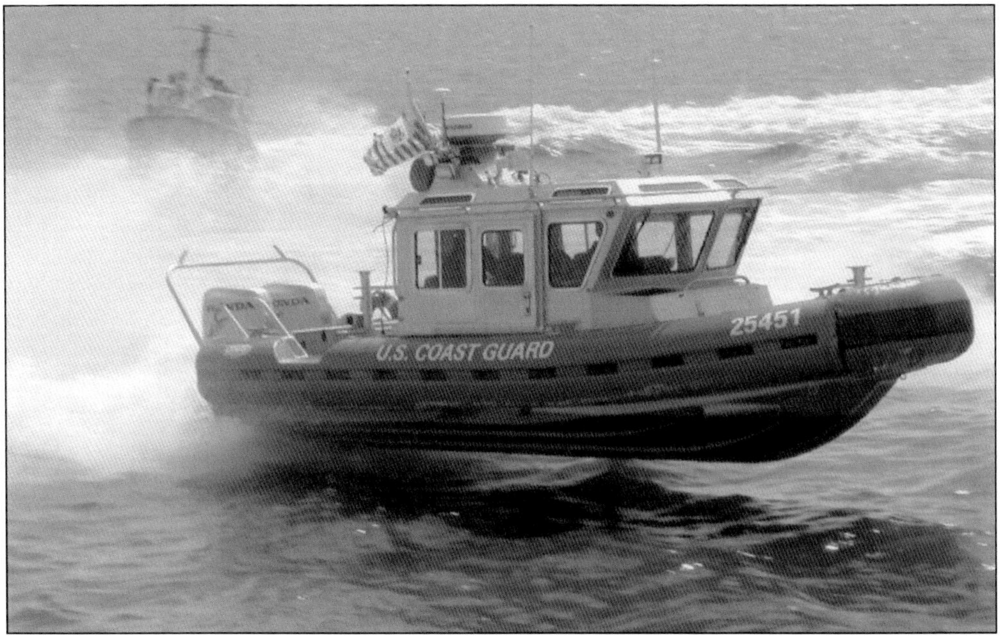

Fast Fleet. The RB-S, pictured above almost airborne, is just one of many fast-response boats produced by Puget Sound–based SAFE Boats International. Established in 1997, the company was awarded a contract in 2002 for up to 700 fast response boats for the US Department of Homeland Security, primarily for the Coast Guard. As of 2010, SAFE Boats had more than 1,400 patrol boats in service with the US Departments of Defense and Homeland Security and other government agencies at all levels. The image below shows eight of the company's boats, led by the Navy's riverine command boat. (Both courtesy SAFE Boats International.)

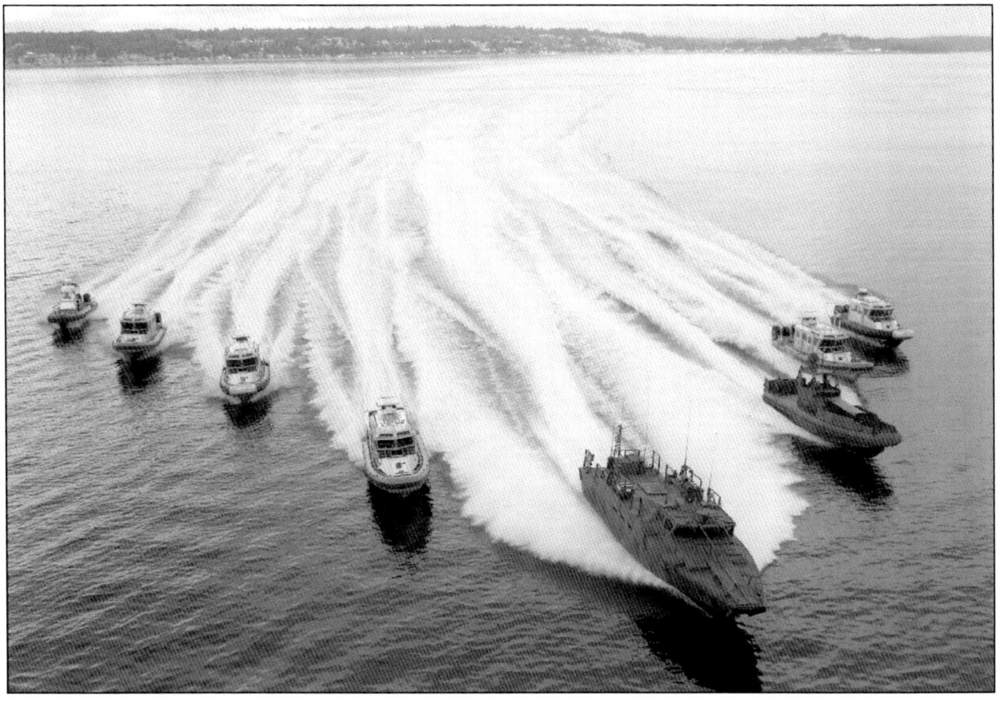

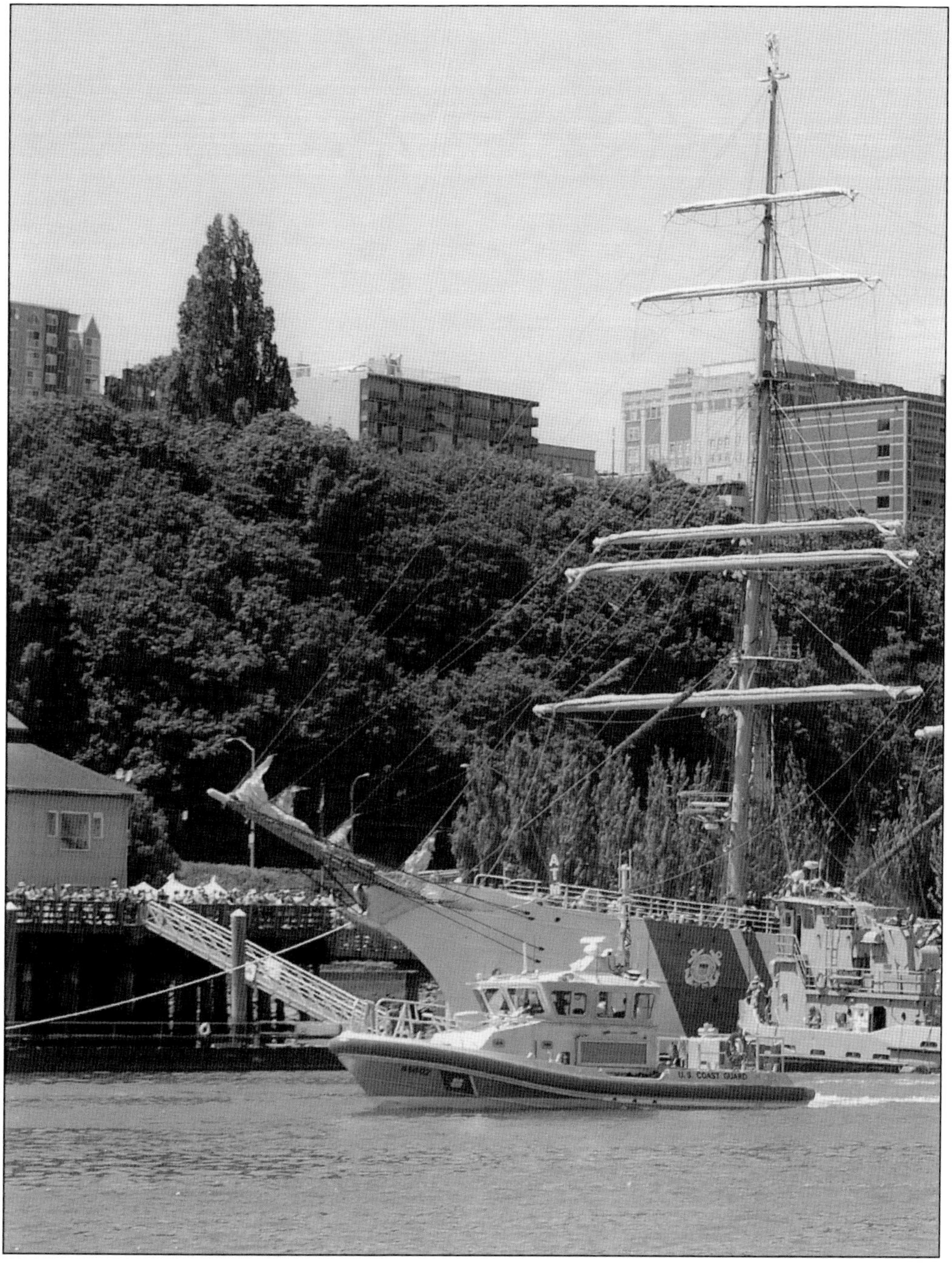

PAST MEETS PRESENT. The second production Coast Guard RB-M (Response Boat–Medium), CG-45502, is pictured passing near the bow of the 295-foot Coast Guard training tall ship *Eagle* when she visited the Tall Ships Tacoma event in 2008. The new RB-M was on acceptance trials in Puget Sound at the time. Prior to her 2008 visit, the more than 70-year-old *Eagle* had only appeared in Puget Sound twice before, in 1965 and 1978. (Photograph by Chuck Fowler.)

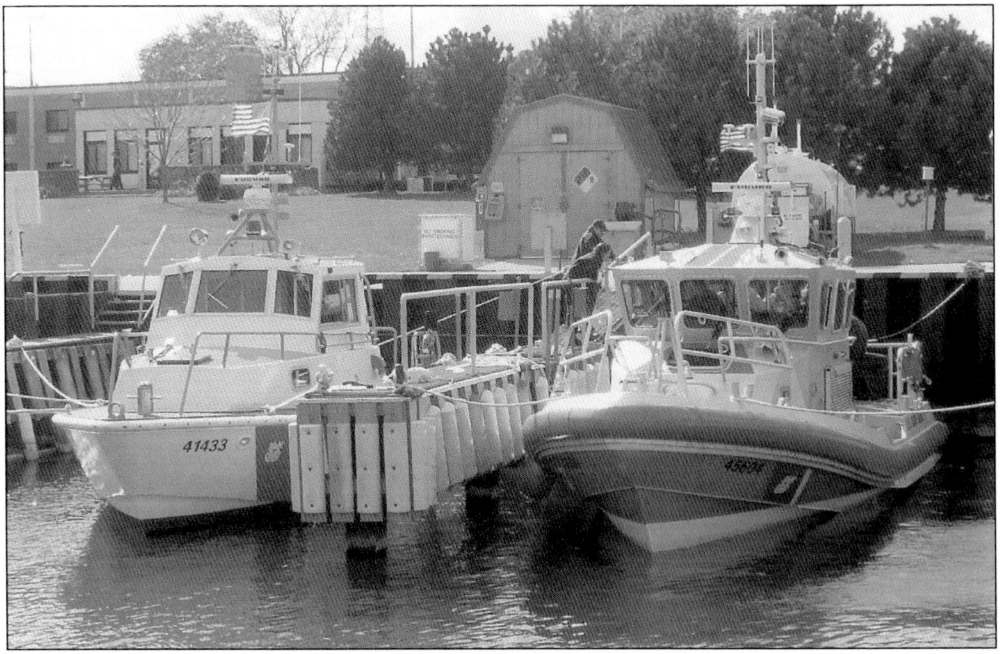

Frontline and Production Line. The RB-M was planned as a replacement for the widely used Coast Guard 41-foot utility boat (UTB), pictured moored at left above. By 2008, the UTB had reached its 25-year maximum service life, with reduced performance and increased maintenance. The prime contractor for the RB-M was Marinette Marine Corporation of Wisconsin in partnership with Kvichak Marine Industries of Seattle, with each company building half of the total 180 boats ordered as of the end of 2010. Full production began in 2008, and the boat shown below undergoing final outfitting was scheduled for delivery in April 2011 to the Coast Guard station at Mayport, near Jacksonville, Florida. (Both courtesy US Coast Guard Project Resident Office, Kvichak Marine Industries plant, Kent, WA.)

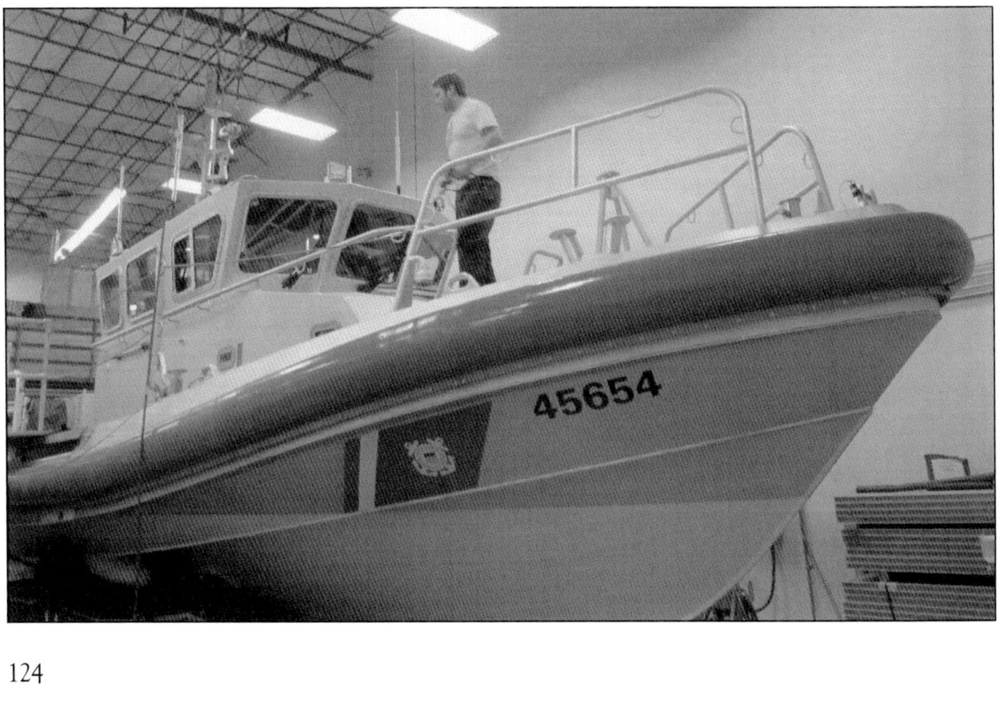

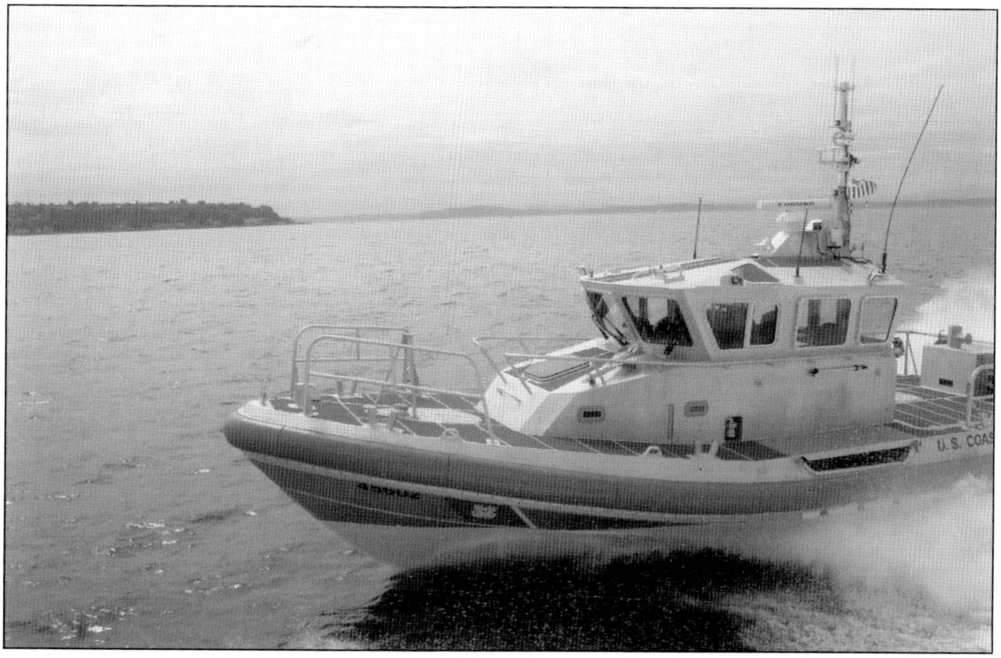

Sea Trials Spray. CG-45602, the second RB-M off the production line at the Kvichak Marine Industries plant in Kent, near Seattle, is shown above at more than 40 knots (46 miles per hour) during sea trials in Puget Sound in mid-2008. In August, CG-45602 was delivered for evaluation to the Coast Guard Station at Cape Disappointment in Ilwaco, Washington, the home of the National Motor Lifeboat School, and she was later reassigned to Port Angeles for permanent duty. At the end of 2010, the first RB-M was delivered to Coast Guard Station Seattle, and two more were scheduled by mid-2011. (Both courtesy US Coast Guard Project Resident Office, Kvichak Marine Industries plant, Kent, WA.)

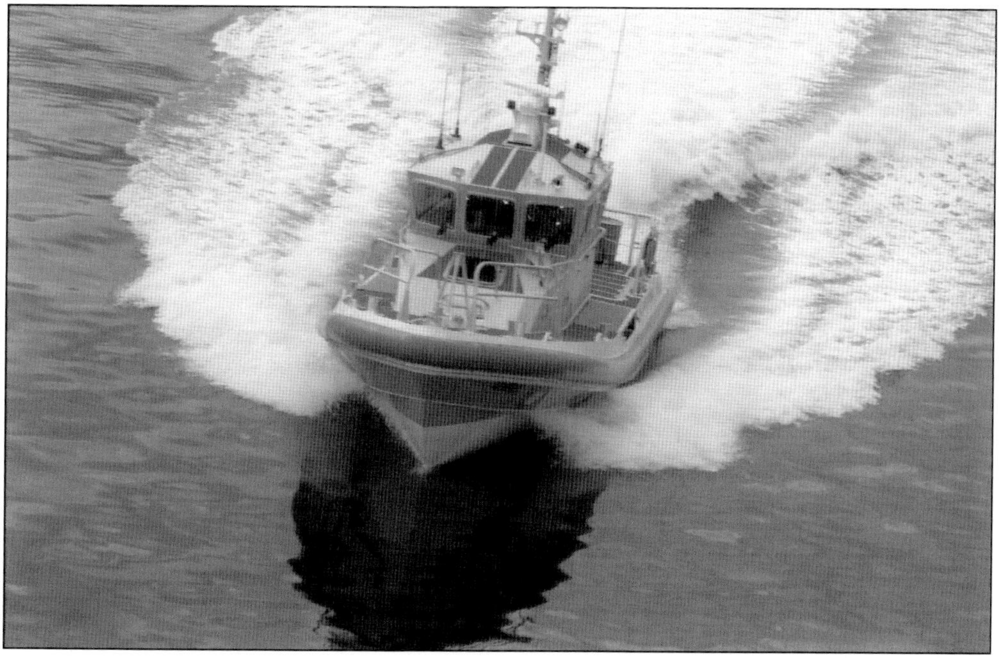

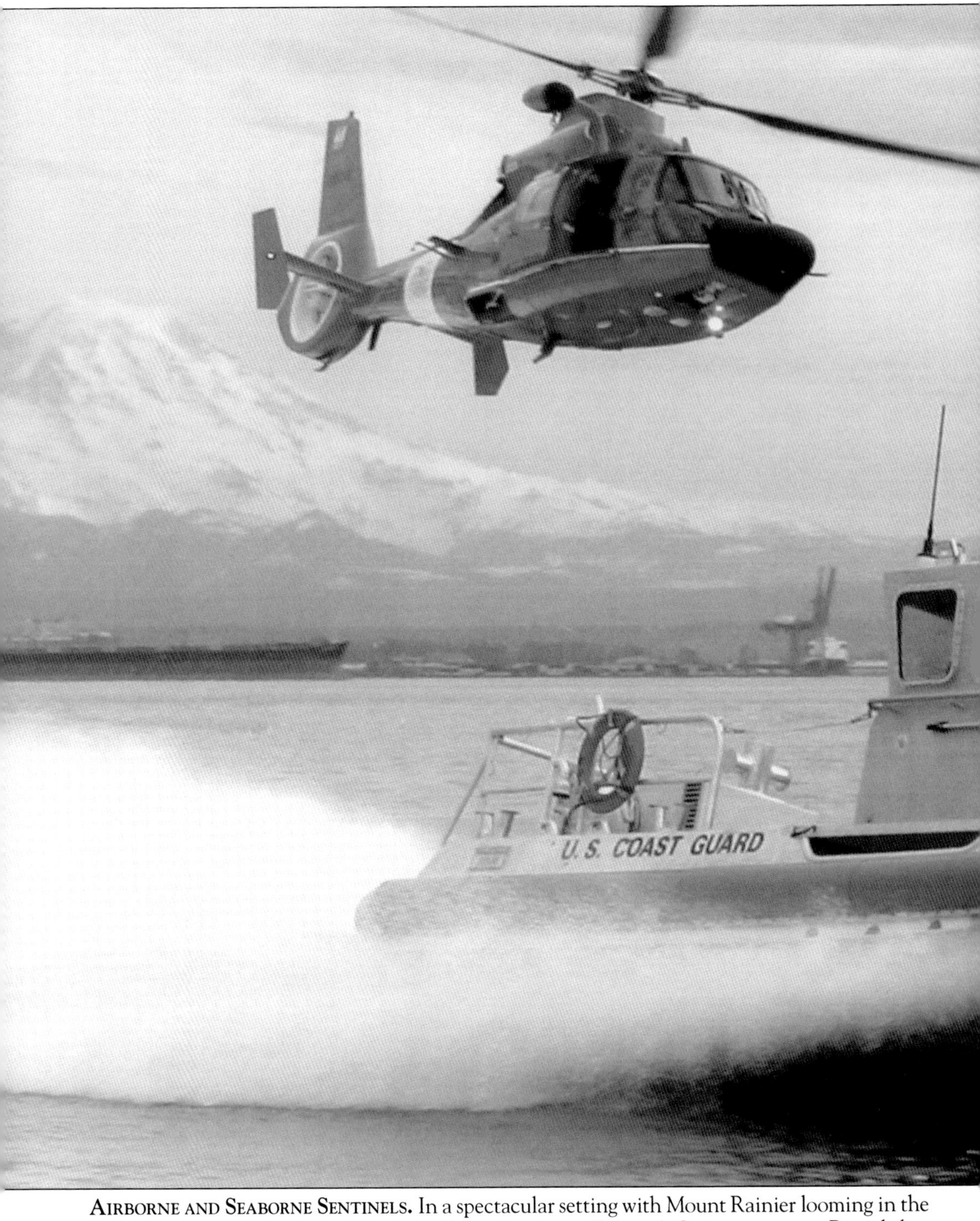

AIRBORNE AND SEABORNE SENTINELS. In a spectacular setting with Mount Rainier looming in the background, a Coast Guard RB-M patrol boat cuts across Tacoma's Commencement Bay while a MH-65 Dolphin helicopter flies escort low overhead. Working together, the fast, high-technology air and sea response craft provide marine security, law enforcement, rescue, safety, and other vital sea services around the clock, day in and day out. Historically, in the greater Puget Sound

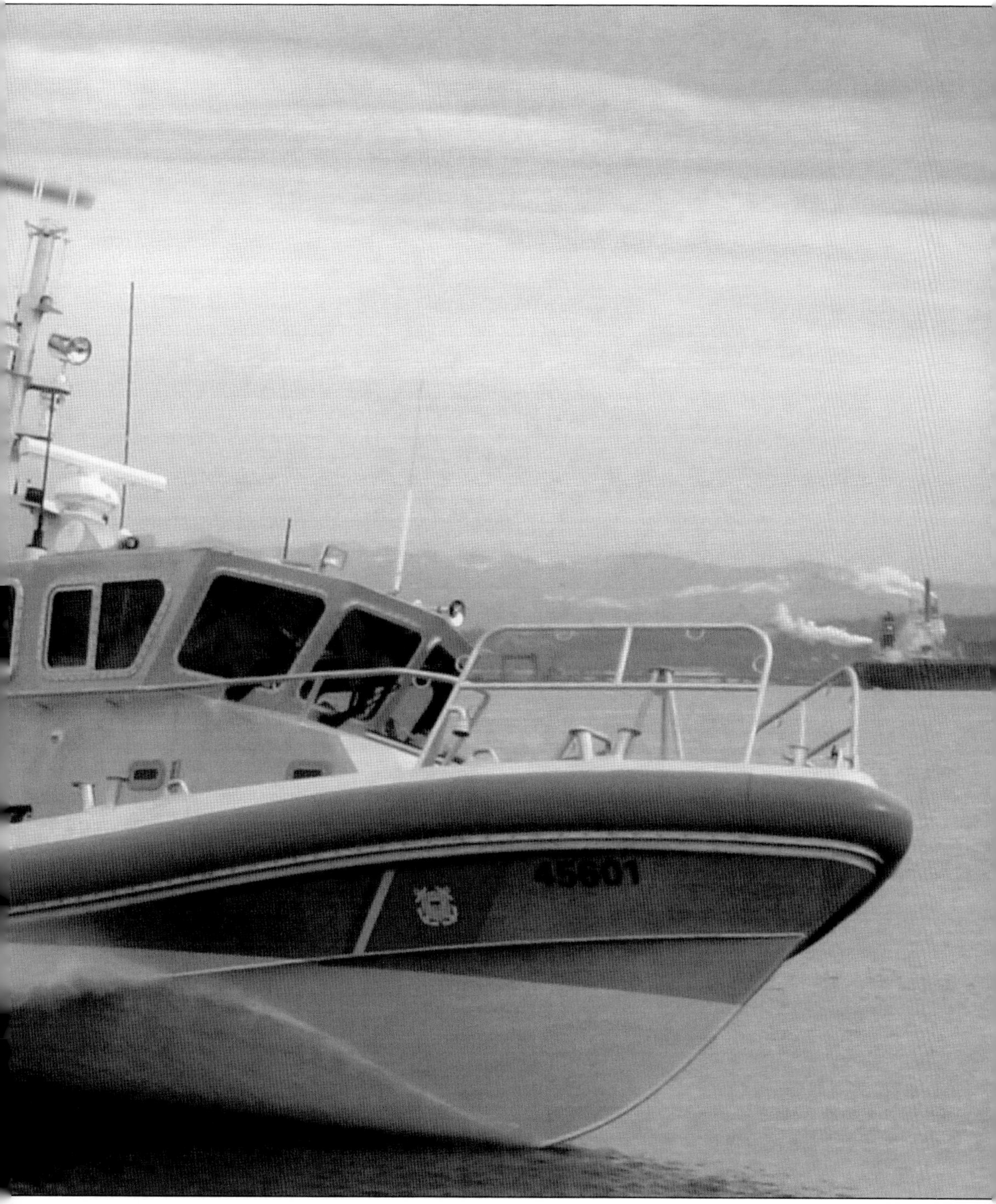

region, the Coast Guard, the Navy, and even the Air Force have used their human, seaborne, and airborne forces, including a vast and varied fleet of patrol and rescue boats, to protect the national values and people of the United States. (Courtesy US Coast Guard Project Resident Office, Kvichak Marine Industries plant, Kent, WA.)